CHRIS DONALDSON

Printed Worldwide
First Printing 2021
First Edition 2021

10 9 8 7 6 5 4 3 2

To my wonderful wife, Julie, without whose patience and support,
this book would not have been written.

GOING THE WRONG WAY

Posing on the bike in Cape Town harbour with the Seltrust Endeavor yacht behind.

CHRIS DONALDSON

Table of Contents

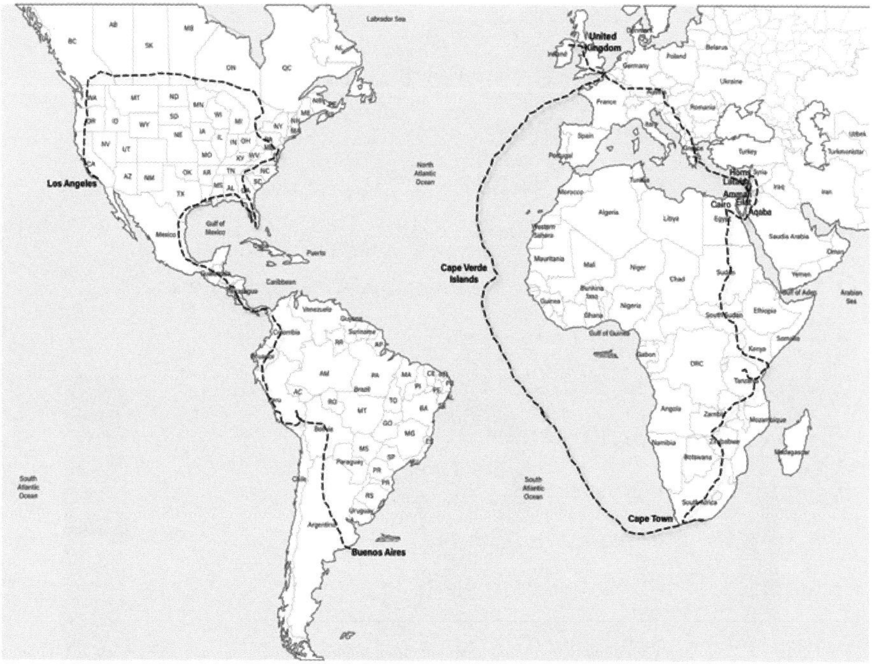
United Kingdom
Los Angeles
Cape Verde Islands
Cairo
Aqaba
Cape Town
Buenos Aires

Belfast, 1979. The James Dean, 'Rebel Without a Cause.'
look is spoilt by the smart crease on my trousers

Rio de Janeiro,1981. After, going the wrong way, to many times!

Author Biography

On his return from South America, Chris joined the family furniture shop in Belfast, which over the years he expanded into London and Dublin. He was UK Master Franchisor for a fitness company, developed a Health & Fitness Franchise, and a Mobile App company in Dubai; where he lived for eight years with his family on a 47ft yacht.

His hobbies include sailing and flying. Following his quest to do things his own way, he built his own aeroplane. He still rides his Moto Guzzi Le Mans, SOI 222, and some years ago rode it to Moscow and St Petersburg with his wife, Julie.

The journey still impacts his life to this day where he continues to go the wrong way whenever he can; a trip to Australia is still a dream.

Chris now works with Ed's son, Jeff Arditti from North Carolina. He sells their furniture in Europe, Russia and Australia.

He now lives in Belfast and is the father of two beautiful girls.

Belfast cemetery has recently noticed some paranormal disturbances at the grave of his old English teacher. Rumours of him writing a book have apparently reached the afterlife.

Foreword

SINCE THE STONE AGE, THE WALKABOUT HAS BEEN AN ABORIGINAL RITE OF passage. It is when adolescent boys wander aimlessly into the bush on a journey with no particular destination. During this time, they make the spiritual transition from boy to man. It's a time for self-assessment and deep thought when he can learn about himself without the influence of his elders, friends, or family. It's a physical and psychological journey.

I didn't look like an Aboriginal adolescent as I set off from Belfast on my café racing Moto Guzzi, but looking back, I see that the same determination drove me to set off on a journey of self-discovery. I was twenty-one and, wanted to go 'somewhere' for 'some time' and, well, for 'something'!

Australian society now views the walkabout with disdain; it encourages kids to avoid risks, to go with the flow and to accept authority. The journeys we take in our modern lives are usually for pleasure. Young people may spend six months volunteering or on a foreign eco holiday, but even these kinds of trips are pre-planned and have been through rigorous health and safety checks.

Should young people, both male and female, learn about themselves on a walkabout now? We talk of "Millennials" and "Snowflakes," young, over-emotional and easily offended adults who are uninterested in anyone else's opinion. Over- educated, overworked and overwhelmed, they are on an organised path from cradle to grave.

This desire drove me to break free from my mediocre, middle-class existence and reach out for the unknown. The demand was irresistible and bound me to an ancient ritual that many young men before me had taken for adventure.

Introduction

March 1981

Any exertion at 13,000 feet is exhausting, but pure torture for a man riddled with hepatitis. Just climbing one flight of stairs had me panting like a rabid dog.

After riding down from the USA to South America, my plan had been to sell the bike to pay for the flight home. But the biggest bike in La Paz was a Honda 50, and no one wanted an 850cc Moto Guzzi. My only option was to beg my parents to send money.

"Buenos Dias," I said to the operator who sat reading a Batman magazine. Great, I thought, my survival is reliant on a retard. "I want to send a telex."

"Estados Unidos?" he said, glancing up at my jaundiced face.

"No, Irlanda del Norte, Gran Bretaña."

Looking irritated, he handed me the message pad; clearly a critical moment in Batman's plan to save Gotham City.

"$5 per line," he murmured.

I printed the words as if it was the last message I would ever write.

"I'm stuck in La Paz, run out of money. Please transfer £500 care of Bank of Bolivia, La Paz, at once."

I watched the ticker tape flick through the machine and wanted to dive down the line back to the comfort and medical care of home. The silence as the spent paper tape hit the floor was deafening. That was it: my last effort spent. I paid and shuffled towards the door, hoping to get some word back the next day.

In Belfast, Ken sat at his telex machine.

"What's happening? Send more info," he replied. The operator jumped as the machine spat back. Responses arrived a few weeks later, not two minutes.

"Hey Gringo, do you want to reply?" My status rose above the Penguin.

"No hay dinero," I said and shrugged my shoulders. I was down to my last five bucks.

"I give you ten words free," he said, excited to be back in the real world.

"Ok, send this."

"Hi Ken, send the money and wait for the book." Well, here it is, 40 years later!

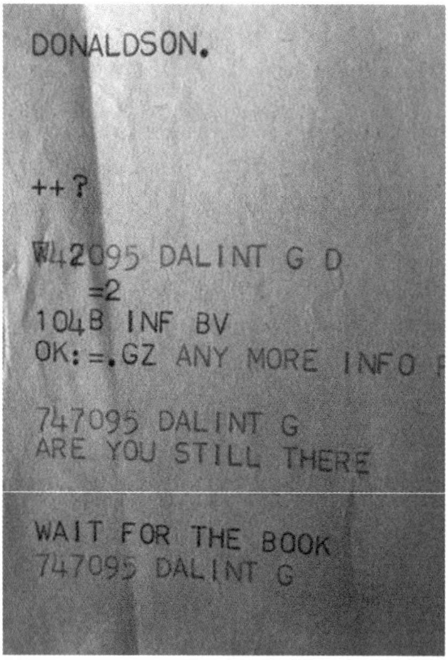

My telex receipt from 1981

CHAPTER 1

Growing Up in War-Torn Belfast

In 1958, Fidel Castro started a revolution in Cuba, Mao Zedong began the great leap forward in China, and I was born in Belfast.

It's well known that the firstborn is special and my parents, I am sure, were captivated. The second baby was still a wonder, but they had seen it all before. By my arrival, the novelty of boys had evaporated. They shipped my eldest brother to boarding school, and number two and I shared a room. We shared everything: hand-me-down clothes and toys. So, by my turn, they were third-hand and done in; it's my excuse for having no fashion sense.

The first and last-born are always parent's favourites, and I didn't resent it. I never would have wanted that adulation and I quietly accepted my place in the pecking order. But this doubtlessly led to my shy personality, where I was always happy hanging around in the background and accepted my number four position in the family.

My clearest childhood memories of our family are our summer holiday road trips. We toured the South of Ireland, then France and Germany. In July 1969, I watched the skies over Switzerland while listening on the car radio as Neil Armstrong stepped onto the moon. Perhaps these adventures planted the seeds of my travel wanderlust.

In August 1969, the first British troops arrived in Ulster to quell the sectarian violence, rather quaintly called the 'Troubles.' The next month, my unconcerned parents sent me to RBAI, a Protestant school right in the centre of Belfast. The 'Troubles' soon escalated into a small-scale civil war. In 1972 alone, the IRA carried out 1,300 bomb attacks and 497 people lost their lives – most of them were innocent civilians in Belfast.

My classroom offered a grandstand view of the bombings. The school would shake violently, as the pressure of a bomb blast reached us. We would rush to the windows as the teacher screamed at us to sit down.

When McCausland's car showroom, just behind the school, was bombed, we didn't even need to go out, as car parts rained down into the back yard. Coincidently, at exam times the school was prone to spates of bomb scares; a high- pitched voice phoned a bomb warning to the headmaster's secretary and everyone piled out onto the front lawn while they searched the school.

Children get used to anything; it soon became the norm to see the destruction and to search the bombed-out shops for souvenirs.

Kids from the Catholic area beside the school threw stones over the wall, and we threw them back; neither side could see what they hit. But we shouted, "Fenian bastards" in reply to the "Proddy fuckers," which made up a little for the lack of any visual gratification.

Some classmates had to walk through a Catholic area to get to school, and the headmaster insisted we wore the bright yellow caps as part of our uniform, which said, "I'm a Protestant, throw stones at me!" The teachers must have thought it was character-forming for the boys to get a damn good stoning.

I took the bus to school and as it slowed at the corner at the front gates, we would jump off the platform at the back, like parachutists exiting a burning plane. Our dash through the traffic saved us a 100-yard walk from the bus stop and earned precious kudos from the bigger boys.

The IRA bombers targeted shops and offices, so the police enclosed the city centre with fences and guarded gates where all the shoppers were searched. However, in the city streets, car bombs continued to explode sometimes without warning.

Then the government imposed internment and imprisoned hundreds of suspects without trial, which only made matters worse. Every night, my mum and dad discussed the deteriorating security situation, but for some reason, they never suggested we shouldn't go to school in the city centre. I often wondered why the adults just couldn't sort it out, and what it was all about, anyway?

One day, a guy walked into Dad's furniture shop and dumped a rucksack on the floor.

"It's a bomb," he said to the bewildered staff and walked off. The manager, Billy McCauley, carried it out to the street where it exploded ten minutes later.

During another attempt a few months later, Billy refused to open the door, so they left the bomb in the porch and the staff cleared out the back. As the bomb disposal officer approached, it exploded, and a steel beam from the shop front flew clean over his head to land behind him. But the shop was soon boarded up and trading again.

One afternoon in 1975, the school shook as a huge bomb exploded nearby. The lessons continued, but after school, I saw the smoke coming from the direction of the shop and ran towards it.

The red-brick shop had collapsed in a pile of rubble and splintered joists. A steel skeleton was all that remained. Mahogany tables and chairs lay in the street, and a steel beam impaled a brown velvet sofa. Shredded floral fabrics fluttered gaily in the breeze. The office girls stood in tears and the storemen cursed to hide their worry about their future. Some had worked there for 30 years.

I saw Dad standing, staring at the wreckage; he looked broken and dejected.

"The bastards have done it this time," he said as he stared at the shattered ruins.

"You can rebuild it, Dad," I said. Kids are scared when they see their parents distraught. I wanted him to tell me it would all be okay. But a few days later, he managed to reopen in temporary premises with the 'Bomb Damage Sale,' signs ubiquitous in the Troubles.

Recently, I found an old advert in the Belfast Telegraph archives for the 13th of April 1973 where my father apologised to the customers 'for the inconvenience,' of his shop being destroyed. Belfast shopkeepers insisted on a 'Business as Usual' defiance throughout those brutal years. The IRA would not beat them - or be seen to.

19 PUBLIC NOTICES 19 PUBLIC NOTICES

DONALDSON & LYTTLE LTD.

Apologise to all their customers for he inconvenience caused by recent bomb damage.

The Company wishes to express its thanks to all for their forbearance at this difficult time.

Until repairs have been carried out

BUSINESS WILL BE CONTINUED

from our Showrooms at

29 GREAT VICTORIA STREET

Telephone 42401

The shop sat between the Europa Hotel and Donegall Pass police station, so every time they got blown up, our windows came in too. And as the Troubles went on, they bombed the Europa Hotel 33 times.

I don't remember ever fearing the danger at hearing the police sirens, at watching buildings burn and excitement at the chance to rummage through the remains of a shattered shop on the way home from school.

As a teenager, I worked at the shop on Saturdays. Part of my job was to search the shop after everyone had gone, as the IRA campaign against G Plan sofas was to place small incendiaries in the furniture. If I found one, I was told to pick it up and put it in a bucket of water. This particular evening, I opened a wardrobe door, and a guy flew out. I made a grab at him but fell over as he dashed downstairs and I chased after him. He shook the locked front door turned like a cornered animal and we stood, sizing each other up as I hit the emergency police alarm. He had an impressive scar on his face, while I had spots.

"Don't move or I'll fucking kill you!" I screamed, although just how I would do that with the scatter cushions at my disposal, I wasn't sure. The police arrived and took him away in handcuffs. I started trembling as I realised the danger of the situation, but the cops laughed and said he was a well- known shoplifter chancing his luck.

I never did very well in school, I spent too much time staring out the window wondering what was over there, always a bit of a dreamer. These days, problem kids have loads of names/excuses for being behind, Dyslexia, Asperger's and so on. In our day we were troublemakers, or just plain stupid. By the time I failed my eleven plus exams, I was already branded a let-down by the teachers, and I knew what they thought: I was hardly your average rebel without a cause. I was not very intellectual, or good at sports, not very confident, and not going anywhere.

I left home at twelve years of age. Well, I joined the Sea Scouts, and they became my new family. The Scouts taught me more than tying knots; it gave me a place to develop friendships and served as a springboard to develop my own personality. We would hike in the Mourne Mountains come rain or snow, sail dinghies and camp on Islands in Strangford Lough, without our parents having any notion of where we were.

The older boys would meet in the church hall after the Scouts, and I would stare in awe as they roared up on their big Norton's and Royal Enfield's; my scouting became more Hell's Angels than Baden Powell. Sometimes they would let me try to kick-start the big single-cylinder engines, nearly breaking my leg.

During one scout meeting, two local hard men came into the church hall, they had been drinking and demanded money. There were twenty of us so I told them to fuck off, not realising that everyone had retreated behind me.

They left after a few obscenities.

"That was brave, Chris!" someone said.

"They didn't look that tough."

"Yes, but they had broken bottles."

And that was the moment I realised I needed glasses! Along with the glasses, my volcanoes of acne, the final calamity was braces. My confidence slid into oblivion, just when I needed it most - the arrival of girls!

Saturday nights in Belfast in the seventies meant hanging out in the street with a bottle of cheap German wine, learning to chat up females. The drink made it less intimidating for me but can't have improved the experience for the girls! We'd go for a song to the music of John Lennon and Simon and Garfunkel.

When I was 16, I read in the Motorcycle News about a bloke who had driven his motorbike to Australia. It lit a fire in my imagination and I bought my first motorbike for twenty quid; it was a BSA Bantam. Not quite Jack Nicholson's Harley-Davidson, but to a spotty teenage git, it was the next best thing; and the full-face helmet hid my acne!

No doubt, the Ulster 'Troubles' added to my eagerness to get away, helped by my geography teacher, Sleepy Sam, who assured me that the world was round, full of strange exotic lands and different cultures, and where, for some reason, they didn't care if you were a Protestant or Catholic.

But my Bantam wasn't going around the world, as it stopped every time it rained, so it had to go. I bought a BSA 250, but it broke down at every traffic light, so it had to go too.

My next bike was a 600cc BMW, which was boring, so I tried to sell it. But it had 100,000 miles on the clock, so I connected a drill to the speedo to wind the clock back. Two days later, a guy on a Honda flagged me down.

"I used to own that bike," he said, glancing at the milometer. "Only 60,000 miles? That's less than when I sold it!"

"OK, I wound the clock back," I admitted.

"Don't worry, I wound it back from 150,000 miles myself!"

Drink-drive laws existed, but the police were too busy chasing terrorists to worry about them. So, when I drove back from the Polytechnic bar after a few pints too many, it was no big deal. I kept to a steady 30mph on the motorway as my friend, JC, was holding my whisky glass, and it spilt if I went any faster.

"Let's stop at the Club Bar for a refill," JC said. The Club Bar had a dubious reputation and had its windows boarded up after a recent bombing. Not confident about my balance with JC on the back, I pulled up and lent the bike against the hoarding. There was a loud crack and the hoarding, the bike, and the two of us fell into the public bar.

A couple of old boys were watching the horse racing on TV and barely gave us a glance as we sprawled across the floor swearing.

"Get that bike out of my bar," said the barman.

"I seem to have spilt the whisky," said JC, dusting himself off.

I picked the bike up and drove out of the hole before coming back in for another drink.

In 1978, over 300 people died in road accidents, while 80 deaths were caused by the Troubles. The police finally caught on and cracked down, and by 2018, traffic fatalities in Northern Ireland were down to 70, less than one-quarter of the carnage of the seventies.

On our last day of school, the headmaster told us we would look back on our school days as the happiest of our lives. This depressed me, as I thought mine had been crap! Life improved when I enrolled at the Ulster Polytechnic. Finally, I got to communicate with Catholics without the use of stones or missiles and we got on fine, but we didn't discuss religion or politics. We knew we had different viewpoints, so we kept conversation to birds, booze and bikes.

Then my best mate, Kenny, got shot in the face. He was studying at home when he heard screaming downstairs. Three IRA men had broken in and kicked his mum to the floor of the hallway.

Ken saw red, sprinted down the stairs and chased them out the door. But as they ran, one swung around and fired a wild shot, hitting Ken on his chin and the bullet got lodged in his neck. They rushed him to the hospital where, not surprisingly, some of the world's most experienced gunshot surgeons worked. It was touch and go, but the bullet had missed his vital nerves by millimetres.

After weeks in intensive care, his mum asked us to sit with him and cheer him up. Kenny was a big guy so normally we couldn't get away with slagging him, but now immobile with tubes and wires everywhere, we poked good-natured banter at him to put a smile on his face.

We left a Playboy magazine lying open on his bed every visit, and because he couldn't move to hide them from the nurses, we creased ourselves laughing.

When he had recovered enough to tell us to fuck off, his damaged vocal cords sounded like Donald Duck, which was even more hilarious. They never caught Kenny's shooter, but he still gives us hell about our bedside manner.

Belfast folk developed a very un-PC sense of humour, making fun of the most serious of situations. A friend who was a policewoman told me that, after a particularly violent riot, someone brought a severed hand into the station and gave it to the Desk Sergeant.

"What's this for?" he said.

"You could always make an ashtray from it!" said a passing copper.

The Protestant UDA fought to stay British and the IRA to be Irish, and neither cared who got caught in the violence. They murdered parents and children in front of their families, intimidated schools and forced them to shut. They killed over 3500 people, including 180 children. No one knows how this breakdown of normal society affected us as children.

Perhaps it made us resilient and stronger? Or perhaps it fucked our heads up? Some kids experienced terrible things. West Belfast was a 'no-go' area for the police, and the IRA punishment squads disciplined offenders by knee-capping them. Sometimes wrongdoers disappeared and were never seen again. There were daily riots and constant harassment by the British army who never tried to 'win hearts and minds.' West Belfast now has a suicide rate three times the UK average for middle-aged men. The 'Troubles' children, now adults, cannot handle the stresses of normal life.

My parents sent me to school in the centre of Belfast, an incredibly dangerous environment, without any concern. People got shot for being the wrong religion or blown up for being in the wrong place at the wrong time. Nowadays we panic if our kids go out without their mobile phone.

I recently watched BBC 'Pop goes Northern Ireland,' on TV. The program is about the Troubles in 1977, to the background of 70s rock music. Between images of carnage and destruction was a clip of a university charity parade, with students in fancy dress and having fun. Suddenly there I was, on the screen, riding my BSA round the City Hall with no trousers on, purple underpants! The Horror; the Horror!

The murder and mayhem were never far away. In the following year's parade, two IRA men disguised in fancy dress mingled with the students and shot dead a soldier and a female security guard.

1978 was a bad year, with twelve people getting burnt alive while having dinner in the La Mon hotel. Most were members of a local Collie club and a junior motorcycle club. The bomb had gallons of petrol mixed with sugar to ensure that the burning petrol stuck to its victims.

Middle-class South Belfast, where I lived, was more stable but the terrorist threat was always there and we learned to cope. It was violence caused by the grownups, the politicians, the clergy, people we should respect and expected to look after us. It gave me a lifelong cynicism for people in authority.

When I watched Narcos on Netflix, I realize how similar the Colombian terrorism was, except that they were clever enough to fight over money and drugs, rather than religion and politics.

When I was 19, I bought a Norton Commando, which had a more authentic mileage than the BMW. It leaked oil, the exhaust blast could wake the dead and the vibration dislocated your corneas, but it cornered like it was on rails.

British motorcycles were noisy and leaked oil. But that was part of the image. They were all about chaos and anarchy.

Then I saw the red Moto Guzzi Le Mans in a shop window; it was love at first sight; one test-drive and I was hooked. The Guzzi had a big V twin. It throbbed like a heartbeat, like life itself. I had to have it. I'd saved up, but I was short £1,000 after selling the Commando. My mum tried to bribe me.

"I'll give you the money for a car, but I'll only lend it if you buy the bike," she said. But I was in love. I worked every weekend and paid her off.

I thought I was King of the Road. One day, I was cruising through town with my mate, Phil, when a big Kawasaki pulled up at the lights. I nodded to him and revved my engine, and he nodded back. We had a drag race! The lights turned to green, I dropped the clutch, and popped a wheelie and screeched up Wellington Place, touching 80mph as we passed the City Hall. I skidded to a halt at the next lights and heard a distant siren wail. Eventually, a Police car drew up beside us.

"You know we were sitting behind you at the lights?" the cop said. As I squirmed in embarrassment, the Kawasaki rider drove past laughing so much that he wobbled! But the police only gave us a caution, probably because we were so boneheaded.

That May, we rode to the North West 200 races, with thousands of other bikes. We stretched our bike's performance, watched a few races, and downed a few pints and everyone raced back to Belfast. We ended up in the pub with a load of bikers, high on the adrenalin from the ride.

"There I am, doing well over the ton," I overheard one biker say. "Then this Moto Guzzi Le Mans screamed past. He must have been doing 130! I gave up!"

"That was me, mate," I said.

Mad wankers, that's what we were.

When I learned that Tom Herron and two other racers had died that day, I regulated my riding style a little. If these guys had killed themselves, skilled and sober, what hope did I have?

One evening, as I rode up the Antrim Road, a crowd stood outside the police station. By the time I saw the British Army at the other end of the street and realised that there was going to be a riot, I was within the mob.

"Excuse me," I shouted to the lads, and I weaved around, as they stood, petrol bombs in hand, like actors in a B movie waiting for the director to shout action. I reached the line of soldiers, standing with shields and Land Rovers blocking my way.

"Excuse me; can you move?" I shouted, and they parted their ranks for me to drive on through.

"You're fucking bonkers!" a soldier shouted in a cockney accent, and a few seconds later the bottles and bricks started flying.

In 2012, at a trade mission in Dubai, I met Martin McGuinness, an alleged former leader of the IRA, he was the Deputy First Minister in the government. He was with First Minister David Trimble, a former hard-line Orangeman. It was obvious they were great friends and cracked jokes together, but I didn't like it. Sure, we have to move on, forgive and forget, but I found their camaraderie sickening. I wanted to ask him if he'd bombed my dad's shop in 1977. But my wife persuaded me it wasn't the time or the place.

I felt my shy personality held me back. A lack of self- assurance can be a self-fulfilling prophecy. To make up, I socialized too much and studied too little. My parents lined me up to go into the family business. I could see my whole life unfold before me with a job, mortgage and old age.

I didn't know why I was going off. Was it to discover myself? Or just to test myself without the influences of my parents, family, and friends?

My dream was to ride to Australia, continue to America, and back home and circumnavigate the world. Did I want to meet new people, learn about different religions, and interesting cultures? Nope. I just wanted to get the Hell out of Belfast.

My maps promised me tarmac roads all the way to India. Burma was closed, so I would board a ship from India to Singapore, then to Indonesia and on to Oz. But with the oceans and politics, the concept of riding around the world was more an illusion.

It should take a couple of months to reach India, then another couple to ship to Australia, I reckoned. With £1,000, about £4,000 at 2019 prices, it would be enough for four months' travelling. I would stay with relatives in Brisbane, sell the bike and fly to America. If I left in September, I should get to Oz in time for their summer.

I tried to sell my soul and buy a BMW, but the Moto Guzzi didn't sell, so I converted it into a touring machine. Off came the sports fairing and low-slung clip-on handlebars. On went a touring screen, comfortable high handlebars, top box and panniers, adjustable rear air suspension, air filters, and a cassette tape music system with speakers on the tank bag. I felt terrible–it was like hitching a caravan on to a Ferrari.

I'd worked on my old BSA Bantam, but would have to learn motorcycle mechanics along the way to keep the bike going for the 10,000 miles to Australia.

What would I need for the trip? Camping gear and waterproofs and… a brown velvet jacket and cream trousers. "You need to look smart at Customs," Dad explained. I wondered what the Iranian immigration would make of this fashion faux pas, but the velvet suit made the packing list.

Then toiletries, my cameras and one book: Zen and the Art of Motorcycle Maintenance, along with maps of Asia, and a First Aid kit. The tools and spare parts were the next dilemma – where to start with these? Sod's Law meant that I wouldn't need the parts and the tools I'd brought, but would need the ones I'd left behind.

I packed a 6-inch divers' knife, which I would never use in a fight, but it would look frightening. Passport and documents were hidden in my money belt, along with my traveller's cheques.

Last, the cassette radio and amplifier: people would hear me before they saw me! Dire Straits, The Clash, The Stranglers, Pink Floyd, The Beach Boys, then Joe Cocker and David Bowie. The cassette tapes took up precious room but would prove indispensable for the long road ahead.

CHAPTER 2

Leaving Home

My departure day was a disaster, I was so disorganised and missed the ferry. The first part of riding to Australia was catching the boat to Liverpool, and I had failed miserably!

I went to my girlfriend's house to say goodbye one more time; we had agreed to split, so it was a confusing farewell. Then the doorbell went.

"I thought you left today!" Colin said. I always knew he fancied my Janet.

"Bugger off, slimeball," I said and slammed the door shut.

"Who was that?" said Janet.

"Some asshole; I told him to fuck off."

But I realised that time and attractive girls wait for no man. Tomorrow I was going, no matter what.

The next evening, as I punched the starter, my mum started crying, and her tears unnerved me. As a cocky twenty- one-year-old, full of invincibility, Mum's crying filled me with foreboding. What if the world outside was full of demons she had forgotten to warn me about? My excitement turned to apprehension; I wanted to shit a brick.

"Look after yourself, boy, and mind those bloody Arabs," warned my dad for the umpteenth time. He'd spent two years in Egypt during the war and had a healthy distrust of Johnnie foreigner, especially the Arabs.

"No worries, Dad!" I shouted back as I roared down the drive like Joey Dunlop, but there was so much weight I hit the hedge and had to stop at the end of the drive to turn to wave. Better to be a caring son than a bungling biker! My mum was still sobbing with her head buried in my dad's chest.

I made my way through the city, past Dad's shop, the Crown Bar, and the landmarks of my humdrum life. I watched the vacant faces of the commuters going home for dinner, blissfully unaware of the impending crisis in their midst, the overburdened bike and the overwhelmed brain.

The Liverpool ferry clanked and groaned in the inky black harbour, and the jaw-like doors devoured me as I drove through and overcame the first obstacle on the way to Australia.

As I disembarked the next morning, the emotion was finally behind me. The sun shone, and my confidence soared, for two hundred yards. The bike still handled like a demented supermarket trolley. My handlebars had worked loose; I hadn't tightened the bolts. Let's forget Sydney and see if I can get to London, I thought, trying to keep the front wheel on the road. I dumped the brown velvet suit in the first waste bin as I tried to lighten the load. Driving along the M1 was terrifying, as the huge juggernauts roared past. Ireland only had forty miles of motorway in 1979. Although I was off to drive around the world, I just hadn't expected quite so much traffic.

I found my Uncle's flat in Vauxhall where I could stay while I got my visas for Iran, Iraq and the countries on the road east.

I tried to get insurance at the AA head office. The young broker listened intently and called his boss.

"The AA will charge you £650.00 for a maximum claim of £1,200 if you die," he said, eventually.

"So, you're giving me less than a 50% chance of survival!"

"Personally, I wouldn't even give you that," he said.

"I'll take my chances on my own."

But I bought a Carnet de Passage, so I could drive the bike through the countries on the way to Australia. It was a legal guarantee that ensured I exported the bike out of the country and the AA could prosecute me if I didn't.

An old school friend, Alistair McKibbin, was studying medicine at St Mary's Hospital. We met up in his local pub in Paddington, with his friends.

"Where are you off to?" one said

"I'm on my way to Australia on a motorbike,"

"Why?"

"Why what?"

"What are you trying to prove?"

"I'm not trying to prove anything," I said defensively. I hadn't worked that one out myself yet.

One of the gang was a sexy physiotherapy student called Angela. She had a cute smile, a dimple on her chin and just what I needed to take my mind off the impending catastrophe.

She lived in a redbrick terraced house in Acton with five other students, and I ended up on the top of a London bus going home with them. Angela's mother was English and her father from Rio de Janeiro. She told me stories of South America and the Mardi Gras and lit another ember in my imagination.

I loved the buzz in London, the iconic sights and the famous places, so familiar from playing Monopoly. I didn't expect the city streets to be paved in gold but it was intoxicating to a wee boy from Belfast.

After calling at the various Embassies, and by the time I got my Iranian visa, it was the 4th of November 1979.

On Angela's TV that evening, a bloke with a big bushy beard shouted, "Death to America."

The American Embassy had been overrun and the entire staff taken hostage. Ayatollah Khomeini had started an Islamic Revolution. The Shah of Iran had been overthrown.

"Death to Western Imperialists!" chanted the students.

I knew Irish motorcyclists were probably in that category.

"Is it bad news?" Angela asked.

"Not bad, it's terrible!"

Angela read my Middle Eastern guidebook: "Iran is the most friendly and stable country in the Middle East."

"Not now it's not!"

The road east was closed as tight as a duck's arse. My plans lay in tatters.

"Stay in London," she said. "You can get a job. It'll be fun." Not what I had been planning for the last four years but very tempting, looking into her big brown Brazilian eyes. But I could imagine the slagging from my mates: I leave for Australia and get as far as London; I'd never hear the end of it!

The Iron Curtain shut Eastern Europe off and winter was closing in. The Middle East was at war and Iran was impassable. And Africa? The Guzzi wouldn't like dirt roads, let alone the desert.

I bought a map of Africa, with a dotted line across the desert, inscribed "road". It looked like my best choice: drive south to the Kenyan coast, hang a left, ship over to India and ride to Australia as planned.

"I'm going to Africa," I announced, as the third bottle of wine hit the bin.

The girls nodded at me with that understanding expression that you give your Granny when she says she wants to drive her Morris Minor to the moon.

"Of course you are, dear, now have another sherry."

Uncle Jim worked in the Foreign Office and was an expert on all things overseas. At the family dinner, he informed me I was insane, and they would never see me again.

"My boy, the Egyptians will steal the fillings from your teeth; there is no road across the Sahara. Sudan is at war with Eritrea, (where the fuck's that, I wondered?). Uganda is at war with Tanzania, the Kenya-Tanzania border is closed. Rhodesia is at war with Zambia and apartheid South Africa is cut off!" (I would have asked what apartheid was, but decided against it, as Jim was in full flow now.)

"The whole continent is a disaster," he roared. "West Africa has a coup every weekend."

"Ok, Ok, Thanks for your advice, Jim, but I'm going anyway," I said.

It couldn't be that bad – could it?

I left that evening; I felt London sucking me in and by the next morning, I might have changed my mind. The black tarmac ahead taunted me. Leaving Belfast was daunting, but this was worse, it was more real – and a shitty real. I was on my way to France, full of uncertainties. Before, I'd planned where to go. Now I had no bloody idea.

I sat on the car ferry with Uncle Jim's voice going through my mind. What if he was right? I had studied my Australia routes for years, with different options and family to stay with there. Now my Asian guidebooks lay in the bin. My act of bravado with Angela and Uncle Jim wouldn't work on myself; I realized that I was bull shitting. I didn't even know what they called the countries. I mean, 'The Sudan' sounded like a car!

I couldn't return to Belfast… I'd be a laughing stock. Go back, re-plan my route – or buy an off-road bike for Africa– and then leave in the spring.... Or London – stay with Angela! Two weeks away and I was talking to myself!

"Hi mate! How's it going?" A middle-aged trucker called Fred sat and told me his life story. His wife had left because he bored her, (I understood her point), but I was an avid listener and the rambling minutia took my thoughts away from my future. After three pints of Guinness, I drifted off to sleep. I could continue, or end up like Fred.

That was that! I was on my way.

In the immaculate war cemeteries that dotted the French countryside, white gravestones lined up like the rows of soldiers they were. Those young men were only eighteen when they left home looking for adventure, as I was doing, but got butchered in the mud of France and they now lay forever in this foreign field.

My grandfather fought in France but made it home. What twist of fate stopped him from ending up in this field? I jumped back on the bike and shivered, filled with foreboding, and continued south through the Forests of the Ardennes.

By that evening, I was near Germany and camped in a damp field. I needed to save money by sleeping rough. I had lost my tent pegs so used my spanners and screwdrivers. A blizzard tried to blow me away all night and by next morning I was suffering from 'biker man flu.'

I stayed in the tent the next day and night. It was miserable, with icicles on the bike and my nose, all alone in my soggy French field. I tried not to think of Angela and the "stay in London" option.

The sun in the Sahara had worried me, not frostbite in France.

Jim warned me that, once out of Europe, I would be an easy target for rogues. If I got mugged in Iraq, they would never see me again. I imagined my parents, with no word for months, phoning the British Consulate to find out where I may have been. Eventually, they would realize that I was dead in a hole somewhere.

God, I needed to get moving!

Every truck that came too close splashed torrents of freezing water at me as I tried to steady the bike in their wake. I dug deep into my reserves all the way to Austria and started climbing the foothills of the Alps; snow began to fall. The only way I could keep going was by calling in to the service station toilets, grabbing all the toilet rolls, then stripping. I wrapped my body, starting with my feet and legs. Roll seven covered my waist, and the next three were wound around my chest. I finished the sexy ensemble with Stretch and Seal and plastic bags wrapped around my feet, to try- in vain- to keep the water out.

"Danker Shun, Chum," I said to the newsagent, who was wondering why a non-German speaker wanted three copies of Die Welt newspaper. I stuffed them in my waterproofs, and he nodded.

They should keep me warm for another fifty miles, before the sleet found its way through again, always starting at my crotch. If I crashed, the doctors would wonder, as they stripped off my leathers, why an Egyptian mummy was riding through the blizzard. By the afternoon, the snow was lying, and the bike was sliding around like a drunken donkey. Then, as it got dark, a real snowstorm blew in. I nearly skidded off the road so I turned off at the next exit.

The road wound down the hill to a small Austrian village and I forgot any thoughts of camping, as the snow lay thick in the quaint but deserted streets. Then I stopped a big guy in a ski-suit as he walked out of a drive.

"Guesthouse?" I shouted.

He motioned "come with me" and I followed him to a large wooden chalet up a steep drive. I followed the big guy into the kitchen and found three generations of the family drinking Schnapps around the roaring log fire. The warmth of the room enveloped me and my glasses steamed up after the blizzard. Only their teenage daughter could speak English, and she gave me a glass as I took off my helmet.

"Do you have a room?" I asked, the Schnapps warming me as it slid down my throat.

"Ja," she said, "We have a room."

The daughter could speak English and introduced the family, Mum, Dad, Fredrick, daughter Louisa and Granny.

The conversation was stilted as Louisa interpreted.

"You stay until the storm passes," Fredrick said. As I stood up to take off my waterproofs; the toilet paper fell in a mess of papier mâché on the floor, and everyone collapsed laughing.

"Only a mad man rides a motorcycle in this weather!" Fredrick laughed, pouring me another Schnapps. My cheeks turned bright crimson with the warmth of the fire, the Schnapps and the wet paper nappy.

"Where are going?"

"To Australia," I replied, and it felt marvellous to say it. It was the first time I was actually travelling.

"I will come with you," Frederick said, slapping my back so hard he nearly took off my head. He looked like a lumberjack.

"No, take me!" Louisa said, which drew a frown from Dad. Louisa was about sixteen, very cute and clearly enamoured at having a wandering biker in the house.

She showed me to the room and gave me some dry clothes; then a dinner of rich beef stew and red wine. After camping in my soggy field, I was in heaven.

Next morning, I threw back the curtains to see the Alps in all their glory. The storm had passed, but the snow lay deep on the road, the mountains glistened across the valley in the sun, and the boughs of the trees hung heavy outside my window. It was stunning.

Louisa knocked on the door and came in with strong black coffee and toast.

"The roads are closed; you may be here for a week!" she said.

"I'm in no rush," I smiled back.

"Let's go skiing then!" she said. "It's the first week of the season and the lifts are just open."

Fredrick threw the skis in the pickup truck and drove us up to the chairlift. I hadn't planned on Dad coming too. Soon I was skiing down the nursery slope in my motorcycle leathers. I had only skied once before, and I flew out of control, ending up on my face in the snow. It was great therapy and took my mind off my worries from the journey.

The next day, Louisa was back at school, so I skied on my own. Motorcycles are not the ideal ski transport, but I converted the Guzzi into my snowmobile, with skis on my feet, one on each side of the bike, like stabilizers. I kicked her into second gear and made my way up the two miles to the chairlift. I parked beside the four-wheel-drive Mercedes with their fashionista ladies in their coordinated ski attire. Not for the last time, my fashion sense turned heads for the wrong reasons.

Over the next few days, I tried to master the art of skiing, and riding on ice, along with long walks with Louisa, under the ever-watchful eyes of Frederick. He showed me his furniture factory where he turned raw planks of oak into handmade antique wardrobes.

They welcomed me into the family like a long-lost relation. We spent evenings in the big kitchen in front of the wood fire talking about life in Ireland, Austria and oak furniture. We drank Schnapps, which warmed my heart while I looked out as the snow swirled round the yard. It was November, and the Alps lay across my path and it got colder as the days passed.

But I was on my way, finally, like a traveller rather than a tourist.

Louisa was four years younger than me, and I could see she was falling for my lone wolf biker character; I should go before she got hurt.

I rang my parents, who couldn't believe I was only in Austria after nearly a month.

"You should be halfway there, son. What are you doing?" my dad said.

"You need to hurry and come home to start work." I had only just left Ireland, and now they were trying to draw me back, to what? A job I didn't know if I wanted. But he was right. I should move on.

Frederick gave me a hug like a long-lost son.

"I hope you find what you are looking for, Chris." His words hit me like a West Belfast brick on the head.

"What am I looking for?" I said.

"You will know when you find it."

Shit! What was I looking for? Why did I set myself this ridiculous task, and why did I not just give up and stay longer? There was something driving me, if only I could recognize what.

The family refused any money for my stay.

"You will need it more than us," Fredrick said. This was my first experience of the special bond that travellers form with people they meet. The family provided hospitality and friendship, and in exchange, they received some tales of my adventure. And a bit of them rode off with me as I left. Louisa was heartbroken. Mum and Dad looked from the window as she helped me pack my panniers, with a tear in her eye. I blew her a kiss and rode away.

Something special happened to me in Austria. It was as if everything that had passed before in my life, my growing up, Belfast, my preparations, was all gone and in the past. The journey finally began.

I wonder if Louisa remembers the strange toilet-roll- wrapped biker who called that day?

But Austria didn't want to let me go yet, as another blizzard blew in as I followed the trucks again, with my feet sliding through the slush.

Soon, the road became too dangerous and, near the top of a pass, I pulled in behind some trucks. Soon a massive snowplough roared up the road behind me, the driver waving. A friendly guy, I thought, and I waved back, but as he thundered past, a bow wave tsunami of snow buried me.

Grabbing a handful of throttle, the bike punched a hole in the drift and lurched forward behind the snowplough and I was soon heading towards Yugoslavia.

The best thing about Yugoslavia was that Greece was at the other end. The concrete slabs on the roads didn't join, so it was like a speed bump every 5 seconds: bedump, bedump, bedump. They named this route to Greece the 'Road of Death.' It was quite normal to come over the brow of a hill and see three trucks abreast coming towards me, head-on, with another car overtaking on the hard shoulder.

I entered a tunnel; I turned on my lights and nothing happened, there was so much mud on the headlight lens. With the full beam from the oncoming trucks and a crazy driver trying to drive up my backside, all I could do was drive. Meanwhile, Mr Crazy blasted his horn inches from my back tyre. I was about to become road-kill.

I was too cold to camp, so I stopped in a half-finished roadside motel made of concrete breezeblocks. The receptionist was short and fat, spoke no English and looked at me with complete disdain for not speaking Yugoslavian. She started shouting as if this would help.

The room was bleak with a bare linoleum floor, an iron bedstead with threadbare sheets and a blanket made from coconut husks. I thought I was in jail. Dinner was grey soup and stale bread.

After two days of riding, I was tired of cold grey things and wanted to be in Greece where it was sunny with bright blue skies. I knew it was; I'd seen the postcards. And at the border the sun came out, the sky was blue and even the petrol pump attendants smiled. It was like turning a TV from a black and white to full Technicolor.

Finally, the bike handled better, and I now enjoyed doing what a Guzzi does best, blasting round fast bends on a silky flat road; I lapped it up.

Near Thessalonica, I spotted a motorcycle with a GB sticker, the rider bent over the back wheel. Jeff, a young Scottish guy, was on an overheating Suzuki Enduro 380.

"Where are you off too?" I asked.

"South; just glad to be out of that shithole Yugoslavia," he replied in a broad Scottish accent. It was a meeting of minds.

As we were both going to Athens, we travelled together. I'd had two days of nothing but grunts, so English sounded good, even the Scottish version. Jeff was the same age as me, untidy, mangled hair like me, and as clueless about where he was going. In two months, he started a new job in the UK and did Europe in the winter, on a bike, so he was also as stupid as me! His small Suzuki slowed me down, his engine constantly overheating. There was no rush, and the sun shone on me.

Jeff had lived in Athens when he was a kid, so he knew his way around town. We found a deserted campsite, with a resident pack of mangy dogs, who took it in turns to piss on our tents, even though some attractive piss worthy trees grew beside the tents.

One of his old family friends owned a restaurant, and we reckoned that his friends would be too polite not to offer us a free dinner if we just arrived at 7 pm. We parked the bikes with the big Mercedes and BMWs and sauntered into the top restaurant in Athens. The cunning plan worked; they insisted we stay for dinner.

Belfast was 2800 miles away. I'd had a momentous struggle to get here. Life tried everything to stop me, but now, I was just a boat ride from Africa.

Jeff's company was fantastic and annoying in equal measures. If I wanted to go somewhere, I now asked someone else's opinion. It was a real pain after being self-centred for so long. Jeff had a tendency to get everywhere as fast as possible, while I wanted to savour the sights and experiences. But my boxes' small locks could be easy to break, and I only tied the tent and sleeping bag on, so an extra pair of eyes was great.

When you travel by car, you watch the world go by through the window, which isolates you from the world. On the bike, you're in the world; you're part of it. You can appreciate the wind going past, smell the smells and, if you put your foot down, you can even touch the road zipping past below. When you stop, people come over to talk to you. Most guys love bikes; they have either owned one, or wanted one, so it's a great conversation starter.

And girls, well, they just can't help finding bikers attractive!

We spent our last night in Europe in a coffee bar trying to chat up some young Greek girls. They spoke no English, but motorcycles speak a universal language of their own, and we took the braver ones for a spin round the block. Innocent sexual energy flew round the table, fired up by the mystery and excitement of our stunted dialogue, our youth and exotic nationalities.

CHAPTER 3

Israel & Cyprus

I PLANNED TO TAKE A BOAT TO EGYPT AND FOLLOW THE NILE TO SUDAN, then take the train across the desert. Jeff said he'd come as far as Egypt, as his job started in the New Year. I wanted the endpoint in our partnership, because, while I enjoyed the comfort that company gave for a while, I would be on my own again.

We drove down to the Piraeus docks.

"Sorry," the ticket girl said. "Egypt boat broke."

"When fixed?" I replied in my perfected English-Greek.

"No now," she replied.

"No, know?" I asked.

"No go," she said.

"Very engine broke. You go Israel. It's beside Egypt –boat go, now!"

That was when I made my big mistake and said, "What do you think, Jeff?"

"Yeah, no problem! It's peace and love with Israel and Egypt, they signed a treaty. We can drive through Israel and mosey down into Egypt."

With that careful planning, we bought the cheapest tickets and drove straight on.

"If this is the best ship, I wonder what the broken one looks like!" I said. The car ferry had fifty years of rust and paint holding it together.

We had bought the "Deck class" tickets, which I thought meant we would sit in the lounge for the two-day voyage. But as the ship picked up speed, an obnoxious Greek purser, wearing a grubby white uniform with big shiny gold badges like medals, threw us out the back.

"Dick means dick, and you paid for dick," he explained. Dick was well and good while the sun shone and we watched the Greek coastline slip away. But then it started to rain. We huddled behind the funnel with a group of impoverished 'Dick class' travellers. Among them were George and Colin, two Irish guys wearing Guinness T-shirts and the same scrappy "travellers'" beards as ours. The scrappy beard was the badge of our common rebellious cause.

Colin said he was trying to help George get over his frontal lobotomy operation, and after a short discussion, I believed them. They planned to work on a kibbutz.

There was John and his girlfriend Alison from Wales. John claimed he was a "real" Hell's Angel. His scrawny beard was an unfortunate bright ginger tone and he said he was on the run from the cops. He wore dirty jeans and a waistcoat with no shirt, so as it was December and freezing, he was either really tough or really stupid.

They rode a Norton Commando, which he claimed was the best bike in the world. I used to have a Commando, and no, they hadn't been the best bikes in the world since about 1950. He claimed it did 140mph and pulled wheelies in third, and also claimed Alison was hot, which was also nonsense. Whatever drugs he was on were clearly mind-altering. Alison stared at John as if he was a Greek Adonis, and spent all her of time squeezing the spots on his chest.

John claimed he regularly bit the head off chickens, an easy claim to make on a boat with no chickens. "Why are you on the run?" I asked.

"Last summer I rode up to Bangor, Wales and took a dog for a walk."

"You got arrested taking a dog for a walk?"

"Well, I was on the motorbike, see, and this old geezer was walking his greyhound. I grabbed the lead on the way past and next moment I was doing seventy. The poor dog couldn't keep up… and greyhounds were supposed to be fast. After a mile, he looked more like a sausage dog!"

Alison was in stitches, although she must have heard the story a million times before. But the local constabulary didn't appreciate the funny side, and he had to get out of town.

After finishing our duty-free Ouzo in the rain, we mutinied and wanted to go below decks, but the doors were all locked.

"Only one thing for it, lads: jump," said John, and he disappeared over the side.

"Fuck, he's gone!" I ran over to find him shimmying down the railings on the side of the boat, onto the next deck.

"Easy!" he shouted.

It was easy, as we could climb down the rails like a ladder. But it would have been easier if the cold black Mediterranean Sea wasn't surging past thirty feet below. But luckily, the Ouzo provided all the prescribed intelligence and coordination that I needed.

A few minutes later, we were in the deserted first-class lounge, perfect for a kip on the sofas, until the security guards found us. We scattered in all directions. At the stern of the ship, I climbed back up sober. Not so easy this time!

John turned up an hour later with a black eye and a massive gash on his face. "What happened to you?" I asked.

"Well, I got cornered by the security guard and his Alsatian."

"Jesus, did he set the dog on you?"

"No, I bent to kiss the dog good night, and the fucking thing bit the face off me!" Doggy karma, I thought, as Alison dressed his wounds.

ISRAEL

The ship finally docked in balmy Haifa. My first time outside Europe, I was excited to get off. The Irish lads left for their kibbutz, and we were now three bikes, as John and Alison wanted to join us. I wasn't that keen, but he said they had a contact in a kibbutz, just south of the city.

John wore one of those old leather skullcaps with goggles that fighter pilots used to use. He looked ridiculous. "What a plonker," I said to Jeff, and he nodded as we drove away from the harbour.

We headed into the countryside, where John took off like a scalded dog-walker, after his bragging, determined to show he was the fastest rider. I wasn't having that and tucked in behind him. He was most upset when he couldn't shake the Guzzi off his tail as we weaved up Mount Carmel. When I noticed a few hundred yards of clear road ahead, I opened the throttle and overtook him, hitting 90mph! But at the next bend, he cut inside and nearly ran me off the road. I eased back and let him past, not wanting to end up in a hedge for the sake of some Welsh wanker. I had made my point and claimed the moral victory, although John was waving his fist in the air like he had won the TT.

We found the kibbutz in some dusty fields and parked up beside the farm trucks and tractors. There were some very solid concrete buildings that looked like they had been built to withstand a nuclear explosion, and some ancient Nissen-type huts with corrugated iron roofs. The land looked too parched for farming. One of the older kids showed us around; he liked our bikes and wanted to know all about them.

"You will now have a lecture about Israel," he said. Sounds like propaganda, I thought, as we were ushered down into a bomb shelter lecture room by two older men, who introduced themselves as concentration camp survivors. They explained that refugees from Russia had founded the kibbutz in 1939, and they still used the original Nissen huts of the camp but had built the new camp with bomb- and rocket- proof shelters after attacks from Syria.

The lecturer gave a blow-by-blow account of the conflicts, right up to the present day. Israel had agreed to normalise relations with Egypt – the first recognition of Israel by an Arab country. The Israeli forces were retreating from the Sinai. This seemed good news, as we should be able to drive to Cairo okay.

After the talk, we mingled with the kibbutz members. Some of them showed their German concentration camp numbers tattooed on their arms.

I wanted to stay and work for my bed and board for two weeks, and they seemed happy enough to have us.

Kibbutzim are run as a commune where everything is jointly owned. So, when three motorcyclists drive up and show the kids an alternative lifestyle outside the gates, it could cause alarm! The next day the committee decided we should leave, as the teenagers loved our bikes too much.

We made our way to Tel Aviv, and Jeff and I agreed that we needed to dump John and Alison. We couldn't listen to his bullshit anymore and I didn't want to be associated with him. As we entered the city, we let him roar off ahead then snuck off at the next junction. We never saw them again.

We stayed near the university and drove to the British Embassy, who told us the border with Egypt was still closed. They weren't quite ready for tourists yet.

To the north, landmines blocked Lebanon and Syria. There was a crossing into Jordan at Allenby Bridge, but it was closed. I was stuck again. Australia was further away than ever.

That evening, we drowned our sorrows near the university and chatted with the barman, Alex, who was studying law and wanted to improve his English. We were about the same age, but something about him made him more worldly-wise.

"Come stay with me. You can teach me English and I will show you round Israel," he offered.

Alex took us to his parent's apartment in Natanya, a small coastal town north of Tel Aviv. It had wide streets and modern apartment blocks. Twenty years ago, it was a sleepy Arab fishing village.

The first thing I noticed in Alex's room was a smashed guitar hanging on the wall.

"What's that all about?" I asked.

"It's my lucky guitar," he explained.

"It doesn't look that lucky to me!"

Alex joined the army when he was eighteen, and by twenty-one, he was a captain in charge of a mobile artillery regiment on the Golan Heights.

"Our guns fire a 155mm shell, forty kilometres," he said.

"A few years ago, during the war with Lebanon, I was off duty in the mess tent, telling jokes and singing songs with my men. I broke a string on the guitar, so I left to get a new one from my tent. I had just reached the door when a mortar landed on the mess tent. It broke my arm and my leg," he said, showing me some scars, "but it blew all my friends to pieces. If it hadn't been for that guitar string, I'd be dead too."

I stared at the mangled guitar in shocked silence and imagined what would have happened to someone playing it.

"I never got it; I should have been with them. I still play guitar, but I resigned my commission to study law," he said. "I want to study, not kill people. I want to learn to be a lawyer … and crack down on the drugs trade!" He smiled as he passed me the joint. "The border with Lebanon has miles of landmines but we still get the best Lebanese black hash," he laughed.

"Other soldiers go off to war, it's in our backyard; it's war for 365 days a year."

Alex's parents were elderly Polish Jews. The Germans had sent his mother's family to Auschwitz, his father's to Belsen – they were the only survivors. They met in a refugee camp in Cyprus and got married two weeks later, arriving in Israel during the Arab War in 1946. They were proud of the concentration camp tattoos on their arms. It was a status symbol, as it was because of their history that the State of Israel existed at all.

"Are you bitter for what the Germans did to you?" I asked his mum at breakfast.

"Yes," she said. "I know it is wrong to hate. Some of my friends forgive, but I can't." She was a frail little old Polish lady with her walking stick, but her face-hardened.

"Fucking bastards," she spat. "I'll never forgive them."

I was not used to hearing little old ladies swear, but then most little old ladies that I knew hadn't seen their families put in a gas chamber.

"When we came here from the concentration camps, we fought like tigers; we will never turn the other cheek as our Rabbis told us to do in Poland."

Alex said later, "They never speak of what happened in the concentration camps. Thirty-five years on it's still too painful to talk about. It will die with them," he said. "The new generation were not in concentration camps. We will learn from history, but we want peace. Lots of Jewish kids lose interest in religion, much to their parent's disgust. Our parents worry we will head to California and leave Israel to the Arabs."

"Will you do that?" I asked.

"Israel has fought for thirty years; there is no end to it." "You sound like an old man, Alex."

"We grow up quick in Israel."

The next day, we drove to Jerusalem, an important place for the Jewish, Muslim, and Christian religions. Jeff and I didn't give a shit. After a quick tour of the city and breakfast at a sweet-pastry café near the Wailing Wall, we made a decision.

"Let's ride to Jericho," I said, recognizing the name from my Sunday school days. And Jordan was only down the road. The landscape we rode through was barren. I wondered why anybody would fight over this place.

I thought the Bible stories were fairy stories. But as you travel through Israel, places like Jerusalem, Jericho, and Nazareth are real, with people living in them. It was as if I had wandered onto a Star Trek set and found out the Starship Enterprise existed! I put my boot down and "allegedly" touched the same path as Jesus had. But while he may have walked on water, he couldn't ride a Moto Guzzi.

Jesus spent forty days in the Judaea Desert. The forty minutes the ride through took was enough. The rocky screes and eroded hills followed us down to the Dead Sea. It was December and still cold, but now the sun came out as we passed below sea level. It looked like any other Sea, with white horses and waves rolling onto a sandy beach. But as we got closer, the white horses became dried lines of salt, and the beach was rock-hard salt, baked in the sun. The waters had receded as more of the Jordan River got used for irrigation. We drove onto the salt beach for a photo. I put my hand in.

"Yuk!" The water felt oily. "I'm not swimming in that!" We stopped in at a roadside café, lured in by two attractive girls sitting in the sunshine. Bergit and Ellen were from Sweden and hitchhiking to Eilat.

"That's amazing, we're going there too! Do you want a lift?" Jeff and I said, simultaneously bursting into fits of laughter. Giving a lift to two girls seemed much more exciting that the dusty walls of Jericho!

Eilat was on the Red Sea, about eighty miles away in the wrong direction. It would be a struggle on our overloaded bikes, but I shifted my gear to make room for the girls and their backpacks while arguing with Jeff who would get the prettiest one. I felt the bike groan in disgust. We were on Highway 90, the lowest road in the world, at four hundred metres below sea level. Little did I know that next year I would drive at four thousand metres above sea level, on one of the highest roads in the world. Flash floods had blocked the road south with sand and rocks, but we weaved past the traffic jams. Eventually, we came to a stretch of road, which the rains had washed away. A river was still roaring through the foundations.

"Wait for the water level to drop," the policeman at the roadblock said. Fine for everyone else, but we had Swedish girls to impress!

"Let's go for it," Jeff shouted. It didn't look too deep, although it would be easier on his Enduro bike. We plunged into the torrent of rushing water and with great splashes and clouds of steam; we surged out the other side to cheers from the onlookers. The girls were less impressed with our riding skills. They were terrified and got soaked on the back!

By the time we rode into Eilat, it was dark and Ellen offered to let us crash out in their rooms. We were getting somewhere and sauntered through the marble-floored reception and the manager took one look at us. "I don't care if you are with our guests, bikers are not coming in."

Bergit said their rooms were only on the first floor and we could climb up. I told the girls to flash the lights while we walked out the back.

"Shit, they are on the third floor," said Jeff, as the girl's room lights flickered. We found some ladders in a building site and climbed onto the second-floor balcony with them and then, using the drainpipes, we reached the third floor. Then it was a simple matter of shimmying across three balconies to their room. Easy!

The fact that we were in the middle of a major terrorist war zone, with armed soldiers patrolling the streets, should have dampened our passion at this stage. But it didn't. A couple were enjoying a romantic glass of wine on their balcony as we climbed over. "Excuse us, we're just going to see our girlfriends," I said.

"Good luck," he said with a smile. We made it to the girls' room for our just rewards, to discover that they were theology students on a biblical field trip. So, we passed the evening discussing Jesus and the Holy Land. Not quite what we had in mind!

The next morning, we worked our way along the balconies to make our way down to wolf whistles from the building site workers who, having seen the girls on the balcony, put two and two together.

After a few days on the beach, we rode back up to Jericho to cross the dismal river Jordan: it was little more than a stream. The Allenby Bridge was now the only road into Jordan. We got past the checkpoint at the Israeli end, but the Jordanians were having none of it and sent us back. The bridge was only for Arab pedestrians; they allowed no foreigners cross. "Those angels aren't coming to carry us over" sang Jeff, as we looked at the promised land on the other side of the river. We were running out of options.

On the way back to Jerusalem, we were stopped by army checkpoints at every town. This was the occupied West Bank.

"What the fuck are you doing here?" a cockney accent asked from behind a gun emplacement.

"Who are you?" I replied. "And where did you get that accent?"

"I'm Captain Lawrence, from the East End."

"Lawrence of Arabia?" Jeff and I said together, laughing.

"Hilarious," he said. "You shouldn't be here; it will be dark soon!"

Captain Lawrence said he had come out ten years ago on holiday and stayed.

"I love the frontier atmosphere," he said, "and I'm not even Jewish! I kind of feel I'm doing something here rather than just paying the mortgage in London."

We pitched our tent behind the guns and had a few beers with the soldiers, eighteen-year-old kids on military service. We showed off our bikes, and they showed us their M1 Carbines and their Willys Jeeps.

Israel was only thirty-two years old and had an air of optimism. The Arabs had attacked from the North, South and East, but they had survived, determined to build a homeland for the first time in 2,000 years. But earlier we had driven through an abandoned village off the main road. The houses were furnished but deserted, apart from some stray dogs. It was very spooky. Lawrence explained that, after the murder of some Jewish settlers, they had cleared the whole town. The residents were now refugees in Jordan.

"Don't go there," he said. "It may be booby-trapped."

"That's extreme, throwing out a village of innocent people because of something one guy did!" I said.

"This is a dirty war," replied Lawrence. "The law here works by retaliation. If an Arab attacks the State, his house will be bulldozed, and the family made homeless. And if the village hides a terrorist, we will demolish the town."

"Not exactly winning hearts and minds," I said.

"That's the way it works. That town will be a Jewish settlement soon."

"Anyway, you guys need to watch yourself. Palestinians don't like Israelis, and you look like Israelis. Nobody in the West Bank has motorbikes bigger than a 125cc, so you stick out like a big Jewish nose."

We stopped for breakfast in the next Palestinian town. But from the dirty looks the locals gave us, we weren't welcome, and we didn't hang around. Lawrence was right; only wealthy Israeli's would be on bikes like ours, and we were sitting ducks on our own.

I had one last chance to get through the Egyptian border; the Israelis were moving back, but with the Sinai Peninsula being a big area, it was taking time.

"Just because no one has tried to cross the border doesn't mean it can't be done," I said.

It was my last hope, it was worth a try, and Israel had been expensive. I had spent nearly £300 of my £1,000 and was still a long way from Australia. If I went back to Greece, I wouldn't be able to afford to continue.

The Egyptian border was a two-day drive, so we stopped in a small Arab town near Ashkelon to get some food. The main street was a dirt track, with a few corrugated iron shacks, and the air smelled of cow dung and human urine. Jeff nipped into a shop while I monitored the bikes.

Soon smiling children came over with their hands out; "Baksheesh," they asked, assuming we were rich–which we were, compared to them.

Soon bigger kids appeared, not so smiley and more aggressive, now demanding rather than asking. I caught a hand in my top box and banged the top closed. Then a kid touched my exhaust pipe and squealed as his hand imprinted on the hot metal. The crowd surged forward, shouting.

I pressed the horn to get Jeff out of the shop. Now there were about twenty teenagers and adults jostling me. Jeff jumped on his bike. "Let's get the flock out of here," I shouted – our favourite Holy Land wisecrack.

"Okay, Jesus." I kicked into gear, and plunged down an embankment, scattering the crowd, then veered onto the road. Jeff popped a great wheelie, and we sped off in a hail of stones.

We found a deserted beach ten miles on. We saw the lights of a settlement a few miles away and tried riding on the beach. But within a few minutes, we were both stuck, so we pitched our tents where we were.

"That was close; those guys were cross."

"The understatement of the year," I said, "but yeah."

I forced a laugh. What would have happened if we hadn't ridden away? We would have lost all our gear and the bikes. Who knows what they would have done to us?

It quite shook the two of us up but, being blokes, we were too macho to admit any fear – but we would have to be more careful.

Travelling with Jeff increased security, and we got on well, but we grated on each other's nerves. Jeff drove too fast while I liked to see more, and he had a habit of revving his engine as he rode past the frequent donkeys and carts. Donkeys would then jump into the middle of the road, as I came behind. Jeff thought this was hysterical! It pissed me off. But the big difference between us was he would go back to the UK soon while I had a longer-term plan.

The tents were damp in the morning, so we had a leisurely breakfast to let them dry. I noticed an army jeep heading our way. "Here comes John Wayne again!" I said. It was an Israeli Army patrol.

"What are you doing here? Do you know the Gaza Strip is just down the beach?" the commander demanded.

"Why? Are the bars worth going too?" said Jeff, thinking the Gaza Strip was some sort of Benidorm bar scene.

"No, it's a Palestinian city with 2 million angry refugees, and they would tear you apart if they found you here," he said, rolling his eyes.

"I think we met a few of them yesterday," Jeff replied. The young soldiers joined us for brew up, and we talked about Israel and Ireland. They were just kids really; they didn't know if the Egyptian border was open or not, but they pushed our bikes out of the sand, and soon we left on our different routes, and paths in life.

We continued south, passing kibbutzim with rectangular fields of fruit trees, stark green in the otherwise barren desert. The road was empty, apart from a few military vehicles and Bedouin camels. Then we were stopped at a roadblock by a bunch of well-armed soldiers.

"We want to go to Egypt," I said.

"You're already in it," one of them laughed. He was right; we had passed the old border marking some miles back. "This is a military restricted zone, and the road is closed."

"We have permission," I lied.

"Okay," he said and lifted the barrier as if to say, 'I don't give a shit'. We drove on, every mile closer to Cairo and further from Tel Aviv. The only people around were nomadic Bedouin wandering the desert with their goats and sheep, as they had for centuries. They ignored the borders, and the wars fought on around them; they had no land, no passports, and travelled to their pastures, whether in Israeli or Egyptian territory.

Soon we passed burnt-out tanks and trucks, scattered, half-buried in the sand. There had been a ferocious battle here and bullet holes pockmarked the ruined buildings; the place was a ghost town. It looked as if the soldiers had gone for lunch. I guess the Israelis didn't bother to clear it up, knowing they would hand it back. As boys, we were dying to jump into the burnt-out Egyptian tanks, but there were "Danger: Land Mines" signs, so we passed on the opportunity.

The military traffic ignored us, assuming that we had permission. The United Nations peacekeeping troops in their white helmets and blue uniforms gave us suspicious looks as they drove past. "The laundrymen," Alex had said the Israeli Army called them. "We leave them to clean up our mess!"

We talked our way through three more checkpoints and I started to get hopeful. The young soldiers were only interested in the bikes, forgetting to ask for papers, and then we reached a large sandbag wall. It was the end of the road and a hundred metres further on, there was a pole with an Egyptian flag on it. At the side was a dugout with machine guns pointing towards Egypt. A huge tank squatted with its engine running, the business end pointing towards Egypt.

An officer stuck his head out of the dugout. He looked at us in sheer disbelief.

"How the fuck did you get here?" he shouted. "Do you want to get shot?"

"Can we get to Egypt?" I said, trying to change the subject. He rolled his eyes.

"Get down here!" he ordered, glancing across no-man's- land. I was sure I saw Egyptian machine-gun muzzles following us as we climbed off the bikes. I felt like we were trying to cross the Somme on the first of July 1916.

The dugout was full of soldiers packing boxes and scurrying around. There was a heavy machine gun facing Egypt through a hole in the wall.

"I don't give a fuck where you go," he said, "but we move back another twenty miles tomorrow, so I don't need any aggravation. They won't let you into Egypt, anyway."

"If they let us in, will you let us out?" suggested Jeff, "You can ask them to let us through?" Unfortunately, he said it in a 'we're not interested in your stupid war so if you let us pass you can go on with your silly games' tone of voice.

The Captain smirked and picked up a red phone, which connected straight through to Egypt. He chatted in Arabic, throwing a couple of glances our way and grinning. Clearly, he was saying: "These wankers want to cross the border; do you want to shoot them or will I? How is your family? Okay? Good. Talk soon. Shalom." He put the phone down and shrugged.

"Sorry guys, he says he will shoot you. Now, fuck off back the way you came," he ordered. "And there is a curfew at dusk, so if you're not away, you'll be shot anyway."

"Power-crazy jerk," I murmured, quietly, to Jeff on the way out.

"Got a big tank, small cock."

"I think he's serious," Jeff said.

"Let's get the flock… you know… out of here!"

We acted as casual as possible under the circumstances and tried to keep some remnants of dignity, but sped back the way we came. It was depressing; the soldiers now had smug looks on their faces, or so I imagined.

That was that then; I was buggered, and it was my own stupid fault. The only way out was going back to Greece. "Silly bastard," I shouted inside my helmet. I would be back in Belfast for Christmas.

We had two days left before the boat sailed, so we took a ride to the Golan Heights. Alex bought me a harmonica, and we practised on the way. He would blow a tune at the back of my helmet, then pass the harmonica to me to play one-handed. We passed through the derelict customs post into Syria and stopped to take in the view.

"Don't step too far off the road," Alex warned. "Piss on the verge, there are landmines everywhere."

We drove up to his old unit, perched on top the heights. The tanks were dug in, their guns pointed towards Syria. Alex was a popular commander, and the guys all shook his hand, clearly pleased to see him. We were on Israel's northern front line, only an afternoon's drive from their homes in Tel Aviv. To the north, south and east lay their enemies, and to the west, the sea.

From the trenches, we saw abandoned villages and more minefields. Somewhere ahead over the scrubland was the Syrian front line, with similar young men facing back.

"There are some smashed World War Two Panzers there," Alex said. "The Syrians got them cheap, but they weren't too impressive by 1973."

The Golan Heights are made up of small hills, and whoever controlled them controlled thirty kilometres into Syria to the north, and thirty kilometres into Israel, back the way we came.

"We can't hand them back," said Alex. "Whoever owns the Heights owns Israel."

"You are handing back the Egyptian Sinai?" I said.

"That's different. We trust the Egyptians, but not the Syrians."

We made our way back to Netanya; it was on the far side of Israel but only a couple of hours drive. Depressed, I saw no way out of the conflict for these guys, and no way out of Israel for us.

On our last night, we went to see the movie Hair, with Alex and his friends. It's an anti-Vietnam War movie about a group of hippies befriending a country boy conscript and leading him astray. I asked the guys afterwards, "What did you think of the anti-war sentiment?"

"We are anti-war; we want to live in peace," they replied.

"The movie has Americans invading Vietnam; we are just protecting our homes," said another.

"The Palestinians may not agree," I said.

"This is our land now," Alex said.

"But what about the Arabs?"

"The Arabs attacked us and lost. If they had won, they would have killed us. Fuck them; the land is ours."

These guys were students and not hardliners, but they had no sympathy for the families who had their homes bulldozed. They were casualties of war, collateral damage. One guy was more direct, and I suppose more honest.

He said, "You can't come here with your European human rights when every Arab nation wants to drive us into the sea. What human rights do they give us? You expect us to be benevolent when they keep trying to kill us?"

The next day we bade our farewells and rode back to Haifa. It was the same boat that brought us here, and the crew were not particularly pleased to see us. But we were very subdued. Had it only been two weeks ago? I decided to get off in Cyprus when I heard there might be a boat to Egypt from there.

Jeff would go back to get some spares and said he would meet me in Cairo in ten days, but I knew he wouldn't. We had shared some crazy experiences, and after our adventures together, it was sad to see him go; we swapped addresses and phone numbers but we would never meet again.

It seems strange now; looking back that after spending so much time together we just went off on our way, with a 'see ya sometime.' We had an intense relationship in difficult situations, where we totally relied on each other, and then parted on our separate ways without looking back. Perhaps we knew that our friendship relied on the circumstances we had been in. That's the way it was with many travelling companions throughout the journey.

CYPRUS

On a desolate Cypriot tourist beach, the wind and rain tugged at my tent. I got up to secure it with stones, but the thunder and lightning kept me awake all night and I slept in, and then missed the last boat to Egypt – by an hour!

It would be another month before the next boat!

At a small café, I got chatting to the owner, Sergio, who had left his farm in Northern Cyprus during the Civil war, fifteen years ago. His wife had since died and his children left to work in a Greek restaurant in London. The British set up the refugee camp behind the café, for the Jewish refugees going to Israel, probably including Alex's parents. Now, the Nissen huts were full of northern Cypriots waiting to go home.

For me, my last choice was a boat to Latakia, in Syria, then drive through Damascus, down through Jordan, drive south to the Red Sea and then take a boat to Suez. I had come so far, that I was determined to make it.

But it was a high-risk strategy; the Israelis had warned me not to go to Syria. There was a civil war going on, but they wouldn't mess with a boy from Belfast, just passing through.

Would they?

CHAPTER 4

Syria & Jordan

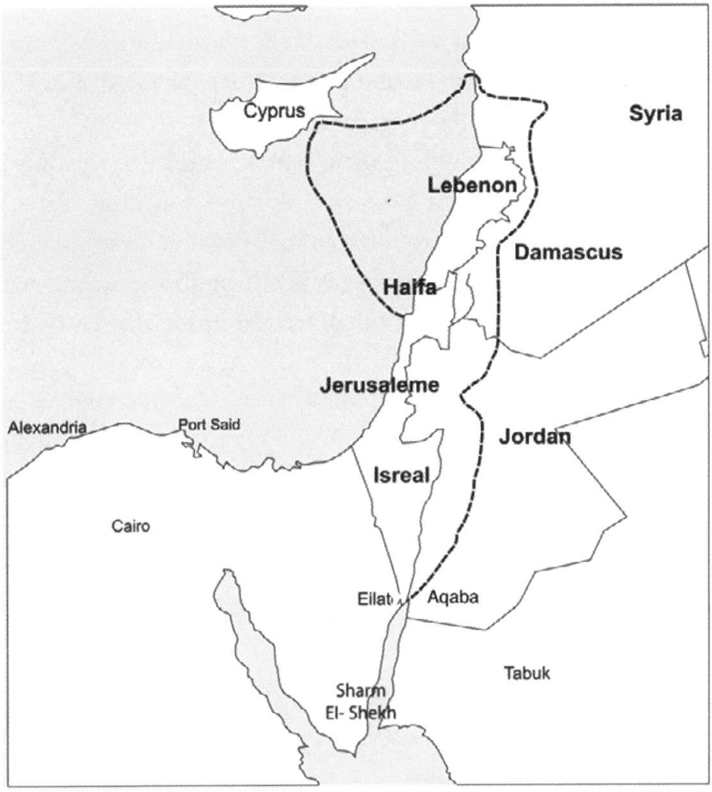

My tyres slipped on the wet steel of the loading ramp, as the wind and rain whipped around my screen to drag me into the Mediterranean Sea.

Car ferries have always attracted me. Our family holidays started with the car ferry and the smell of steel and heavy machinery, the diesel fumes and the massive steel doors closing brought back the excitement.

The Latakia ferry was like a shabby old tramp steamer with streaks of rust down the yellowing paintwork, and it smelled like a damp bonfire as if it had caught fire recently.

In fact, they had burnt three passengers to death a few weeks ago and the back of the ship was still black with soot.

They were repairing it as we sailed. Well, two painters attempted to cover the blackened steel with white paint, which blended with the soot into an ancient yellow, like the original finish.

The passengers were a rough-looking bunch, and I was the only Westerner. As the ship sailed into a gathering storm, I stayed near the Weetabix lifeboats, held together with fifty years of paint. The seas were choppy, and the boat creaked as it corkscrewed through the waves. Most of the passengers were throwing up, but I arrived in Latakia early the next morning.

The port can't have changed since the Crusader's time 1,000 years ago, with sandstone ramparts along the seafront. There was a half-sunken ship in the entrance to the harbour. The waves swept through the open windows and doors of the submerged superstructure.

Then the immigration officers boarded and set up tables in the smoky canteen, and the passengers lined up. I stood out like a vicar in a whorehouse in my black leathers amongst the Arabs in their white robes. When I handed over my passport, the officer looked at me like I'd passed him a piece of dog shit.

"You emigrate to Syria?"

"I don't, I just want to pass through."

"Why? Don't you like our country?"

"I'd really love to stay, but I'm in a bit of a rush," I said, smiling.

He was wearing a shabby black uniform, all shiny at the elbows, and he had a great big moustache. He must have filled his cigarette with some tar he had scraped off the road. It stank.

He spoke to the others in Arabic, and they knew, that I knew, that they were talking about me, and I didn't have a clue what they were saying, so they could intimidate me. It was working. If Jeff had been here, we would have pretended we weren't scared by whispering cocky remarks and laughing.

"I'm travelling to Egypt, through Syria and Jordan,"

I added in explanation.

"You go to Israel?"

"I go to Jordan," I repeated. But a lie detector needle would be off the chart. Armed guards sat with their feet up, trying to look tough, but their boots didn't have laces, which made me think at least I could outrun them.

"Why you have a motorcycle?"

"Why you want to go to Jordan?"

"Why you not get visa in London?"

I answered as best as I could between each new demand, but he was uninterested in my response.

"Wait over there," he barked.

I tried to act casual as I examined an imaginary spot on the back of my hand, while they processed all the Arab workers.

I reckoned they had already decided to shoot me and were just arguing about how to dispose of the body.

They seemed to think my story was implausible and, in their shoes, I would have had to agree with them. But they stamped a piece of paper, and they directed me to the Customs desk.

They stamped more forms, and I paid more fees and they finally told me to go.

Three guards blocked the exit gate. They wore a combination of civilian clothes and army uniforms; they looked like mercenaries and carried an assortment of weapons.

"Where is your spare wheel?" they demanded. "Every vehicle in Syria must have a spare wheel."

"What?" I stammered.

Their insistence on health and safety seemed a little silly, considering that Syria was in the middle of a civil war. There was more chance of getting my throat cut than getting a puncture. But eventually, they accepted that my spare inner tube would do and let me go.

I popped out of the port like a racehorse at the starting gate, and, I was on my way, with only two days to get to Aqaba for the last boat to Egypt!

It was the 16th of December 1979 and Syria was in the middle of a civil war. Radical Islamists were engaged in a tit for tat murder spree with government forces. Anyone was a target, and everyone was nervous.

Brought up in Belfast, we had our own civil war, so I was used to it.

I would put my head down and drive before they realised I was there.

No bother.

In Latakia, it was still 1940 and the main form of transport seemed to be the donkey. But old ex-British WW2 motorcycles burbled along in a remarkable state of preservation.

The main road to Homs was like a country lane, through pretty countryside and villages, rather than a main thoroughfare. They had built it when the biggest vehicle was a horse and cart; now juggernauts ripped up what was left of the tarmac.

In the villages, the petrol stations had manual hand pumps. The petrol was ancient too; the Guzzi spluttered to start after a fill-up.

It was like the west of Ireland with the odd Crusader castle thrown in. The Syrians didn't wear the Arab white dishdashas, and they looked more European. They wore old double-breasted pinstriped suits - a Brian Ferry look, but without the cool.

On the outskirts of Homs, when I stopped to ask two guys directions, they took out two submachine guns from under their jackets. Not quite the reaction a tourist expects when asking for directions!

"Police … Papers," they demanded.

I would have asked who they were but decided the machine guns gave them the authority they needed.

"You are Israeli?" one demanded, before spitting on the ground in my general direction.

'No," I assured them "I've never been there in my life."

"Where are you going?" they demanded, "You an Israeli spy?"

I wasn't too worried, as I had made sure not to get an Israeli stamp on my passport so I had nothing to hide. I unpacked all my bags, and they searched through them.

They saw my camera and started shouting! All spies have cameras, don't they?

"Ah, camera," they said as if it was as good as a signed confession.

"No, no, I'm a tourist," I said, pretending to take pictures of the landscape while smiling inanely.

"We will develop the film to check what you have been taking pictures of," the sidekick said.

That wiped the smile off my face. I had forgotten the pictures taken in Alex's army camp, his big guns pointing into Syria.

SHIT!

If they developed them, it was proof to anyone that I was a spy! They would shoot me!

One of Alex's comments flashed back.

"We don't mind the Egyptians or Jordanians, or even the Lebanese. But the Syrians we hate. They take no prisoners, so neither do we."

"But tourists take pictures of your beautiful country," I told him, smiling idiot-style again, but now shitting myself at the same time.

And smiling and shitting simultaneously was a new skill. I panned around my pretend camera, looking for a Crusader castle but finding the army camp across the road.

My interrogators were not impressed.

"I'll take your picture if you like," I suggested.

"No, not allowed," they said, although, they seemed to quite like the idea. A truckload of soldiers came and joined the action; the new guys shouted questions, again, trying to catch me out.

Either they wanted to be witnesses to me being shot, or maybe just beat me to death. I was panicking, as no one knew I was here. I hadn't told a soul I was in Syria. They could lock me up for years.

The officer barked.

"Go, keep your camera away. Go. Go!" I left before they changed their minds.

The roads were a nightmare, and the bike bounded from pothole to pothole, even when I slowed down. Old Russian Army trucks thundered by, inches from my shoulder. The road deteriorated until the surface had so many potholes, it was like a honeycomb, with small strips of tarmac between them.

The bike was shaking to bits, and I stopped to re-tighten bolts as they vibrated loose. Just as the road seemed to disintegrate, it turned sharp right and became a brand new four-lane motorway, starting from a field in the middle of nowhere! Surreal! Soon I was sitting at 80mph in the fast lane.

I spotted a donkey cart coming the wrong way in the fast lane, so I slowed a bit. Motorway regulations seemed to be fairly lax.

Every time I stopped for a break or petrol, a crowd of locals would gather, and a guy with a gun would appear as if from a crack in the pavement. And the interrogations started again, so I kept driving as long as I could.

"How do I know you are the police?" I asked one well- armed Brian Ferry.

He pointed at my luggage boxes with his gun. I didn't know if he was saying "My gun is my badge" or "I shoot your luggage if you're cheeky."

I opened the boxes, keeping the camera well hidden. Most didn't speak a word of English, which was more menacing, I just kept saying,

"Tourist…Ireland…Jordan…. Leave Syria…tonight… please" and they waved me on as if I was more trouble than I was worth.

What I didn't realize was that, as security had broken down in Syria, so each region now had its own independent militia to protect their local populations. They were as nervous of me as I was of them.

I had had enough of double-breasted suits and submachine guns, so kept going to the border. The contents of my camera were too damning!

By dusk, I reached Damascus, and I watched the sunset over the oldest inhabited city in the world. I had wanted to spend time here, but fear took precedence over curiosity, and I kept going.

The road climbed and deteriorated again as I approached the Jordanian border. The rain froze on my visor, my fingers were numb and I was nearly out of petrol.

The border post was deserted, so I drove straight through. The road deteriorated into a dirt track, and there were no streetlights or buildings; it was pitch black, and desolate; I was in no-man's-land.

Through the drizzle and mist, my headlight beam suddenly lit on two soldiers standing in the middle of the road wearing balaclavas and old-fashioned WW1 greatcoats. They were armed with sub-machine guns, of course.

Bloody hell! I slammed on the anchors to skid to a halt just in front of them, but they didn't flinch. Unshaven and gaunt, the taller one shouted at me then prodded me in the chest with his gun. I produced my passport and all the other papers I had.

He kept shouting and poking, but finally, I'd had enough machine guns for one day!

"So, what the fuck do you want?" I shouted back!

After a moment's silence, they burst out laughing and whacked each other on the back! I stood mesmerized, not knowing whether to laugh or cry, while the Guzzi burbled between my legs, trying to calm my nerves with its steady beat.

"I am sorry for my friend," the short one said, "He likes to make a joke with you!"

"Ha bloody ha," I said, too sarcastic for own my good.

"Most people bloody scared at his joke; you bloody brave," he laughed again.

"No, I bloody scared too."

"You go now, you bloody good sport," he said grinning, "We hope you have enjoyed our country."

"It's been a blast," I replied, and drove off.

"You guys are twisted," I shouted back when I was well out of hearing or range. It would be a while before I saw any funny side.

JORDAN

Two buildings appeared at the Jordanian border, and someone was locking up for the night.

"Hi, are you open?" I said.

"No, but I will stamp your passport."

The Customs officer introduced himself as Said. He was smiling, spoke excellent English, but above all, he didn't have a submachine gun.

"Come back and stay in my parent's house," he said, "you have dinner with my family."

After the day I'd had, I was as happy as a turkey in the summer.

Said was obese, and he hoisted up his immaculate white dishdasha up to his thighs and climbed onto the pillion. His fat legs stuck straight out each side, a comical sight, as we trundled down the dirt road to the village.

"Welcome," he said, proudly showing his independence from his parents, who lived in the house next door.

His "house" was a bare whitewashed room with a mattress on the concrete floor, and it had a Primus stove in the corner.

"Very nice," I said. Not quite the Hilton, but a roof for the night, and it was raining again.

We sat cross-legged on a rug on the floor and drank sweet black tea, ate some bread with a bean stew, and we discussed Middle East politics.

The Jordanian version of the war differed greatly from the Israeli one. The 'Arab invasion in 1967,' was now a 'War of Liberation.' There could be no attempt at peace; they must drive the Jews into the sea.

I could understand their point, as I had seen the abandoned Palestinian villages, and understood the hatred caused by the Israeli occupation of the West Bank.

But religious discussions are never won, as people never alter their opinion, and 99.99% of the time they just follow their family's religion and views.

"You are my guest, you must sleep in the bed," Said insisted. "I will sleep on the rug."

The bed was just a large straw mattress, and the floor was concrete, so I ungraciously accepted. After a rainy day on a motorcycle in a freezing cold wind, I was still shivering. But after a few minutes, Said climbed onto the mattress.

"It is too hard on the floor," he said, and I now felt uncomfortable. I gave him the benefit of the doubt, and it was a big mattress, but I was just dozing off into blissful sleep when I felt the hand on my thigh.

For fuck's sake! I thought and pushed his hand away. I don't need this shit after the day I've had!

"No Said, I am not interested," I said firmly. Homosexuality is illegal in Arabia and the men socialize together without women, who live in a different part of the house.

So, in a society without women, all sorts of things will go on.

It was common to see older men holding hands with young boys; in fact, in traditional areas, it's seen as a status symbol to have a "Bacha bazi" or boy for play.

So, while sex before marriage with women was out, they turned a blind eye to boys. And to be accused of sodomy, there must be four independent witnesses, so as long as you don't shag your boy in the middle of the High Street, you are okay.

I'd accepted hospitality from a Customs Officer, who was clearly after my body. And while it was comforting to know I still had my boyish charms and wasn't over the hill at 21, I was in no mood for this shit.

But Said wasn't taking no for an answer and thrust his hand forward again. I had had enough.

"Said, no means no, so piss off!" I shouted, grabbed my bag and opened the door to go.

Fuck! It was snowing! I don't believe it, I'm in the bloody Middle East and it's snowing. I'm caught between a blizzard and a hard-on!"

Shit, shit, shit.

Said followed me across the room; he was a big guy, over six feet tall, and he was getting annoyed, but so was I.

I eyed him up, not sure if I could take him on in a fight. "Maybe you like?" he said, "Nobody will know."

There was no response from my groin, only revulsion of this fat slob.

"I'm quite sure, now fuck off," I said and pushed him back. I threatened him with my clenched fist. He made a grab for my balls.

"I gave you dinner, what you give me?"

"You're not fucking me for a cup of tea and some beans," I shouted, pushing him back.

That sounded embarrassingly like he wasn't getting sex without paying for a proper dinner. 'Maybe if he had offered a glass of wine and a steak…!'

He backed off but kept eyeing me up and down and murmuring to himself.

Bugger it, I'm out of here and I walked out. The snow was swirling around the bike.

I brushed the snow off the seat and punched the starter. Click- click – click! Shit! The battery was flat.

Said was at the doorway, smiling in expectation, knowing I had to go back.

I pushed him back, closed the door and took my big sheath knife out.

"One step and I'll cut your balls off," I said.

Now, I'm not the sort of guy to knife anyone, but with Said, well, there's a first time for everything. But the big, shiny blade was enough to persuade him to keep his own weapon away.

Realising that he would not pull tonight, he was soon asleep on the mattress, while I sat against the door keeping one eye on him all night.

At first light, I crept outside; it had stopped snowing. I pushed the bike down the hill from the house before I bump- started the engine. I wanted to put some distance in before he woke up, in case he tried to report me.

My still-virgin bottom was blissfully back in the saddle. "Fucking homosexual border guards. Give me guys with submachine guns any day!" I shouted to myself, as usual, getting no response but the sound of the wind.

The road wound down through the ochre mountains, as the sun warmed my body. Soon there was golden desert sand each side of the road and my spirits lifted.

Just after Amman, I stopped for petrol, and four shifty- looking Arabs came over with the usual questions, where are you going, where are you from, but very pushy and aggressive.

"What's in the boxes?" one said, poking in my open top box.

"Nothing for you, mate," I said and snapped it shut. They went back to their van glancing at me. I didn't like their attitude and quickly left.

A few miles further on, I was at a T-junction when I suddenly heard an engine screaming. Glancing in my mirrors, I saw a white van approaching fast. I just swerved, shouting "Blind bastard!", but as he sped by, I caught the driver looking straight at me. He was trying to hit me! I skidded to a halt in the ditch, with the engine stalled, and I nearly fell over.

The van screeched to a halt twenty yards ahead, and the four Arabs from the petrol station jumped out and ran towards me. They didn't have daggers between their teeth, but they may as well have. I punched the starter, and gunned the engine, dumped the clutch and the bike charged forward, scattering them as I passed. I caught one of them in the crotch with my boot and I turned to see him buckling, but the others jumped back in the van to race after me.

"You have no chance," I said to myself and clicked down the gears, hitting 80, then 90mph. "Good to have a Le Mans still!"

That was the second time I had nearly been "rear-ended" this morning.

I could see the ferry sitting in the docks as I approached Aqaba, and I was ecstatic. I had made it!

Eilat and Aqaba are just two miles apart, but I had travelled over one thousand miles to get from one to the other.

I could see the Israeli border post in between, where only two weeks ago, I had been drinking beer with two Swedish girls!

CHAPTER 5

Egypt

THE FERRY SAILED AROUND THE LOW DESERT HILLS OF THE SINAI PENINSULA, and hung a right and travelled up a very blue Red Sea to the port of Suez. The boat was a big improvement on the Syrian one, if only because no one had burnt to death on it; but it was still a rust bucket.

Hundreds of migrant workers walked around with huge ghetto blasters on their shoulders. Arabic rock music is a serious assault on the eardrums, but this cacophony of sound could drive a man insane.

The only other Europeans on the boat were four Dutch hippies. They were driving their minibus to Kenya, taking a boat to India, then on to Australia. After the stress of the last few days, it was nice to talk to someone who thought my route to Australia was possible. It was also nice to meet someone who wasn't trying to shoot me, shag me or drive up my ass.

The ferry docked with the usual bedlam of tugboats and shouting required to get a ship berthed.

I started my engine, but as the bow doors opened, a wave of humanity surged up the ramp. The new passengers charged on before the old ones had disembarked. It was chaos! With horns blaring, I tucked in close behind the Dutch minivan and pushed through the throng.

In the huge corrugated-iron Customs shed, hundreds of passengers emptied their bags of pots and pans, radios and roasted pigeons onto the tables. Chickens were running around with small children chasing after them. Some people stood shouting their heads off for no particular reason. Behind each table sat three uniformed Customs officers, two of them drinking tea, while the third stamped pieces of paper with great enthusiasm. There was a fee for every form. First, the disembarkation form, landing form, an arrival form, immigration form and so on… The whole thing was a big scam.

But none had a submachine gun, and while it was a rip- off, it was quite jolly, as the Egyptians ripped us off with a big smile.

"You will pay," the grinning officials replied to my protestations. I assumed this to mean: 'You have more money than us, so give us your cash.'

"You buy Egyptian number plates," one guy insisted handing me a metre-wide huge cast iron plate.

"Too big!"

"OK, but you pay anyway."

At 5.00 pm, suddenly, the officials got up to leave. "Tonight, you can sleep here,"the Customs boss announced, pointing to the dockside as if doing us a tremendous favour.

We parked beside the silent dock cranes and creaking mooring lines. The Dutch Renault campervan had pictures of Bambi, Peter Pan and a map of the world painted on the side.

On top sat a wooden platform for a two-man tent.

Pete, his girlfriend Eve, and their friends Bent and Freddie had all gone to college together.

We listened to my David Bowie, smoked some hash that the police had sold us, and drank warm Egyptian beer.

Back in the Customs Hall next morning, the Egyptians continued their redistribution of wealth policy, with more forms. It was hot, and tempers were getting frayed; this time the officials got up to leave for lunch.

"Enough!" Pete parked the campervan across the door and blocked the way out.

"You finish our papers," he ordered. "And we are not paying another penny."

They realized that their scam was over, and with one last stamp, they took the whole bundle of forms and dumped them in a bin.

"You can go," they said, having the last laugh. Exasperated, we finally drove through the gates and we set off for Cairo, one hundred miles away. It was like getting out of jail, and great to have the wind in my face, to be free and riding again.

In Africa!

The petrol station made me even happier, it only cost ten pence a gallon. (In the UK it had cost £1.25 a gallon). Maybe I would like it here.

The two-lane road to Cairo was deserted.

"Are you hungry?" Eve shouted out the side window of the van as we drove.

"Yes, starving!"

I passed my helmet through the window and Eve handed me a sandwich which I devoured as the slipstream tugged at the cheese.

Twenty miles from Cairo, the traffic backed up, a mass of old Chevrolets, buses, donkeys and carts, horns blaring, with the overpowering odour of diesel and donkey dung.

The Egyptians have had no driving lessons since the Pharaohs were in town, and dents covered every car. Some Egyptians had a secret passion for stock car racing, and others the dodgems. Passengers travelled on the roof of the buses or hung out the windows. I kept behind the minivan to get some protection, but suddenly the bike shunted forward, rear-ended by the car behind. An old man in an even more ancient Austin smiled and waved his hand at me to usher me forward; he had pushed me forward to keep the traffic moving!

It was getting dark, and we had nowhere to stay.

"Go to the Pyramids," Freddie suggested. "Sounds like a good idea."

Being a cultural philistine, the Pyramids were the only Egyptian thing I knew. They were south of the city in Giza, and we reckoned that the biggest tourist attraction in the world would have a campsite nearby.

It was dark and deserted but the gates were open, so we snuck in and followed the track and found ourselves in the shadow of an ominous wall of stone blocks.

"This must be it," someone said, as we peered into the inky blackness. "Let's camp here."

My tent pegs wouldn't go into the 4000-year-old sandstone, so I improvised and tied the front corner of the small tent to my handlebar, then strung the back corner to my rear indicator, and pushed my luggage inside to the four corners of the tent to hold the shape out. Voila! - a motorcycle- framed tent, with the added advantage that no one could try to steal my bike without me noticing!

But the ground was as hard as an iron boat deck, with a few marbles thrown in.

The boy from Belfast had finally made it to Cairo. I drifted off to sleep with a surge of satisfaction. I wondered if it always took a hard struggle to achieve something meaningful. The next morning, the African sunlight hit my tent, and the temperature rocketed from zero to 30 degrees in seconds. I opened the zipper.

"Jesus H. Christ!" I shouted.

Twenty feet away was the Great Pyramid of Cheops. A wa
mous blocks towered 500 feet above, and 750 feet along from

And a few hundred yards away, the Sphinx sat in silent vigil, its crumbling body in stark contrast with the hardness of its stare.

"Who put that there?" said Freddie.

"I'm not sure we should be here!" I said. It was like camping in the front garden of Buckingham Palace.

"This has got to be the most exclusive campsite in the world," announced Pete.

Eve made tea while we ate breakfast of flatbread and feta cheese, as Bent read from his guidebook.

"The Pyramids were the tallest buildings in the world for three thousand eight hundred years," he began, "and made of two million blocks, each weighing two-and-a-half tons."

We sat in silence, taking it all in.

A policeman came over and asked Freddy who gave us permission to camp.

"Mohammed Ali," said Freddie.

"Who is he?" said the Policeman.

"Oh, he is the greatest," said Freddie giving him a few more Piasters, and he walked away.

I'm not sure how we did it, but we stayed there for a week without being moved on.

That evening, I rode to the Sphinx and the other pyramids. It was eerie and magical; my twenty-one years of age were totally insignificant amongst these buildings that had been there for eternity.

Some thirty years later, I revisited the Pyramids, along with thousands of Chinese tourists and their selfie-sticks. They parked dozens of coaches up our lane, and tacky souvenir shops lined the place; it was like ancient culture meets Disneyland. I walked past our old campsite; still expecting to see my oil stains from the bike.

My clutch was sticking, and I dismantled it where, 4000 years ago, the Pharaoh's charioteers had greased their axles. It looked simple. I had to unbolt and remove the back wheel, the rear suspension and swinging arm assembly. Next, the battery and the carburettors would come off, which would give me access to the gearbox. The gearbox would slide off the back of the engine, to let me clean the clutch plates. But, after an hour's work, I suddenly came over dizzy, and dropped a carburettor, breaking the petrol inlet connector.

SHIT! It was a vital piece, and the engine wouldn't run without it.

But I made one by glueing a plastic Bic pen top onto the carburettor, but only a trial run would tell if it would work. Suddenly, a massive stomach cramp hit me and I knew I had to squat quickly as something terrible would happen. I sprinted to the nearest excavation, which was a tomb of some King, with an armed policeman guarding the entrance.

"Stop!" he shouted,

Neither wild horses nor a Pharaoh's curse could have stopped me; I had my pants halfway down as I jumped into the hole.

The copper stuck his head over the edge just as my bottom erupted like a small thermonuclear explosion, nearly blowing a hole in the ground.

"Allah Akbar," he exclaimed and made a tactical withdrawal.

I sat shivering and sweating.

"Dysentery," Eve announced, as my bowels performed somersaults, and I vomited as my temperature shot up to 105 degrees. One minute my arms were so heavy I couldn't move, next so light I floated around the tent in a cloud. I hallucinated that I was being chased down the road by trees with branches for arms and roots for legs.

I slept on top of the camper, but I had to climb down the ladder to go to my toilet tomb, slipped, and landed on my back with a groan; with my shorts still around my ankles.

Freddy heard the noise and came round to check. "Are you okay?" he asked.

I must have broken my back and was about to give birth to an alien, vomiting and shitting myself at the same moment.

"I'm bloody fantastic, mate, just fantastic," I groaned. As I recovered, the guys started running bets on how long it would take for me to shit out whatever Eve was feeding me.

"Twelve minutes from eating to shitting!" shouted Freddie, "That's about a metre a minute. Or at sixty metres an hour…" as he worked out the average length of intestines.

"It must be a new world intestine speed record!"

I laughed and cried at the same time. It took two days for the fever to burn out enough for me to put the bike back together.

The Dutch were now my best friends in the world. Pete and Eve were like the mum and dad of the outfit, with Bent the practical eldest son and young Freddie, the joker.

They would drive off sightseeing in Cairo as I convalesced, with Eve monitoring my movements. In the evenings, we sat and talked about life, the universe and our travels.

I told them about Said, the Customs Officer in Jordan, and they had their own tale of sexual deviation.

They had met a respectable middle-class family in Jordan who invited them to stay over. The family, which included three generations, lived together. They enjoyed a traditional dinner, with the conversation on various Western and Arab topics. They gave them the guest room, but after they retired to bed, there was a knock at the door. Freddie answered and found the four brothers standing in a line. They wanted to know if the guys had finished fucking Eve yet!

Freddie tried to explain that it was not like that; Eve was in a relationship with Pete, and the others were just friends. But the brothers started getting annoyed.

"It is our right to fuck her," They insisted. "A woman sleeping in the same room as three men is a whore."

Freddie and Bent closed the door, while Pete and Eve escaped out the window and drove to the police station.

The brothers broke the door down and beat up Bent and Freddie, then threw them onto the street where they made their way to the police station on foot.

But the police were not very helpful, as the family had reported them and wanted them arrested. Eve had broken the law by sleeping with a man when she was single.

"They tried to rape Eve!" they complained.

"Any man would do the same!" the sergeant said. "She is a slut."

The police let them go with a caution, and they drove out of Jordan as quickly as they could.

"They have different moral codes," Pete said in that empathetic way, that only the Dutch could have.

"It was just a clash of civilizations," said Bent.

"That's civilization," I said, 'trying to rape your dinner guest!"

One problem with camping by the pyramid was that tourists wanted their photograph taken with us as if we were part of the attraction. To this day, pictures of me fixing my bike in front of the Great Pyramid adorn hundreds of mantelpieces in Japan.

It was a privilege to camp there. Tourists came and took photographs and returned to their Western hotels, but I was living the experience; not just the sights, but also the local people. Once the Arabs knew we were not rich tourists, they gave us some respect and became friends, so I got to know the local culture and the ancient monuments.

The camel drivers would come over for coffee, fascinated by my bike. I took them for rides around the pyramids, in exchange for a ride on the camels. Freddy learnt how to beg with the local kids. It was funny to see the tourists' confusion when a bunch of scrawny Egyptian kids and a fair-haired Dutchman asked them for 'baksheesh.' The kids loved it as their turnover shot up. Even the police smiled and left us alone.

On Christmas Eve, the Dutch left for Aswan. We had known each other for a week but I was emotionally empty after they left. They took the tourists back to their hotels that Christmas evening, and I had the place to myself, with some Egyptian brandy, beside the oldest buildings in the world. The stars were out, and the moonlight bathed the Pyramids. That night, the ghosts of the Pharaohs swirled around my tent.

On Christmas Day I phoned home. I needed to tell them where I was going, in case I disappeared.

The Main Post Office was built back in colonial times with marble floors, mahogany panelling and solid doors to keep the great unwashed out. The antiquated Egyptian phone exchange had wires plugged into holes in a mahogany panel. I sat in a wooden phone booth and waited… I was eventually connected.

"Hello, Mum," I said, "Happy Christmas."

"Where are you? When will you be home?" she shouted.

"I'm in Egypt," I said. I could hear the family having Christmas dinner. Suddenly, I was alone and homesick and two thousand miles away. I longed to be at the party. It was my first Christmas away.

"Where are you going now?" Mum still shouted although I could hear her like she was across the hall.

"South somewhere… maybe Kenya," I replied

"Kenya? Why are you going there, for God's sake?" my dad chipped in.

"I don't know. I'll tell you when I get there," I said, getting annoyed at this questioning of my plans (or lack of them). But for my middle-aged parents, travelling without a destination was incomprehensible.

"Why don't you come back home and start work? Enough of this messing about!" Dad barked down the line. In a flash, I was just a wee boy again, being told off by my parents, instead of a seasoned world traveller.

The five minutes seemed like five seconds; suddenly the operator pulled the plug, mid-sentence. My Christmas treat was finished! I sat dejected in the dark cubicle, staring at the inert black Bakelite phone. Half of me longed for the normality of the Christmas party at home, back with the security of my friends, and my family. My other half was annoyed at my vulnerability. As I fought with my emotions, the next customer banged on the glass door. I stormed out, nearly knocking him off his feet.

Rather than give peace of mind, the phone call created confusion. I had left to discover myself, get away from my parents and their control and all the call had done was pull me back to being their wee, quiet boy. Irish mothers didn't like their sons to grow up and leave home. They don't want to lose the emotion of being a mother. Irish fathers did very little fathering; they worked all week and played golf at the weekends. And if the kids were still up when he got back from the nineteenth hole, that was a bonus. It was the way parents were, back in those days.

But I was my own man now! I didn't need anyone! 'Grow a set,' I thought. What had annoyed me was that no one was interested in my travels; all they wanted to know was when I would be back, to fit into their life plan, not mine. I strode back outside into the wall of noise and chaos of Cairo and two shoeless kids came running over.

"Backsheesh, give me money!" they demanded, pushing their grubby hands in my face.

'Bugger off, why don't you," I swore at them, as they turned to shuffle off, heads down. I was in no mood for beggars, but suddenly I was Scrooge, killing the spirit of Christmas.

"Hey guys, take this," I shouted after them, handing them a bunch of coins.

"Happy Christmas," I said.

"Shukran!" they shouted and ran off with the loot. Hell, it worked! It made me feel better.

'Fuck them all, I can do this,' I thought, 'Let's just take it a day at a time.'

I resolved not to phone home again, as my reality was Egypt and I was heading further from home every day. There was no point of thinking back; I had to concentrate on the task ahead. It would be many months and miles before my parents would hear from me again.

Victorian explorers didn't receive any news from home for months. A hundred years ago, when Stanley found Livingstone in the middle of Africa, he had been out of contact for six years.

I would be one of the last generations of travellers to be alone in this way. Now with the iPhone, email, and Facebook, it is impossible to be without contact. Travellers are never alone now. That isolation has gone forever.

I had to find some brake pads and Khalid, one of my camel guys, said he would take me to his cousin who would make them for me. He jumped on the back and directed me through the back streets of Cairo. It was like entering a labyrinth.

Cairo pulverizes the senses like a pneumatic hammer. It's a city designed for two million but inhabited by about twenty million. The peasant population of Egypt was moving in, and the town expanding by building shacks on top of shacks. People were crammed into rickety hovels everywhere. It was hell on earth as far as town planning was concerned.

Human sewage ran in the gutters along with the horse and camel shit. Drinking water was from a tap at the end of the street or delivered by a horse and cart. Cairo had reverted to the middle ages.

The streets were only wide enough for a motorcycle or donkey, while the upper storeys hung over the alleys. There were rats the size of cats, and as brazen. Children ran naked in the sewage, and mangy dogs snarled at us as we wound our way through the maze.

The workshop was just a shed with old bits of engines lying about. I was unimpressed.

"Welcome," his cousin said as he looked at my old brake pads. A crowd of children stood looking in. I felt like the Queen doing a state visit. The nearest thing he had to Guzzi brake pads were some half-worn ones from an Opel Cadet; he clamped them into his lathe, and in minutes he had them cut down to the perfect size, and all for a few pennies. In Egypt, they threw nothing out when it could be useful again.

On the third floor, Khalid's fifty-second cousin had a carpet factory. I climbed the rickety stairs past dark landings with old women sitting around smoking pipes. The Dickensian factory had a dozen wooden frames leaning against the walls. Strung inside the frame was the weft of the rugs, and on the floor sat dozens of six or seven-year-old children, cross- legged, tying the knots in the woollen threads. There was an old picture torn from a magazine of a completed rug for them to use as a pattern for the new carpet.

When I entered, they glanced at me, before the boss shouted at them to go back to work. This child slave labour shocked me.

"Why do you use children for this?" I asked.

"Their fingers must be nimble; children make the best rugs with the finest threads," he said, showing me a completed rug. It was exquisite.

"This is wrong; kids should be out playing." The dilemma of this hit me. Would these kids be better playing in the shit in the street?

"If they do not work, their families will starve," the owner said. "In a few years, their fingers are too slow, so this is best."

His logic was hard to argue with, especially in this city. But this was still slave labour; the twist to the story was that they would sell the finished rug to Western tourists to take home. Westerners wouldn't put up with child labour in their own countries but have no qualms in taking advantage of the cheap goods. You sit in your cheap clothes made in Bangladesh sweatshops, on a chair from China, drinking coffee from Brazil without a qualm.

"You will buy a rug?"

"Sorry mate, I live on a motorcycle," and I hurried away.

It was Boxing Day, and I'd had enough of the gagging pollution and poverty of Cairo, so I followed the Nile south into the open countryside. It doesn't rain much in Egypt, and for millennia all the life-giving water had come from the mighty Nile. This was some of the most fertile lands in the world, washed over with the soils of Ethiopia as the floodwaters made their way to the sea. I drove along the highway, which seemed to act as the frontier between two great forces of fire and water, the golden desert sands on one side, in stark contrast to the verdant green of the fields on the other.

I stopped for a brew and took out my gas stove. I'd lost my matches, so I lit the stove from the spark plug lead, wondering if it was a good idea to light a naked flame beside my petrol tank.

Palm trees lined the river, and an old paddleboat lay, rusting and overgrown with creepers spreading over it like a fungus. It would never sail again. A large wooden felucca drifted past so slowly it hardly moved, its triangular sails hanging lifeless in the air on the 'A' frame mast. It was shipping sacks of grain to the city. Life would go on; women washed clothes while the kids played and swam, and I could hear the slow thump of an old diesel pumping the water to irrigate the fields. In contrast to Cairo's pollution, the river was a breath of fresh air.

A breeze blew sand across the road, just enough to show the desert's presence. It lay in the road like spindrift waves and made small dunes edging out onto the road. I loved it. This was the Egypt I had come to see. It was great to be back on the road, and I could finally relax a bit; life felt good as I basked in the morning sun.

For the first time, I enjoyed not knowing where I was going. To travel is always about going somewhere, for a purpose, but now I was just travelling, just for the sake of it. What a strange feeling of contentment, I thought, staring at the felucca as it moved an inch further. I was alone in a foreign land in total control of my own destiny, with no one else to consider when deciding what I wanted to do. It was a defining moment for me.

In Europe, there was the uncertainty of where to go. Once in Israel, I had just needed to get out, and Syria and Jordan were nuts. Cairo had been chaotic, and I had been ill, but now, finally, I was at peace with the journey, and myself.

In the field, a young couple cleared irrigation trenches, so that water would reach every inch. They worked with old wooden hoes to move the mud, as the ancient Egyptians would have done. The young farmer was wearing a dirty galabia, the loose-fitting white robe that Arabs wear. The girl was wearing a once-spectacular pink chiffon evening gown, cut off at the knees, from some charity shop. It hadn't seen a dance for many years. Her face was beautiful with big soft brown eyes and high cheekbones.

As I packed up, my eyes caught hers, and we smiled at each other. I waved, and she waved back.

"As-salamu alaykum," I said, in my pidgin Arabic.

"Wa alaykumu salam," she replied, smiling again.

I wondered at the dismal poverty of their simple life, as they started working again. I must have looked like an alien creature from outer space in my leathers and big red motorcycle. Our lives were so different, just crossing for an instant but both enjoying the moment; we moved on in our own directions again.

I wonder if she still remembers me.

As I drove along, it was like I'd been here before, with the desert, palm trees, flat roof, square mud-brick houses, donkeys and carts, camels and Jesus-like bearded Arabs. I've seen this scene in pictures in Sunday school; it was unchanged for thousands of years.

I continued for about 200 miles down the bumpy tarmac road, then I turned off the road at the Temple of Karnak. The principal temple in Egypt, and four thousand years old, I deemed it worthy of my attention, as I was a bit of a heathen with antiquities. The site was closed, but I snuck in.

It was just me, and the Gods. This temple sat, magnificent in its silent splendour. I wondered what the now redundant Gods, such as Zeus, thought of the newer, sexier versions like Jesus and Co?

Could there be a 'Gods retirement village,' where they sat in orthopaedic Parker Knoll chairs, watching gardening programmes and looking down at the Gods of Money that now rule the Western world?

In Egypt, where someone always wants to make a buck, a teenager suddenly appeared from the ruins, trying to sell me 'genuine' artefacts.

"You buy ancient Egyptian money?" As he checked over his shoulder, he produced a bag of corroded coins.

I rubbed the grime off; I could see it was a 1972 French centime.

"God loves a trier," I said, handing it back. Charcoal of the fires from a village nearby drifted over the statues, now bathed in the pale evening sunshine.

I needed to set up camp before dark.

Cairo driving was terrible, but in the open country, it was ridiculous. It was late and the road was empty when out of the darkness, a truck suddenly blasted on his lights at full beam! Dazzled, I swerved into the ditch as he passed tooting his horn and waving gaily out the window.

An old steam locomotive crept across a level crossing, like an exhausted dragon. Wagons were loaded high with sugar cane, and a dozen dirty workers with machetes over their shoulders followed. Two guys ran over to shake my hand, and they grinned as they walked around the bike touching it in amazement.

"Come, smoke hashish," one said and produced the biggest bag of marijuana I had ever seen. For some odd reason, it seemed safe enough to go with them, so I had soon set up my tent in their compound.

They produced cornhusks, which we roasted on the charcoal fire and sat drinking sweet Arab tea. They produced a homemade hookah water pipe; we smoked hash and honey- scented homemade shishas into the night.

"Why do the trucks drive without lights in the dark?" I asked.

"Oh, that is to save petrol," they said.

Well, they didn't actually say that, as no-one could speak English. But after an hour of me pretending to be a truck driver, sign language, drawing lines on the earth, and an Egyptian charade, that was the message communicated to me! It was great entertainment.

Yes, it's great to be going nowhere, I thought, as I drifted off to sleep.

After three days drive, I reached the city of Aswan, on the southern border. The town was full of mud-brick, flat-roofed houses, with the odd Colonial-style hotel and a few classy sixties-style office blocks thrown in for bad measure. Aswan was the cultural border between Arab and black Africa.

They quarried granite used for statues in the pyramids here and shipped it down the Nile in sailing boats. The mines were long abandoned because of the downturn in the pyramid-building business, and a discarded cracked obelisk still lay imbedded in the rock.

The Aswan Dam created Lake Nasser, so I would have to travel by boat to Wadi Halfa in Sudan. I would take the train to Khartoum as the desert road was bad, and my front wheel had gained more dents from the potholed road from Cairo. My arse thought a jackhammer had pounded it all week; a float on a boat would give it time to heal.

Most travellers camped in the grounds of the old run- down Victoria Hotel. My Dutch friends were busy building a plywood house on top of their campervan; it now looked like a psychedelic double-decker bus. It was great to see them again after a week on my own, and we caught up on news of what lay ahead on our journeys.

For some travellers, it was the end of the road, but others were preparing to make the trip down through Africa. Everyone was young, in their early twenties. It was the end of the 70s so all the blokes had beards and long hair, while the girls wore tie-dye cheesecloth pantaloons.

Parked beside me were Bert and Miffe from Denmark, in an orange VW Kombi with their fair-haired five-year-old son, Nicki. He looked like he had lived in a campervan all his life. They planned to go as far as Khartoum. Their Kombi was old and battered.

Luke and Theresa, from Belgium, had arrived in a brand-new Kombi, all set up for the rigours of Africa, equipped with toughened springs and chassis. Jealous of these residences on wheels, they made my bike a pitifully basic home from home.

An ex-British army Land Rover roared up, and onboard were John and Charlie, two English public schoolboy types. Still sporting schoolboy haircuts and rugby shirts, they had only left England ten days ago and were heading for Kenya, to sell the Land Rover. Typical Brits, loaded with enough tins of baked beans and corned beef to make them self-sufficient.

"And it's taken you two months to get here?" John asked me.

"Long story; I had a diversion."

"Where are you heading?"

"Australia."

"You're going the wrong way, chum, it's a way over that- a-way," he said, pointing east.

"Long story!!!!"

In the campsite's corner was a huge German ex-army truck with two blokes, straight out of Rommel's Africa Corps, who goose-stepped around the site. They were also going to Kenya to sell their vehicle. They ignored everyone and set up in a separate corner of the camp, with another German couple in a Mercedes four-wheel drive. But as we were all going the same direction, I tried to do a deal with them.

"If you take my bike on the back of the truck I will contribute to the diesel," I suggested.

"Ve haf no room. We have to carry eight oil drums of diesel," Fritz explained.

"OK, up to you," I said, but I could have packed ten bikes on the back of the massive truck.

Next day, Fritz knocked over the bike when he was reversing the truck. I shouted at him to mind where he was driving, and he told me to mind where I parked, no damage done, so we averted WW3.

But I laughed to myself at how everyone seemed to live up to my stereotyped national characteristics.

From the posh English with their baked beans, to the arrogant organized Germans, and Dutch stoned off their heads every night.

Lastly, a middle-aged couple turned up in a little Datsun Cherry. Margaret had greying hair tied in a bun and wore a buttoned-up cardigan and Art wore pressed trousers, patent leather shoes and a raincoat. They had a little poodle called Percy held on a leash. It was the oddest sight to see them roll into the campsite as if they'd been kidnapped mid-dog walk in suburban Vancouver and deposited here by some alien force.

Margaret, who was a lawyer, and her doctor husband, had been everywhere. They had sold their house in Vancouver three years ago and had driven their Datsun down the USA to South America, and over to Europe and India. South Africa was their last stop before home.

Just as everyone fitted into my traditional preconceptions, these two blew my theories apart!

While other travellers had cars and vans to hide behind, I was outside and part of what was going on around. I had no privacy and everyone came over to talk motorcycles; we would chat about where we were going, or where we had been.

It was great to have the company, but tiring too. The only time I had any solitude was when I was actually on the bike, riding, that was my only escape.

To add to my woes, my oil pressure light had flashed on and off, which could show a major problem, such as a main bearing failure, or something as simple as a bad electrical connection. Either way, it needed sorting. I took off the engine sump and changed the oil filter. I lay on my back and looking up into the engine, I could see the crankshaft, the con rods and the workings of the engine; this was the heart of the machine. All looked good.

In the UK, engine oil comes in a sterile plastic bottle with the manufacturer's brand label, but not in Egypt. The tall Negro mechanic filled up two dirty plastic milk bottles from a big 55-gallon oil drum, which lay in a puddle of oil.

"Hey Mister, there is still milk in the bottom of these bottles," I said to him.

"Don't worry, it will stay in the engine's bottom," he laughed.

The oil cost five pence a pint. I started the bike up, but the new oil and filter didn't seem to make any difference, the oil light still flickered back on.

Pete came over to see what I was doing; he knew something about engines,

"There is only one way to fix it,' he said.

"How's that?"

"Disconnect the light bulb!" He pulled the wire out, and of course, the light popped out.

"So, all sorted," And to all intents, he was right, the problem had disappeared.

"It's like life, you see a symptom and imagine there is a problem. Sort out the symptom, and the problem goes away!" he laughed.

Simple Dutch logic.

"It's all in your head!" he said.

"What about the oil pressure, though?"

"If the engine is sick, it will tell you." Pete put one end of a screwdriver against the engine casing, and the other end hard against my ear. I could hear the bearings whir through my skull. It sounded sweet. And he was right; the oil pressure never gave me any problems after that and I would forget we had disconnected it. A good lesson in mechanics and for life itself.

Everyone knew where they were going apart from me. Would I hang a left in Kenya, and take a boat to India and Australia, or continue south to South Africa? But I had no friends or relations there, and no way to get back.

Best to think short-term I decided, so let's get to Kenya first; that would be a challenge on its own.

I would take the boat to Wadi Halfa, take the train to Khartoum and go by boat to Juba in South Sudan. I would have to bypass Uganda, as Idi Amin was at war with Tanzania.

The next morning, I made my way up through the Rocky Mountains to the Aswan Dam, which ran across the valley, blocking in the world's longest river.

At the docks, I drove into the Customs Shed, as a line of vehicles queued for the Egyptian, 'you will pay' pantomime.

Resigned to being ripped off, I handed the police the import documents. Suddenly the officer looked at me like I had just accused his mother of being a Jewish hooker.

"What is this?" he shouted, holding a small piece of paper, "This is in Hebrew!"

"No Shit!" I said.

I had made sure not to let the Israelis stamp my passport. Instead, they stamped a separate piece of paper, and it must have got mixed up with my other papers, as Arabic and Hebrew were all Chinese to me!

"You are an Israeli spy!" he shouted, as the other coppers all looked over.

I panicked.

"I don't know what that is," I grabbed it back and tore it up with as much contempt as I could muster.

"You have been to Israel."

"No, I've not. Check my passport; see, no Israeli stamp," I said, my hands shaking as I pointed to the pages. He shouted to the soldiers, who came running over. Holy shit, this was not good!

"Look, no Israeli stamp, a spy would have an Israeli stamp on their passport, wouldn't they?"

The officers got excited and tore through my luggage. All my bags were emptied, and my pockets searched for other documents. I sweated like I had a rainforest under each armpit, as I remembered about my camera full of Israeli photographs.

"Israel is scum; they are our enemy!" The captain spat, his bushy moustache inches from my face. I could smell his falafel lunch. I wanted to explain that they were not his enemy and that since the ceasefire they were actually best friends… but stopped myself short.

"Yes, they are dogs!" I agreed, "Egypt is the best!" Trucks behind started tooting their horns at the hold-up.

The boat was only fifty yards away, beckoning me; I wanted on that boat more than anything.

Some soldiers found contraband on a truck and started arguing with the driver, forgetting about me for the minute. They were unloading boxes of radios, but the driver started putting them back. My guy went over, smelling a profit from what they could steal. Everyone was shouting and pushing at each other now. It was pandemonium.

"Excuse me, can I go now?" I said, seeing a chance.

"Don't come back, or we will arrest you as an Israeli spy," he snarled at me, writing my name in a book, and snapping it shut as if to seal my fate.

"I won't, I promise," I called and made for the boat. I had had enough of this crazy fuck-wit place to never want to come back!

But it also meant that it blocked my retreat, and I wasn't coming back this way.

The Aswan Dam enabled the Nile delta to flood twice a year, doubling food production for Egypt's population. I was in no doubt that if the Pharaohs had built the dam instead of the pyramids 4000 years ago, Egypt would still rule the world.

But the dam had no dock, so they loaded the ferry with two wooden planks from a rocky embankment. They gave me one plank for the wheels and one for my foot to dab it down, with a drop of twenty feet below, fast enough not to wobble and trying not to look down. The dockers all gave a cheer as they grabbed me before I fell in and pulled the bike on board. I made my way to the front of the boat.

The lower deck was for vehicles and animals, mid-deck for the goods and passengers and a plywood roof, open to the blazing sun, for the Sudanese workers.

The half-naked African porters were as black as the Nile waters. With bandy legs and nappy-like shorts, they struggled up the gangplanks with huge sacks on their backs, while their Arab masters shouted obscenities at them. The hierarchy of race was very plain; the darker your skin, the poorer and more subservient you were.

On the middle deck were black-veiled women, screaming children, and a few mangy goats, tied to a rail, were stood pissing on the floor. The porters loaded on grain sacks with the 'Save the Children' stamp, but each time, they poked a hole in the sack and poured some rice into their pockets. Occasionally, a policeman stopped them and produced a bag and demanded his portion. Not a great distribution system for Save the Children, but that's Africa for you.

Most of the Arabs wore white Arab galabias, but the trendier ones had 1970s skin-tight flared jeans, tank tops, and four-inch-high platform shoes. I had discovered where out-of-fashion European clothes ended up.

We all congregated at the front of the boat and made a barricade with the vehicles behind us. That evening, the boat moved from the dock at an iceberg's pace; two hours later we could still see Aswan a mile away.

In our enclosure were John and Charlie in the Land Rover, the Belgians and the Danish in the VW Kombi, along with Margaret, Art and the dog in the Datsun. My Dutch friends had stayed in Aswan to build the house on top of the Renault and the Germans were busy getting organized.

Charlie produced a bottle of Egyptian brandy.

"Do you know what day this is?"

I had long ago lost any idea of the date. "It is New Year's Eve!" He grinned.

"I know," said Bert and produced a pipe and a massive lump of hash!

We had the makings of a party!

We toasted in the New Year in Egypt, Belgium, Denmark, the UK and finally Canada. As Belgium entered 1980, the barge shuddered to a halt, knocking some grain sacks onto the bike. We had run aground! Bert ran to the bridge to check what had happened, while I dug the bike from under the sacks. As I bent over, an agonizing pain seared down my back. I had pulled a muscle, and could hardly stand up.

But the Egyptian brandy seemed to dull the pain effectively.

Bert returned, smiling, "The Captain is terrified of sailing in the dark and has run aground!"

"So, he has run aground on purpose, so he doesn't by mistake?" I said.

"Well, yes, apparently he likes to relax over his dinner!" Bert said laughing.

Above the top deck, a million stars twinkled in the clear, black sky. Without the light pollution from the city, they seemed close enough to touch. I saw the Plough and the Bear and remembered watching them in the back garden a few months ago. It seemed ridiculous that they were the same stars as the ones in Belfast, a world away.

The Sudanese passengers lay on the top deck like corpses, wrapped in their shroud-like galabias; an old Arab tended to a charcoal brazier brewing sweet tea and cooking flatbreads for breakfast.

Years later, the ship had caught fire and over 300 people died. Apparently, it had been caused by coal falling out of a brazier.

We arrived at Wadi Halfa two days late, because of our warp factor 2mph maximum speed, and the scaredy-cat captain. By the time first-class disembarked, it was 5 pm and the Customs guys had closed; they moored the boat offshore to make sure no one could jump off.

The following morning, the boat's engines wouldn't start and the chief engineer had gone off to town with a Sudanese prostitute. It took Bert to discover they had switched off the fuel pump. The engines sputtered back to life and finally, we moved to the shore to disembark.

Riding the bike off the ship was worse than getting it on. They threw wooden boards onto a pontoon and over onto the rocks; passengers walked the plank.

I was halfway across when, with a loud crack, the plank broke, and the bike plummeted onto the steep rocky bank five feet below, but luckily landed upright. But just as I thought I was secure, the bike started to roll back into the water! The onlookers surged forward for a better look at my watery demise, but I gunned the throttle, and roared up the bank and scattering everyone like skittles. Finally, on flat ground, I inspected the bottom of the engine sump where it landed on a boulder. The only damage was a chunk in the sump cooling fins.

Wadi Halfa was a shantytown of mud huts and dusty streets. When they flooded Lake Nasser, the original town disappeared underwater, and a new one was built, or half- built, I should say. This was the start of the railway to Khartoum and the gateway to Africa. Lord Kitchener had built the railway eighty years ago to get his troops across the desert to retake Khartoum. No one had done any maintenance since then.

But by the time we cleared Customs, the only train had left, and it would be a week until the next. This was a disaster.

"We will drive; come with us," Charlie said.

"Sorry guys, they build Moto Guzzi for the motorway, not deserts!"

"We will go," said Bert, "and if we can do it in a Kombi, you can on a Guzzi."

"You haven't done it in a Kombi; you are merely intending to do it, which is altogether a different matter!"

"Do you want to stay in this shithole for a week?" asked

Luke.

'Ok, I'll give it a go."

CHAPTER 6

The Nubian Desert

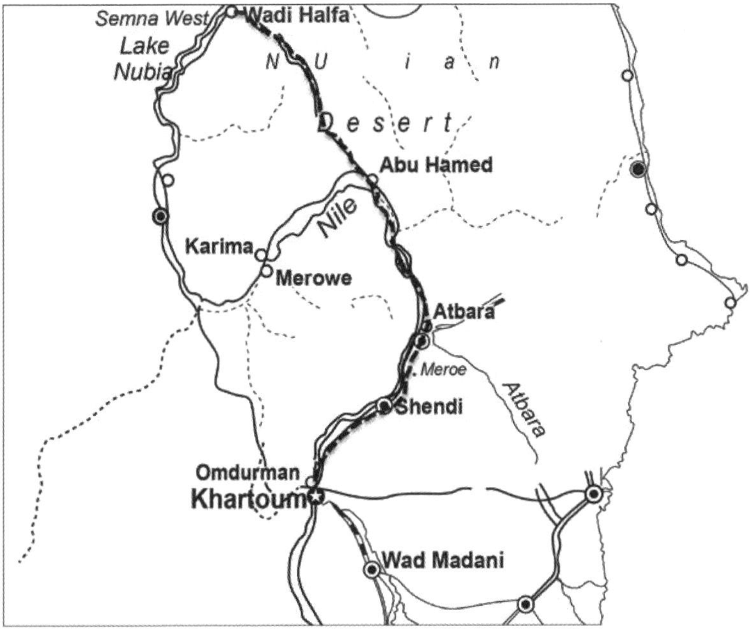

WE COULD FOLLOW THE NILE AS IT MADE A LARGE U BEND TO THE west, or go the more direct route with the railway line. On my Michelin map, a dirt road followed the railway.

The Land Rover was desert-equipped, but two VW Campervans, a Moto Guzzi Le Mans, and the 1200cc Datsun Cherry were completely out of place!

I knew a motocross scrambler with off-road tyres, with a lightweight engine, a high clearance sump guard, and a long suspension would suit the desert. The factory designed my Guzzi with the exact opposite characteristics. With a heavy, low-slung engine, slim road tyres, and a short firm suspension.

What the hell was I thinking?!

The whole town came out to give us a raucous send-off, with lots of waving and high-pitched cheers. We drove past two random pyramids, then the track disappeared in a melee of tyre ruts that crisscrossed in the sand. We all stopped.

An old guy on a camel walked towards us.

"Where is the road to Khartoum?" I asked.

He waved his hand at the desert with a… 'Can't you see it, arsehole?' look on his face.

The trouble was that in Sudan, the word 'Road' is merely the general direction you should go; it makes no premise of any prepared track on which you may travel!

"Let's go for it," shouted Charlie in the Land Rover, and with a great roar of assorted engines, we drove away. The Guzzi skidded and fish-tailed across the sand. I dabbed the ground with my feet to stop me falling. Then, even the ruts disappeared, as the desert wind filled in the tracks. We were lost. Well, not exactly; we could still see the town 200 yards behind us, our fans still waving, but we struggled on, too mortified to go back.

A few miles later, we all got stuck, apart from the Land Rover. The Guzzi sunk up to the engine sump, the front wheel buried to the axle and the rear wheel spinning.

As we set up camp, I knew the smart money was on going back and waiting for the train; we had all failed the first test miserably.

None of us had done any off-road driving apart from the English lads, who spent a wet afternoon in a muddy English field.

We were a motley crew of five vehicles, five nationalities, and all very different people, but all equally despondent as we set up our tents.

"Lambs to the slaughter," I thought to myself.

As the sun sank behind the dunes, no-one spoke; they only worried about the desert ahead.

A canopy of millions of stars shone in the crystal-clear desert air, with not a speck of dust to spoil our view. The silver moon rose, as bright as day, but in black and white and grey. The silence was deafening, not a bird chirping or an insect buzzing. It's hard to find somewhere, where there is absolutely nothing. Perfect silence. I had never experienced this.

I popped two painkillers; my back was still aching after injuring it on the boat when it hit the island.

"Did anyone let their tyres down?" Charlie asked. "You need to let your tyres down to 15 PSI to drive in sand."

The most basic lesson in desert driving, but I didn't know!

"What difference does that make?"

"It increases the contact area, and stops the wheel sinking."

"Ok, I'll see if it helps tomorrow."

I'd decided I would drive 500 miles across the Sahara Desert on an Italian café racer; I was 21 years old and thought I was invincible.

I'd had no thought of what I would do if I broke my leg or smashed the bike, with no motorcycle or medical insurance, and miles from any medical facilities.

But young men use their balls as brains, for risk and adventure. Generals knew this when they ordered them 'over the top' and into near-certain death. Pride and honour drove Kamikaze pilots to eternity. And suicide bombers believe they will go to heaven with 72 virgins. But ask a middle-aged man to do that, and he will refuse. He knows that one virgin is of little use when your cock lands a hundred yards away from your testicles.

But I lay thinking about the day ahead and that night I hardly slept. I felt as though tomorrow I would fight the school bully, a fight I couldn't win.

But I was young, dumb and male; I had to go for it!

I lay awake and watched the sunrise. The wind-blown dunes stretched out forever. It looked peaceful and calming and gave no indication of my baptism of fire ahead.

"I don't know if I can do this, mate," I said to John. "They built my Guzzi for speed, not sand. We've only gone one mile with five hundred to go! That's like driving from Edinburgh to Dover, all on frigging sand dunes!"

"Let's do some mods," John suggested. Moto Guzzi had fitted an interlinked brake system, which would make the front wheel lock up when in the sand, so I jammed it by placing a penny in the plunger. I took off the front brake lever, as I didn't need it and it would break off when I fell.

We lowered the tyre pressure from 32 PSI to 12 PSI. The tyre was nearly flat, but the wide tread now sat flat on the sand.

John put the panniers in the Land Rover and I was ready; as I ever would be.

I looked at the dunes and shuddered at the prospect. I gripped my clutch lever as if my life depended on it. Ahead lay 500 miles of the most extreme riding in the world.

"Let's roll!" shouted John and moved off. I reluctantly released the clutch, and the bike wallowed on the flat tyres, but didn't sink and stayed upright.

An hour later, the Land Rover stopped. It was getting hot.

"Wadi," said John, nodding ahead at a wide gully in the sand that stretched out across our path.

It only rains once every ten years in the desert, when it falls in a deluge for a couple of hours. Instantly, rivers roar across the desert before they dry out to leave a gully or wadi, full of very soft sand.

The Land Rover made it across first, kicking up clouds of dust, but the VWs and cars promptly sank up to their axles.

Charlie shouted at me, "They're too slow, Chris, give her lots of welly!" Nothing else for it, I thought and charged down the bank with the back wheel fishtailing, as I wrestled with the handlebars. Full lock left, then right, as I fought for control. But even with the throttle wide open, I slowed and the tyres sank into the sand, then stopped, the rear wheel spinning. I started digging.

The Guzzi moved better on the flat tyres, but the cars had one big advantage - they didn't fall over.

We made good progress until late afternoon when Bert's Kombi got stuck. Even with the metal sand ladders placed under the wheels, the Land Rover couldn't pull him out.

"We'll use a sand anchor," announced Charlie, producing a small winch and a length of wire cable. Twenty yards in front of the Kombi he said, "Start digging!"

We dug a metre-deep hole and dropped a spare wheel in it. Charlie parked the Land Rover on top then connected the wire between the wheel and the Kombi axle. We took it in turns to pump the small handle, which pulled the Kombi out inch by inch. After two hours of digging, it was clear, but still, the van would not move. One of the drive shafts was spinning inside the hub; the groves had worn away, giving no traction to the wheel. It was a disaster.

"Looks like I'm buggered," said Bert.

The sand and heat had destroyed the VW suspension. The desert separated the weakest from the rest of the herd.

Bert hammered a bolt through the spindles, but it would only be a matter of time before it sheared off.

"Looks like I'll have to abandon the van." But John came up with a plan.

"If we get you back to Wadi Halfa, you can get the boat to Egypt. I'll come with you in the Land Rover."

"What about you, Chris?" said Bert "Are you giving up?"

"I'm fine, I'll drive on," I said, my mouth working totally independently from my brain. It knew I was talking shite.

"Fuck it, I must do this!" I thought to myself.

But the threat of the abandoned VW scared me, and

I knew I should go back with them.

Even with a minor spill, or if I sprained an ankle or wrist, I would have to abandon the bike in the desert. My back was a borderline case already, and I only managed the pain by popping painkillers. If I broke a bone, the nearest hospital was at least five days' drive, plenty of time for gangrene to set in.

The right thing was to go back for the train.

But something wouldn't let me. This challenge was suddenly the most important thing in my life. I failed at most everything else, from sports to exams, to relationships.

There was a stubborn gremlin on my shoulder saying,

'Man up, Chris, you're not backing out of this one, go for it!'

"One down, four to go," Charley said as we watched them drive away.

The next morning, the Land Rover returned with Bert and Eve as passengers. "John towed us the last mile." Bert smiled from the passenger seat; they would come for the ride to Khartoum and take the train back later.

As I started the engine, I said to myself,

"I will take every hour as it comes. I will not crash today!"

I would break the 500-mile ride down into bite-sized pieces, no, nibble-sized pieces, one mile at a time. Once I had done a one-hour ride, I would think about doing another, as each hour without a crash would be a victory over the inevitable.

The ride was all-consuming. Nothing mattered before today, and nothing would matter after, as if I screwed up now, there wouldn't be a tomorrow.

I asked Dr Art what he recommended for my sore back. "Two weeks' total rest," he said in his quintessential Canadian bedside manner.

"Some chance in the middle of the desert," I said as I popped more painkillers.

We passed a burnt-out vehicle. We would see many more, and they usually marked a treacherous part of the desert.

The next day, the ground was firm for a few miles then we reached the first wadi. I stopped to watch the cars crossing first. When they hit soft sand, they hit the gas, rear wheels spinning, as the sand sucked the energy out of the screaming engines. And one by one they stuck up to the axles.

Then it was my turn, the guys stopped digging to watch. Apparently, I was great entertainment.

I gathered my thoughts, like a diver preparing to go off a high board. I pushed off, not too fast, or the front wheel would lose contact with the surface, not too slow, as I needed momentum to stop me sinking. When I hit the soft sand, I twisted full throttle; the big V twin roared and charged forward, wheel spinning. It was a cross between riding a bucking bronco and water-skiing.

I hit a small bush, and the back end kicked out, first in a slow-motion 'tank slap' but then faster as the momentum built and the rear wheel tried to overtake the front.

I wrenched at the handlebars to counteract, kicked the ground to stay upright, but kept the throttle wide open with the engine screaming. I kicked into 1st gear, the back wheel spun as the bike lost momentum, and stopped, stuck up to the engine sump again. I turned off the white-hot engine.

It was hard physical work riding a café racer through the desert. The guys gave me a round of applause before we dug each other out again. It took an hour to cover one hundred yards.

On the first day, we only covered twenty miles, the second sixty and the third fifty. We would be in the desert for weeks at this rate.

The next casualty was Luke's Kombi; one by one, the shocks exploded in a cloud of smoke as the oil splashed onto the hot exhaust. The Kombi bounced along like a demented chicken trying to fly.

I drove down the railway line for a bit. The wind filled the space between the sleepers with sand so it was flat. But at every 10th sleeper, there was a joint in the ancient tracks, which made a hole. The bumping soon had my back in agony, but at least I was moving.

The British engineers made railway bridges that crossed the wadi with two long steel girders spanning stumpy brick pillars. Then the wooden sleepers lay across the girders every half-metre, with the railway tracks bolted to them. In between the sleepers was nothing but fresh air and a thirty-foot drop to the desert. It was frightening looking down through the gaps.

I started over a bridge, driving down the middle of the tracks, with wheels bouncing over the sleepers and my feet astride the bike, sliding along the rails.

My concentration was intense, as the bike bumped over the sleepers. I knew one slip and I would fall off the bridge, landing on my head on the desert below. I had to move fast to stop the wheel from getting stuck, but too fast and my feet bounced off the tracks.

My back was in agony and the hammering rattled the fillings out of my teeth. It was torment, but I made it. Feeling relieved and pleased with my new skill, I walked down to help push the others out of the wadi.

With a dozen crossings like that, each one became easier until I got cocky. On the last one, the bike bounced off a broken sleeper, and my boot slipped off the rail. I plunged over towards the side, just reaching a sleeper with my foot to kick myself upright again. When I got to the far side, I was shaking.

Then the Datsun tried it, but the wheels got jammed on the tracks as the radius was too small for the gaps; it took us all an hour to drag it off the bridge, but luckily the train only ran once a week. Margaret drove off the embankment and plunged straight into a deep culvert, taking off the exhaust assembly and pushing the floor of the car up a couple of inches. As we pushed her out again, the rear window fell in. My shocks spewed out oil, as the seals had blown, and it was only a matter of time before they seized completely. I made a mental note to write to Moto Guzzi Customer Service to complain that their bikes weren't suitable for driving down railway lines!

By the afternoon, we had reached a gravel plateau; I could speed along at 70 mph with the Land Rover racing beside me.

"The last one into the next town is a poofter!" I shouted at Charlie, (it was 1980 - they allowed us to say that then!)

The speed was ecstasy after days in second gear, but not clever with the tyres at 12 psi. In forty minutes, we covered as much ground as in the last two days.

Abu Hammed station was up ahead, and a railway junction crossed our path on a fifty-foot high embankment. The Land Rover powered up the steep slope but wasn't going fast enough and slid back down sideways, wheels spinning and engine roaring. It nearly tipped over in a cloud of dust.

I took it faster but overcooked it, taking off at the top, and as I crossed the railway track, my centre stand caught on the signal wire. There was a loud clunk as the old wooden signal changed from stop to go! Oops.

I drove down the track and into the station, where the confused station-master wasn't expecting a train for another two days.

"The 10.20 is leaving for Khartoum!" I shouted. "Everyone aboard!"

He stared at me as if I was crazy, as I rode down the line hooting my horn.

I was like a big kid on my red choo-choo train! He shouted a few obscenities and shook his fist.

Then Charlie and John appeared in the Land Rover, honking their horn.

The stationmaster shook his head in disbelief. He waits one week for a train, then two arrive in ten minutes. Typical!

We waited in the town's only street for the others to catch up. The whole population came out to see us; this was a big day in Abu Hammed - white folk entering!

We shook hands with every one of the 200 or so inhabitants. They crowded around young Nicki, whose long blonde hair intrigued them, and they all wanted to touch it.

The town had a few dozen mud-brick shacks and the railway station but it was right in the middle of nowhere. Why would anyone live here? It was bleak, and there was no food in any shops, apart from stale bread and Tate and Lyle's golden syrup. I found this all over Africa; Tate and Lyle had the golden syrup business sown up!

A shopkeeper gave me a plate of bean stew and refused any money. Such generosity was a surprise after the Egyptian rip-off culture. Everywhere in Egypt, the people wanted money, while the Sudanese looked pleased to see us. They always gave us small glasses of Arab tea supersaturated with sugar whenever we stopped. The desert people sat serenely, sipping tea to keep them hydrated, their bodies acclimatized to the desert, their pores closed. They could survive on a couple of small glasses a day. We drank copious amounts of water, and sweated like Prince Andrew at a disco, while the Sudanese didn't perspire at all.

But the children looked half-starved, with big bellies and skinny ribs. They came over pleading, hands outstretched, heads over to one side. There was nothing I could do. I had no food to spare and gave them a few coins, guilty at my obvious wealth. I was spending my money on some frivolous quest to travel Africa when these families could survive a year on the price of a clapped-out VW.

Art made friends, as word got out that he was a doctor. Mothers stood in a silent hope of a cure for their kids. Many of them had eye infections and malnutrition; he had little to give them but advice.

"Most of them need a good feed and some disinfectant,"

he said, as we sat around the campfire.

"Why are they here?" I said.

"The desert moves south at about ten miles every year, so the farmland these people had years ago is now sand," Art said. They had nowhere else to go.

Until Roman times, the Sahara had been a grassy savannah, and wild animals roamed there. Global warming had gone on for many years before oil, and now overpopulation quickened the process.

But I felt uneasy at the lack of empathy we had for the villagers. Was it because they were Africans that we were accepting of their plight? I had seen starving African children on TV, but now we saw them in the flesh. Well, no surprise there then; I was hardened to it already.

Strange.

When we set up camp, we parked the vehicles in a circle, wagon train-style. I don't know why; it seemed like the thing to do!

We lay on the sand, exhausted, but happy at how our teamwork kept our vehicles moving.

That evening, Margaret opened her map.

"There's a road from here to Khartoum. We will get there tomorrow!" she said.

"I'll believe it when I see it," I said.

"No, there's a good road."

"Whatever you say." I didn't argue with her as she was cracking from the pressure, and would bicker with Art or anyone who came near.

The next day, we drove the first few miles on firm sand; we flew along until we saw it - the widest wadi ever - it must have been 300 yards!

We all got stuck. It took four hours of digging, pushing and shoving to get to the other side. The heat sucked me dry, leaving scarcely enough moisture to lubricate my joints and allow my brain to function.

By evening, we had covered forty-five miles after ten hours' hard driving and digging. I heard Margaret crying in the car. I wanted to have a good cry myself, as my back was wrecked, and my ass was as red as an English post box. My belly ached from the pounding on my organs, like I had fought ten rounds in a boxing ring.

The Datsun was taking a battering; the continuous banging onto rocks pushed the floor upwards so much that the Canadians' heads now hit the roof. It was a miracle of Japanese engineering that it kept going, with the exhaust, most of the chrome trim, the mirrors and door handles all gone. The interior trim and the back window lay in the boot, but they slept in it every night;

"To stop anyone from stealing it!" Margaret insisted. Luke's Kombi wasn't much better: the engine was tied down with rope, it blew out great clouds of smoke, and ran on two cylinders. Gravity was the only thing holding the van body on the chassis. All the suspension mounts had ruptured, the exhaust was long gone, and the shock absorbers broken.

The spectre of an abandoned burning VW was never far away.

Margaret's main concern was for her dog, Percy, although, at one stop they drove off and left him standing in the desert! John picked him up and put him in his Land Rover. An hour later, the Datsun screeched to a halt, and Margaret jumped out screaming, "Where's my Percy!"

It was funny at the time but with the stress of the driving, tempers got frayed.

Margaret and Art drove too slowly, so got stuck, and then stood by as we dug the car out while she gave us advice. Charlie told her to fuck off politely! Perhaps because I was on my own, I had become the peacekeeper when there was a row between nationalities.

But the strain of keeping each vehicle running in the heat was immense, especially for a mixed bunch like ours. But usually, everyone got on, apart from the persistent pain in the ass, Margaret.

Monday the 7th of January.

Every morning I announced my mantra over breakfast; "Today, I will not fall off," and they all laughed, but it had worked. I hadn't fallen once.

Everyone wished each other luck and started up our chariots, ready for whatever the desert had in store for the day. We travelled closer to the Nile now, and the dry riverbeds were filled with fine sand.

We followed a routine; drive to the next wadi, try to cross, get stuck, push and dig, rest, then drive again. The team would make me cross first so they could watch my heroics. My new routine was to jump off and run alongside and push at full throttle as the wheels bogged down.

The sand dunes had gone, replaced with dry dusty bushes and razor-sharp rocky outcrops, which ripped into my deflated tyres.

Air-cooled engines rely on the 50mph breeze blowing past them to keep them cool. I was hitting a top speed of 15mph, and as there was a following wind of about 15mph, there was absolutely no air going past the engine. The low octane Egyptian fuel pre-ignited in the cylinders with a ping, ping noise, which increased the temperature in the engine to that of molten lava.

It would seize at any moment.

One morning, Margaret and Art disappeared for three hours, and we had to drive around looking for them. Eventually, we found them hidden in a small gully having tea.

"Where have you been?" Margaret demanded, "We've been waiting for ages!"

"You stupid bitch!" Luke swore, and a full-scale shouting match developed. The strain was showing and someone was about to crack.

I had detoured away from the river looking for firmer sand when I noticed something move behind a bush. Suddenly, I heard barking and turned to see a pack of twenty wild dogs running behind me.

Holy Shit! Shit! Shit!

The size of Alsatians, they had huge angry jaws. To them, I was meals on wheels.

As they closed in, I imagined one jumping on the back seat and chewing at my neck, like the wildlife programs when the lions chase an old buffalo, before one falls and gets devoured.

They ran at about 20mph, which was faster than I could drive. I hit some rocks and went airborne. They gained ground, snarling at my heels. One slip, and if the crash didn't kill me, the dogs would rip me apart.

A mangy mongrel snapped at my heel and I swung my boot out at him. The bike swerved as I nearly came off.

The shock absorbers crunched and crashed as I drove like a maniac. It seemed an eternity before the dogs tired, and I pulled ahead. But they still kept following me at a trot, waiting for me to let my guard down so they could jump me again.

I didn't stop until they were well out of sight, and I was still shaking when I found the convoy parked beside the river.

I collapsed on the sand and explained what had happened, but got little sympathy.

"A dog chased my bicycle once," laughed John. "Was it a couple of Labradors?"

"Bastards, I hope the crocodiles get in your tent and bite your knob off!" I said.

Charley called me 'dog food' all the next day.

After days in the desert, the riverbanks appeared strangely green and teemed with wildlife and birds.

"Welcome to the longest sewer in the world," said Luke, as we swam in the river while a random Arab shat in the river just upstream. Why would people want to dump here when they have the whole bloody Sahara Desert? I wondered.

That next afternoon something moved up ahead, like a mirage of hot air wafting on the horizon. An enormous camel caravan crossed our path. Like a huge caterpillar, it floated along, so slow that the camels should fall over. Loaded with packs, the hundreds of camels looked serene, that was until we got close enough to smell the sweat, urine and shit. And that was just from the camel drovers. The camels smelt slightly better. They continued on like an oil tanker that would take too long to get moving again if it stopped.

One drover jumped off his camel and ran over to me, gesturing for a ride.

"Jump on!" I said. He held on tight with his knees up around my waist like a jockey and squealed like a child. The other drovers whooped and yelled with excitement as I rode right around the caravan.

I had made his day and his decade. They rode on, the same way they had done for centuries.

We were some of the last people to see this stunning sight, as Toyota Land Cruisers would soon replace them.

At dusk, we found the Nile again and made camp, watching herders water their camels while the sun went down.

We all skinny-dipped in the river, apart from Margaret, who was still wearing her woollen cardigan, even in the desert's hottest days.

The cool river washed the grime off our bodies. "Watch out for the killer snails," Luke shouted as we splashed about. Parasites like Bilharzia lived in the water and could burrow into your skin and enter your bloodstream and attack your internal organs.

But we couldn't resist the urge to swim in the river. However, we didn't dare drink it and we rationed our drinking water to a litre a day.

I loved the desert's savage beauty; the magical evenings while shadows lengthened across the sand like giant ripples on the beach; the silver moonlit shades of grey against the black skies which held more stars than I had seen in all my life.

We drank tea, smoked some hash and recounted the day's events, while listening to Dire Straits, Joe Cocker and the Clash. My collection of twenty tapes now sounded very repetitive.

But you just couldn't cross Africa with today's musicians, Katie Perry or Ed Sheeran. Not a chance! Although, I guess Pink and Beyoncé could have got me through.

Some forty years later, I still can't listen to Pink Floyd 'Dark Side of the Moon' without thinking of those nights under the Nubian stars.

I was no longer scared of the desert; it was now a challenge, and I enjoyed the contest. I wasn't trying to conquer it, just to survive and cross it. If I succeeded, it would be down to a strong bike, a little skill, and a large measure of luck.

On the 9th of January, we finally rolled into Atbara, our first large town.

We had taken so long that the weekly train from Wadi Halfa had beaten us, but we didn't care. It was the hardest thing any of us had ever done. All we'd thought about was drinking a cold beer at the end of the trip, like the scene in "Ice Cold in Alex," the famous John Mills' war movie. Even the Belgians knew of it!

The film was about a small group of British soldiers who drove through the desert to escape the Germans. In the final scene, they arrived in a bar in Alexandra and contemplated the condensation on their pints of Carlsberg.

Back in our world, the only bars in Atbara protected the windows of a beer shop; it had a small plastic table and stools on the roadside. A wizened old woman sat behind the bars and passed out bottles of beer with a camel on the label.

I popped the top, and foam spewed out. The beer was cloudy and warm. We tried our best to drink them but it tasted rotten, and the moment was lost.

"If it looks like camel piss, and smells like camel piss, it's probably camel piss!" I said.

I needed to stop and rest. Six days of continuous desert riding, digging, pushing and shoving had drained me.

I'd been on the road (and sand) for three months, had ridden 6650 miles from Belfast, more or less without stopping, and I was physically and mentally exhausted. My brain needed to catch up with my wheels. Every morning for seventy days I had opened my eyes and thought, 'Where the hell am I?'

This had been the hardest week of my life, the biggest thing I had ever done. I needed a few days to relax, contemplate, and just strut around town in my leathers!

The rest would drive on. We had only known each other for two weeks but it was an emotional farewell. I would even miss Art and Margaret's continual bickering… well, maybe.

We hugged and exchanged addresses;

"See you in Khartoum," I said.

They disappeared in a rather comical cloud of smoke, clunks and rattles from their clapped-out machines, with 200 miles still to go.

I was suddenly alone after all that action, as if their departure sucked the life out of me, like being dropped into a vacuum.

The single-story mud houses were all painted a cool Mediterranean green and blue, all very jolly after the drab desert dwellings.

I found a hostel for twenty pence a night and I could bring the bike into my bedroom.

The room had four iron bedsteads with straw mattresses, two Australian guys, Gregg and Andy, and a tall black Dinka tribesman, whose name I couldn't pronounce. There was a fan on the ceiling but no electricity.

"Don't sleep on the beds," the Aussies warned, "They're alive with lice."

A few hours later, I recognised the familiar Datsun exhaust rumble. I ran out to the street.

"What are you doing back?"

"They all left us!" screamed Margaret. "They drove off and left us!"

"That's bullshit! You drove off!" shouted Eve, who got out of the back.

"Calm down and tell me what happened," I said before they came to blows.

"We couldn't keep up with the others. It's a nightmare out there, with tracks in every direction! The others drove off and left us, so we came back here!" insisted Margaret.

"That's a lie; you freaked out and turned around for no reason!" Eve shouted, but Margaret was away down the street pulling Art behind.

I sat Eve down with a coffee and she explained. She was riding in the Datsun for a change. After a few miles, with the Land Rover leading, Margaret suddenly screamed, "We are all going to die!"

She made Art turn and go back to Atbara as she shrieked and wailed, having a total meltdown.

Eve was frantic as her husband was in the other cars. They would be searching to find them. It was a disaster. Margaret had finally had her nervous breakdown.

Eve and I walked to the police station to report that they had arrived safely, then explored the tea and coffee houses.

The evening, tea was topped up with hot camel's milk, lots of sugar, spices and with thick skin on top. The dark coffee had a lump of ginger added and was equally as good.

Some bars had fruit juices, with guava, banana, and oranges with lots of sugar and crushed ice. We kept off the beer and gorged on the sweet honey pastries and sponges until we felt sick and returned to the hotel. The police had left the message that the guys would wait in the next town. They could travel in a convoy in the morning.

The torrid heat of the town had replaced the cool desert evenings. I discovered that the reason there were no flies in the desert was that they all lived in Atbara, where the biting was better. That night, squadrons of mosquitoes buzzed around my sleeping bag, where I lay sweating like a camel's scrotum.

Next morning, bites covered my face, arms and legs. I hadn't taken my anti-malaria tablets, so I swallowed a double dose. I looked like a flea-infested dog.

The hotel toilet was a tin shed with a hole in the floor, the fumes so putrid they would suffocate a donkey. There was no toilet paper, just a brown glass bottle of water. I couldn't get my head around using this, so I bought some shiny Arab newspapers for the job.

The bike had taken a pounding; the shocks oozed oil, and two weird boils about three inches long had formed on the side of the tyres. If they exploded, I was finished, as I had no spare.

Atbara had a mile of tarmac road and a large railway siding full of old British steam engines which sat forlornly in the desert.

The streets were a maze of high walls and dusty lanes, with old wooden doors leading to the courtyards of windowless houses. Everything was designed to reduce the effect of the sun's heat. They built houses of mud bricks, with the ceilings made of wooden rafters covered with some coconut thatching and topped off with a waterproof covering of cement-like mud. Good insulation.

All the locals shook my hand as I walked about as if I was a celebrity. In the evening, dozens of men would call to my hotel room to inspect the bike and offer advice, with helpful hints such as, "Petrol here," and "Brakes here". Some would actually kick the tyres, which I expected to burst. Then they would grab a part and shake it vigorously or twist the throttle and go vroom, with a very earnest expression.

I was the top of Atbara's entertainment world.

No women could be seen, only men and boys. Or should I say, men with boys, some holding hands. What would be child abuse anywhere else in the world, was justified here as protecting the sanctity of their women.

By noon, it was 40 degrees plus, and everyone slept. There was no electricity and the ceiling fans were just for decoration. In the evenings, I walked around drinking sweet tea, often invited back to some small courtyard. I smoked some hash and became fluent in Arabic; well, everyone nodded as I jabbered away.

Eventually, I floated back to my room, and all was good in the world.

I met with some schoolteachers and made the mistake of asking what they thought of the American hostage crisis that was still going on in Iran.

"The Ayatollah is the will of Allah. Whatever he does is right."

"But he is a Shiite and, you are Sunni," I said.

"The Ayatollah is the will of Allah. Whatever he does is right," they repeated, trance-like. Strange how a religion stops independent thought. Their opinion is supplied by the Vicar, the Priest or Imam.

The Sudanese took their identity from religion rather than nationality. In Ireland, people did both and had years of killing to show for it.

In Sudan, Islam gave them their beliefs, their customs and their Shia Law. Any sign of individual thought or freedom of expression got you locked up or killed.

Pain still shot down my lower back when I moved, so I decided to take the train to Khartoum. The railway station had seen better days; doors hung off their frames, all the windows frames had long departed. A bare light bulb hung from the ceiling in the stationmaster's office, and an old Bakelite phone sat on the table.

I arrived at 9.00 am for the 10.00 o'clock train, to find the ticket office closed.

"Where can I get a ticket?" I asked the stationmaster. "The ticket office is closed; he will be back after two hours."

"But I'll miss the train."

"Then you take the one tomorrow," he said.

"But I want to go today!"

"How can you go today, if the ticket office is closed?" he repeated, as if he was speaking to a half-wit.

As I rode back to the hostel, I bumped into the Germans who had just arrived in their monster truck. They wanted to leave for Khartoum straight away, so I joined their convoy and gave them some of my luggage to carry.

But by the time I got the bike repacked, they had disappeared. I sped after them through the town's only tarmac road, which stopped at the magnificent wrought-iron gates of a mansion. It wasn't the main road south at all; it just the driveway of the wealthiest man in Atbara.

Shit, where had the convoy gone?! Tracks ran off the tarmac road and spread out in a fan of deep ruts in the sand, as Eve had said. I headed out in the general direction of Khartoum but the sand was a nightmare!

After hours of hard riding, there was still no sign of the Germans. 'Bastards!' I thought, they should never have left someone alone in the desert. I had just enough petrol but was short of water. I only had my small plastic water canteen. Cursing them, I continued on. I realised that one fall and I was fucked, as I was on my own.

Small bushes and palm trees grew beside the river, and one minute the ground was gravel, the next hard dried mud.

All along the way, the remains of burnt-out trucks and cars helped me concentrate my mind.

'Easy how you go,' they seemed to say, 'or you'll end up like me.'

Towards evening, as the huge sun turned red on the horizon, I found an old WW2 landing craft that took me across the Nile to a small village. When we reached the other side, all I could hear was the steady thump of an old diesel, pumping the waters into the lush green fields.

An Arab in a white dishdasha walked up the track from the river.

"As salam alaykum," (Peace be with you,) I said in my best Arabic, "Is there a guest house in town?" I continued in Belfast-English.

"Wa alaykumu salam," (and also with you,) he looked at my bike and said, in perfect Queen's English, "My name is Omar and my house is your house. Come with me."

"No, just a guesthouse," I said. I was nervous of single men, after my Jordanian Customs' cock evening.

"My friend, the desert tradition is that we turn away no traveller from shelter. We will share my house with you, I insist."

I was too tired to argue.

The house had a magnificent view out over the Nile. We drank tea while the sun did another sensational performance; (if you want a good sunset, go to Africa.)

Omar introduced himself and his charming wife and three kids. So, they had women here!

Dinner was a smorgasbord of dishes: hummus, bread, olives, chicken, dates and pastries, and it was delicious. We sat on the floor with the food laid out in the middle of the carpet. Their kids behaved politely and were well-mannered. They were the first Arab kids I'd met who hadn't asked for baksheesh!

He explained that in Arabia, guests can ask their hosts for anything during the first three days of their visit.

I relaxed in Omar's hospitality, and later he took me for a stroll into the village. The haze from the cooking fires lay over the small town like an opaque blanket.

At the centre was a small courtyard with the town's latest acquisition, a black-and-white TV set, powered by a small generator. It was surrounded by farmers. While it rather spoilt my romantic view of the village, for the locals, the TV distracted them from their basic existence.

But for tonight, I was the entertainment as I gave them a talk and Omar translated and boasted about my travels with great enthusiasm.

This was another unique traveller interchange; they gave me a bed for the night, and I gave them my adventure stories of foreign lands. They had questions about Ireland and Europe; the snow in the Alps brought applause, as most had been no further than Khartoum. They reacted to my words with oohs and aahs. It made me feel very special.

After seeing the world through the television, some young men said they would go to Egypt. I thought they would end up in the slums of Cairo, with their children on the streets, or in carpet factories, all because of a TV set. I wondered if the technology made anyone happier, or just created a want for material things.

The next morning, Omar asked me to take him on the pillion to the train station. We arrived late as we had stopped to talk to everyone on the way, and the diesel train was pulling out.

"We've missed it," I said to Omar.

"No, no, follow that train!"

I belted down the track after the train, like Butch Cassidy and the Sundance Kid. With no six-shooter, I tooted the horn, and Omar stood on the footpegs screaming, "Stop!" By the time the guard brought the train to a halt, we were in the middle of the desert.

After kisses on both cheeks, Omar jumped on the train, which slowly moved off. I sat in amazement in the middle of the tracks, waving at the crowd hanging out the windows. British Rail has a lot to learn. It was another unique African moment.

Still 100 miles to Khartoum, and the only sign of the mystical 'road' was giant wheel ruts baked hard in the mud.

As I drove along a trench-like rut, I held my feet up in front to stop them catching on the ground. Suddenly, I flew over the handlebars and landed on my head. I spat out a mouthful of dirt and I struggled for breath, the wind knocked out of me.

Shit! I've crashed! Damage control! Arms okay, legs okay. The bike?

I looked behind me. The Guzzi stood like a petulant pony that had refused a jump. The side crash bars had jammed into the sides of the ditch and stopped the bike dead and it was still standing wedged in the rut. It took an hour of digging with my spanners to get it free.

Then a few miles later, I got stuck up to my engine in the sand. A man on a donkey appeared, from nowhere, and gave me a push out. It was a miracle! He even looked like Jesus. An hour later, my prayers let me down, and I spent another hour placing flat stones across the wadi, then rode across. I knew this desert driving would be hard, but I didn't think I would have to build my own road!

A Land Rover, containing a fat police official and his driver, stopped near me.

"This road is very hard, my friend."

"I know. I've driven from Wadi Halfa."

"I am impressed."

We had a glass of tea together. He was a local Police

Commissioner, on his way to Khartoum.

"We could travel together; you could do me a big favour and put some of my bags in the Land Rover!" I said, "My suspension is suffering."

"No, I am a very important man, in a big rush," he said.

You wanker, I thought, waving as he drove off.

Ten miles on, I caught up with them with the driver under the bonnet.

"Have a problem?" I asked, trying not to snigger.

"Yes," he said. "The radiator is leaking. You must give me a lift to the next town."

I looked at his enormous belly and shuddered at the thought.

"You may be very important but you are also very fat," I said and roared off before he could respond! One wrong turn deserves another!

Just before Shendi, I found the Meroe Pyramids. They looked much smaller than the ones in Cairo, but quite remote. To come across them on my own sent a shiver up my spine, as if I was the first person to discover them.

My track in the sand would be gone tomorrow, but these pyramids would be here in another 4000 years. I drove on, in awe of the power of the ancient kings buried here.

I had long forgotten all thoughts of reaching Australia. Getting to Khartoum was my only goal now. The front of the bike was a disaster area, the shocks splashed out oil and made a horrible grinding noise, like a castrated Pogo stick. The front tyre had a massive bubble pushing out the side. I had to let more air out to stop the bulge in the tyre hitting the forks.

A thick sandstorm blew up as I approached Khartoum. One minute the town lay just ahead, and the next I crawled along, seeing only a few feet in front as the sand swirled into my eyes, choking my carburettors.

SHIT, I've run over someone! I stopped with something slimy under my boots! I had squashed some melons! I sheltered behind a wall.

Twenty minutes later the storm cleared. I had driven through someone's garden and nearly into the back door of their house.

The farmer opened the door and stared at me as if a space shuttle had landed in his vegetable patch.

"Khartoum?" I asked.

He nodded. I'd arrived - by the rear entrance.

I had survived crossing the desert by concentrating on the task and not thinking of anything else. Home, family and friends were now a lifetime ago in a different world.

CHAPTER 7

The Sudanese Express

KHARTOUM WAS AN UGLY MESS OF OLD CRUMBLING COLONIAL BUILDINGS and ugly concrete offices.

The city sits where the Blue Nile and the White Nile join to form the boring plain "Nile." But neither one was Blue or White. Just the Muddy Brown Nile and the ever so slightly darker Muddy Brown Nile.

The Governor's Palace was still there, where 90 years ago General Gordon had met his end by the Mahdi rebels, the predecessors of the modern Taliban.

My history teacher said that General Gordon was a hero, murdered while defending the British Empire.

To the Sudanese, he was an aggressor who tried to convert the Muslim Sudanese to Christianity. One man's hero is another man's terrorist.

Back in 1980, no one knew Sudan was sitting on vast oil reserves; the country was broke and people starving.

The travellers stayed at the Youth Hostel, a large compound with half a dozen dormitories and an outdoor café. Ful Medames, a sort of kidney bean stew, was the only item on the menu; it would be my staple diet for the next month, breakfast, lunch and dinner.

I commandeered the ladies' laundry as a bike workshop and the girls didn't seem to mind me fiddling with my gearbox amongst their bras and knickers.

I attempted to rebuild the forks, but it was useless as the shock absorber plungers had broken up inside.

The front tyre had slashes and cuts and the sidewall came out like a giant boil in two places. I put a piece of metal between the inner tube and sidewall, but it made no difference. Then I tried chunks of wood, which only worked when I lowered the air pressure. The only other option was a Honda 50 wheel!

I found the Germans at the hostel and called them a shower of bastards as they moaned they had shredded their new tyres.

"Serves you right, wankers!" I told them. They looked at me as if I was deranged. Which I was, a bit.

The rest of my desert team had gone on. Bert and Eva had caught the train back to Wadi Halfa and to Europe. Charlie and John had already left for Juba in the Land Rover.

The VW and the Datsun planned to drive the 900 miles to Juba, through "The Sud," an inhospitable region that becomes totally impassable when the Nile floods. With no petrol stations along the way, it meant I would have to carry over 100 litres of petrol, which was ludicrous for the Guzzi.

The only riverboat had broken down, so my only choice was to take the train to Wau, in south-west Sudan, then drive 600 miles to Juba. Still three times my normal range, but just about doable.

At the local garage, they changed the oil, and it shocked me when they threw the old oil into the sand at the back of the yard. I guess that's where it came from.

I asked the British Embassy for advice. George introduced himself as the 'Travel Expert.'

"Can I travel through Uganda?" I asked.

"We don't recommend it."

"Which way do you recommend, then?" I asked.

"You can't go to Ethiopia to the east, Uganda to the south, or Chad to the west, so best you go home the way you came, old chap!"

I don't think he had been outside the embassy walls since he got here from South Kensington. I would get better intelligence at the hostel breakfast table. Before the internet, the way to find information was to ask travellers who had been there.

The Arabs in the north had taken control over the southern Christians after the British left. A civil war broke out between them and had lasted for 30 years. It would be another 30 before the south finally got its independence. Millions would die from famine and genocide.

In Ethiopia, a revolution had broken out, and millions would starve to death, and to the south, Uganda was at war with Tanzania. To the west, the countries in Central Africa started a revolution every bank holiday weekend. After all my trouble to get here, I was stuck. Again.

And, I didn't have a map south of Sudan.

The only place I could sell the bike was South Africa. If I didn't make it there, I would have to abandon it. It wouldn't attract many buyers in Sudan with about twenty miles of tarmac in the entire country.

Bloody Hell, Uncle Jim in London was right; the whole continent was a disaster zone! It looked like a boat to India was the best bet.

I bumped into a couple of Australians at breakfast and the conversation turned to motorcycles.

"Fuck me," one said, "Yesterday I saw someone riding around town on a Moto Guzzi Le Mans; the crazy bastard must have driven it here!"

"Well, that would be me," I said.

"You're fucking crazy, Irishman," he said, and I believed Him.

I met a young French Canadian, called Michel, who was also in Africa by accident. I was twenty-one, he was twenty, so that made him young. He was hitch-hiking in Greece when he stopped in a café and went to the toilet, and the guy drove off with all his belongings and money.

Pissed off with Europe, he took the boat to Egypt and made his way to Khartoum by train. We bonded through our ignorance of all things African.

One evening, we walked to a Palestine Liberation Organization meeting at the nearby university.

They were the guys who had kidnapped and killed the Israeli athletes at the Munich Olympics. They had blown up various airliners and committed other indiscriminate murders. The PLO terrorists had been the ISIS of their day and a very nasty bunch.

I wanted to hear the Palestinian point of view. But the object of the meeting was to recruit new terrorists, not talk about their philosophy. They had a load of Soviet-made RPGs and assault rifles on display, with photographs of guys making bombs.

The local leader, Mohammed, was friendly but became infuriated when I kept calling Palestine, Israel.

"There is no place called Israel; it's all Palestine," he insisted.

"Surely it's the other way round?" I said, "I didn't see one road sign for Palestine, but lots for Israel!"

I told him I was pulling his leg, but he didn't get the joke. "We will never accept the Jewish State; the Jews must leave!" he shouted.

"Surely there is room for Arabs and Jews to live there together?" Michel asked.

"Never!"

"Not a lot of love going around," Michel whispered to me. I had met similar guys in Ireland, both IRA and UDA activists, who all wanted to talk and never listen. They always thought they knew better because they believed 'passionately' in their cause.

Society doesn't think about what religion they want to be. It's not like they decide to be a doctor or a lawyer. If you're born a Protestant, you live and die a Protestant, the same with a Muslim or Jew. Where is the thought process behind that?

Who gets to the age of 18 and says, "Well, I don't want to be Jewish anymore, I want to be a Free Presbyterian"?

We just follow our family. Some people become non- religious or atheist, but rarely do they switch sides.

But the PLO guys had no interest in discussion and they got pissed off when I didn't go along with their opinions.

We left early, for our own safety!

As we walked back through the darkened lanes, a brick hit Michel between the shoulders. A dozen teenagers started pelting bricks at us.

"Fuck off, white man, we don't need you in Africa," they shouted.

"That's debatable; this shithole needs some serious help," Michel shouted to me as we ran, and stones rained down. They didn't follow us, but we didn't stop until we reached the compound.

Khartoum was another dead end, and somehow, I needed to find a way out.

I had patched up the bike, and my internal organs had settled back to their original locations. So, I would take the train to Wau and then drive east to the Kenyan coast. Michel would come on the train but then go west into French- speaking West Africa.

There was a petrol shortage in Wau, so I filled up two jerry cans and drove down to the station.

"You can't bring the bike or the petrol," the clerk said.

"Why not?"

"We need space for supplies for the Civil War in Eritrea"

"Eritrea is the other direction!"

"That's regulations," he shrugged.

Luckily, the stationmaster arrived and relented.

"Ok, put the bike in the goods' wagon and take the petrol with you in the carriage."

The tickets cost £3.50, a bargain for the three-day trip, I thought, until I saw the state of the carriages.

"They robbed us!" I said.

"We will get a flavour of Africa."

"I'm getting the stench of Africa!"

The wooden carriages had no glass in the windows and had hard wooden benches. The toilet was a hole in the floor, which resembled a small volcano of hardened piles of shit built up from the guys with a bad aim.

The stink was disgusting, and I regretted having a shower that morning, as people don't smell so bad when you're stinking yourself.

Our more astute travelling companions had prepared for the trip by not washing for weeks and sat quite oblivious in their own stench!

"The train is extremely overcrowded," I stated the obvious to a very smelly passenger.

"Oh no, Sir, the train is only half full. There will be more passengers to get on at Wad Medina."

Brilliant!

"The journey could take five days. Something always breaks," he smiled.

The passengers looked friendly and seemed to be from the same tribe, with the same scars on their faces. They all looked very fit and chatted away, happy to be heading home.

On the luggage racks lay sacks of grain, bundles of clothes, a few spears, bows and arrows and a couple of hatchets.

They offered us food, which we accepted out of politeness, as it varied from tiny roasted baby pigeons to something that looked and tasted like putty.

"I hope you like your taste of Africa," I said to Michel. Three hours later, the train picked up speed and finally, a breeze wafted in through the wooden slats. The train only moved at about 20mph, but it shook and rocked violently from side to side.

Conversation slowed as everyone settled down for the journey, and I dozed off.

Then a squad of police pushed through the train, emptying bags and shouting abuse. They ignored the spears, hatchets, the revolver and ammunition, but took exception to my two jerry cans.

"Who owns these?" they demanded.

"I do," I said, and they dragged me off to the rear carriage with the cans.

"What's the problem?" I said.

"No petrol allowed."

"What about the friggin' guns!"

"We allow guns, not petrol. Sit there!" the sergeant instructed as we reached the rear carriage.

This is a joke, I thought, but not a funny one; these guys looked scary.

"I have permission to bring the petrol cans. Why am I being arrested?" I protested.

They ignored me and started playing cards.

I sat in the empty wagon with the four policemen, as the train rattled down the track. They wore green fatigues and mirrored sunglasses. If the cops wanted to look intimidating, they had done a good job. I was crapping myself.

No one spoke, and then one passed around cigarettes to everyone but me, which I thought was discouraging. But then again, in the movies, they always give you a cigarette before you get shot!

We sat for two hours, and I started to relax; I was getting a bit bored. Why had I been arrested or had I been? Only one way to find out.

I stood up and walked towards the door, and all four policemen jumped up and unceremoniously shoved me back to my seat. Well, at least that answered that question!

But after an hour, they told me to go back to my seat, but not leave the train.

"I'm not allowed to jump off the moving train!" I told Michel.

"Well, that's good news; I thought they had thrown you off," he said, laughing.

"Thanks for your concern, mate!"

But our attempt at frivolity fell flat, as we couldn't hide our fear. The rest of the passengers were in a different mood now too. The guys who shared their lunch turned their backs to us.

Around midnight, the train stopped at Wad Medina, and more coppers got on, including a fat officer who looked like Idi Amin. I always thought wearing mirror sunglasses after dark was a fashion faux pas, but refrained from offering my opinion. I stood up, but they kicked the sleeping Michel in the ribs.

Never, ever, wake a French Canadian with a kick. Michel grabbed the boot, the cop fell on top of him, and then all six cops jumped on top, punching, kicking and shouting, as I tried to pull them off.

It was a short one-sided fracas; they dragged us off the train and frog-marched us to the station police post. It was dark and humid, with both of us crapping ourselves as the seriousness of the situation sank in. Everyone on the train was staring out the windows.

"You took petrol on the train, and assaulted the police,"

announced the interpreter.

"He kicked me first!" Michel said, rather childishly, I thought, given the circumstances.

We must confiscate the petrol and fine you for resisting arrest."

"Resisting Arrest? I was fucking asleep, for fuck sake!" said Michel.

"And I was told I could bring the petrol!" I said.

I had paid a lot of money for this petrol and I knew there was none to be had in Wau, so I would be stuck without it.

Michel wanted to be a lawyer, and this was his chance to test his powers of persuasion.

"Leave it to me," he said, turning to the interpreter. "Now listen here, you have no right to take the petrol.

We have permission from the station master to carry it on the train. You have no authority to take our belongings from us, and also we would like to complain about the shoddy way your officers have treated us."

The interpreter only spoke two words to the Police chief, probably, 'They're wankers.'

Michel was furious, they had cut short his splendid speech, and he demanded the interpreter tell his story word by word.

But the interpreter shrugged and threw a few obvious Arab insults our way.

Michel wanted his speech translated, I wanted my petrol, the police wanted money and the petrol, so everyone was shouting.

Then the train whistle blew. Bloody hell! It will leave us in the middle of nowhere!

"If we can't take the petrol, I want my Jerry cans!" I said and grabbing them, I started pouring the petrol onto the sand.

That was like pouring petrol on a fire, and all hell broke loose again, as we wrestled for the cans and the petrol gurgled out. But it was four cops against two of us.

The train whistled again and started moving.

"That's our train!" I shouted. "Leave the fucking petrol," and we dropped the cans and ran, as the cops were shouting for us to stop.

Like fuck, I will! We sprinted as the train gathered speed. The cops seemed too busy arguing to chase us. I reached the second last carriage and grabbed the door handle. It jerked me up, and my feet flailed wildly for a foothold that wasn't a revolving piece of train. I found the step and hauled myself up.

Michel was slower, and the train was getting away. "Grab it," I shouted, and he did, catching the last handle, which jerked him like a dog on a lead. He pulled himself up.

We clung on, breathless, as the train rocked along like a drunk with a limp, lurching from side to side. Telegraph poles swept past out of the darkness, missing our heads by inches.

"Jesus Christ, that was close," I shouted anxiously, as if we were finally out of danger, while hanging on to the outside of a speeding train.

I tried to open the door, but it was locked. I nodded for a guy inside to open it, but he didn't move, not wanting to get involved with criminals. He knew better than to mess with the cops.

By the time we got to the next station, my fingers had locked solid from holding on to the handle. When we got back to our carriage, we sat persona non grata, as all our old 'friends' ignored us, terrified to be associated with us.

Totally exhausted, we tried to sleep, and sat and talked about home, family, and plans for the future. We just needed to talk about anything.

In Kosti, more police came on. They took us off for questioning in the stationmaster's office. The story had spread down the track.

"What is your name, where are you going, and why are you here?" they demanded.

"We are journalists for Time magazine," Michel told them, in an effort to make us important, so we shouldn't just disappear.

"Our friends are waiting for us in Wau," we lied.

"Why you fight with the police?"

"Fighting, no, no, no. There must be some misunder- standing!" we said and looked as innocent as we could.

They told us to go to our seats.

I didn't like the journalist story.

"What's the problem?" he said.

"Time magazine would never use 20-year-olds as journalists, and when the police find out you lied, they will arrest us as spies!"

"You worry too much!" he scoffed.

"Well, if they arrest us again, I'll tell them you are CIA," I said, digging him in the ribs.

But we had heard many stories of travellers just vanishing. One day they would meet their friends, the next they would never be heard of again.

This was a lawless land. If the police arrested us for ten gallons of petrol, they would kill us if they found out we had hundreds of dollars in our wallets.

Then I spotted a couple of guys watching us, wearing dirty T-shirts, but wearing smart leather boots when everyone else wore sandals or bare feet. They followed us everywhere.

But the further the train travelled, the cockier we got. Every time the train stopped, we got off one side, ducked under the wheels then doubled back to our seats. We laughing as the cops panicked and ran round to find us. But they couldn't say anything, as that would have given them away.

Eventually, they left, as we had crossed from the Arab north to the Christian south.

The landscape had changed from desert to scrubland, with small trees and bushes in the sandy soil and it was getting hotter with every day. We saw our first Baobab tree. They have thick trunks and spindly branches that look like roots, so they look like an upside-down tree. They grow slowly and are sacred in African cultures.

Round huts with conical thatched roofs replaced the square flat-roofed Arab houses. This was real Black Africa now. Instead of the Arab burkas, the women wore nothing but a rag skirt with their saggy breasts swinging down to their belly buttons. I preferred the burkas!

Young warriors looked fit and armed with bow and arrows, and ran along the tracks at the same speed as the train for miles. Older men appeared wizened, but still lean, as they lopped along at a leisurely pace.

The train would stop in the middle of the bush for prayers, but within minutes kids would be at the windows selling mugs of dirty water. I had run out of iodine tablets but was so thirsty I drank it anyway.

There were only some smelly boiled eggs and stale bread to be found. This was a new experience; hunger and thirst.

The stops attracted beggars from nowhere, malnourished, and diseased, with wounds and disfigurements. Leprosy was rife, gnarled stumps where feet and hands should be. It was shocking, but every time you handed out a few pennies more beggars would appear from the bushes.

On the third day, we had to change trains as a derailment blocked the track. It was chaos to get the bike lifted down onto the ground with about 40 porters, ten to lift it, and thirty to touch the bike so they could claim to have helped. Then they all shouted for payment. I picked the biggest guy and gave him a dollar and told him to sort it out.

I rode up the line passing the wrecked carriages lying on their side. The sleepers had collapsed into the sand foundation and thrown the train off the tracks. I understood now why our train ride lurched violently from side to side.

Personal possessions and some clothes lay strewn around the ground, but nobody knew if it had killed anyone. Even at slow speed, the crash would have been deadly to the crowded carriages.

At the new train, I organised eight men to lift the bike after persuading them that six on one side, and two the other, was not the best way forward.

Then the other thirty guys who advised still wanted paid, but I was getting used to shouting, "Fuck off," in African negotiations. The shy boy from Belfast was learning how to stand up for himself.

This replacement train was half the size, and the carriages were jam-packed. A rush-hour London tube in 40 degrees heat would be sheer luxury. It was impossible to get inside, so we climbed on top of the train with the other passengers.

Children clung to their mothers, and we all hung on to the vents in the roof as the train lurched. It would only be a matter of time before someone fell.

Dehydration was now extreme as the hot sun and the dry wind sucked every drop of moisture from our bodies. At the prayer stops, I now drained the mugs of muddy water without a care as the sand and grit washed through my teeth.

I got chatting with a young army officer, who said that they had a flat-bed wagon with two trucks on it and we could join them. The trucks kept the sun off as we lay under them, but it was terrifying as they rolled and banged against their chains just inches from our heads.

The train's arrival was a big event in Wau. Women ran alongside screaming high-pitched shrieks, and a large crowd gathered. I picked eight men to lift the bike off, as the normal thirty looked on, then again, they all insisted they had helped. Exasperated, I paid the eight men and rode to the station police post to register our arrival. But the horde followed and pushed into the police station behind me, claiming that I had not paid them.

I could feel my head boiling; it was midday, I had been sitting on top of a train all day, and my brain was completely fried.

"These people did nothing," I explained to the copper. "I paid the guys who lifted."

But the sergeant poked his finger in my chest. "You must pay them all," he demanded, "and I fine you ten pounds!"

A red mist came down and my head exploded. I grabbed him by the throat and pulled him towards me until we rubbed noses.

"I have spent five days getting fucking arrested and sitting on top of a fucking train. You can fuck off!" I shouted, "And you can all fuck off too!" I screamed at the crowd, as Michel tried to pull me off the sergeant.

It was pandemonium, with a short one-sided scuffle, as six policemen shoved me into an iron cage in the corner, still screaming "useless copper mother-fuckers."

Luckily, Herbert, my army officer friend, pushed his way through the crowd.

"What is this commotion?" he demanded of the desk sergeant.

"That slimy bastard tried to fuck me over!" I shouted from my cell, pointing to the policeman.

"Chris!" he said, "It is too early for this nonsense; go away and calm down!" as he opened the cell door.

Outside, Michel stuck my head in a bucket of water. My brain sizzled as it cooled, and steam came out of my ears, as the pressure inside my head subsided.

"Who got out the wrong side of the train roof this morning?" Michel said, throwing the bucket of water over me.

Everyone had a breaking point, and I had just found mine.

"Greedy bastards!" I said, as we got on the bike and sped towards the throng of porters at the gate.

"Let me do the financial negotiations from now on," Michel quipped from the pillion. I was still swearing and cursing them all.

But the porters moved aside to let us past; a few even smiled and shouted "Jambo" for hello.

I think we had gained some respect in Wau.

CHAPTER 8

The Road to Hell

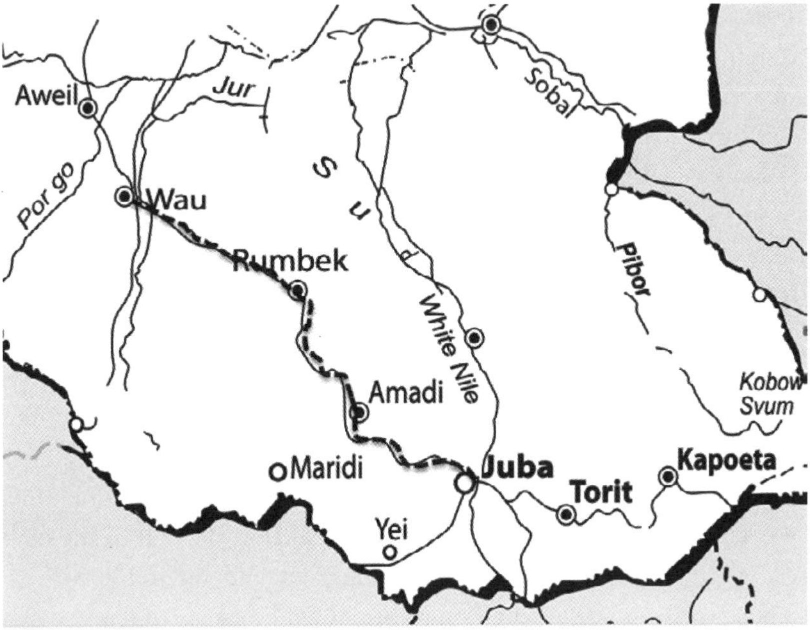

THE WAU YOUTH HOSTEL WAS A SHACK WITH A TIN ROOF AND WAS ALIVE with insects. Bugs would drop out and land on your bed when you slept. All the bed frames sat with feet set in cut-off tin cans. You filled the tins up with paraffin to keep the bugs from climbing up the legs. The strategy had two problems;

1. There was no paraffin.
2. The bugs slept in the beds so the tins stopped them getting out!

I drove the bike into the room and screamed as I got my ankle jammed between the doorframe and the exhaust. It sizzled like a steak on a hot grill and blistered up before bursting. Soon it was bright purple and irresistible to the flies. The Africans let the flies walk over their faces, but I knew the little bastards wanted to get inside my wound and lay their eggs!

The South of Sudan was Christian, while North Sudan was Muslim.

But when they discovered oil in the South, the Arabs took control and imposed Islamic law. The resulting Civil War led to two million deaths and four million refugees. Finally, in 2010, South Sudan became a separate country. It took fifty years and millions of deaths to put the border where the British should have put it at independence.

Wau was a Christian town and the local tribes were tall and very black, their faces and bodies scarred to denote their tribes. The business owners and the government officials were all Arabs.

It was the regional capital for a region the size of the UK and was full of refugees. The main street was a poor attempt at an asphalt road, made of large rocks glued together with a hint of tar; it had a brick church and a few single-storey, red brick colonial buildings. The houses were mud huts with thatched roofs, and the streets were dusty dirt tracks.

The shops were open, but with empty shelves, apart from dried milk powder, stale bread and some dried black beans. At the end of the main street was the 'Jur' river, whose brown waters meandered to the Nile.

There was a modern single-span bridge gifted by an Italian charity. With modern stainless-steel railings and designer lamp posts, it was totally out of place in Wau. The lamp posts had no electricity.

An old hippo lived under the bridge, and every evening it would roar in indignation, as the local kids threw stones at it. Tribal drums would beat long into the night and I heard the animals in the forest across the river shriek, in fear or anger.

Wau was full of stuff that didn't work. Yugoslavia had given them a diesel generator, and when they cracked a piston, they couldn't get a new one so made one from mahogany. The engine could run, but with less power. One thing about Africa was its endless ingenuity. There was no petrol, only diesel and one African mechanic tried to persuade me that my engine would run on a 50/50 mix of petrol and diesel. I would need to prime the carburettors with pure petrol to start the engine. I would leave that as a last resort.

We walked past the Town Hall, and Michel decided he would report the police harassment and theft of the petrol.

Still pretending to be journalists, we talked our way right up to the Chief Commissioner's office.

The room looked decrepit, with faded shocking pink velvet curtains and bleached wallpaper. Behind the mahogany desk piled high with papers, sat the Chief with all his medals, and behind him, the obligatory portrait of the President. Michel started telling him about his corrupt police force, but the Chief cut him short; he was in no mood for listening to a jumped-up Canadian brat.

"The police are corrupt," he shouted. "This is Africa, what do you expect? The policemen probably haven't been paid for six months because government officials steal their wages. They rely on fines to feed their families."

"Stick that in your stupid magazine and fuck off before I have you arrested!" he shouted. We left with our tails between our legs.

"That went well," I said.

"Oh, fuck off too!" Michel said.

It's strange how you adapt to situations and such luxuries as a plate of beans, and a solid crap gave you so much pleasure. The conversation at the breakfast table could be "how was your shit this morning?"

Your 'poo' gave you a sign of your state of health. Diarrhoea, dysentery, worms, and other parasites were rife, so it was essential to watch it. There were no doctors so if you caught a fever you just sweated it out.

And there was no respite from the heat, no air-conditioning or fans, and at night I sweated like a scoutmaster in a sex offenders' line-up, as I listened to the mosquito squadrons form up for another attack.

The next day, there was a military Jamboree and the Vice President was in town, so Michel and I rode out to the army base to watch.

The big competition was to see which soldier could swing their arms the highest. Then a dozen trucks drove around in circles very fast, in a military manoeuvre not used since General Custer's last stand. But it was the African spectators who were the real entertainment to me. The natives shrieked and wailed in amazement at this impressive show of force.

At the end, an old DC3 flew over, and a dozen paratroopers jumped out; a couple even landed near the camp, but most probably ended up in neighbouring countries.

To a man who carried a spear to work, it was an awesome show of strength, clearly meant to say;

"We are in charge, so don't mess with us."

After the show, when I pretended to make a speech at the Vice President's lectern, an officer came over. I thought he would arrest me, but he wanted to chat. Captain Robert said he was a Muslim, as most of the officers were, and only the soldiers were black Christians.

"The blacks need us; they are not good soldiers," he claimed. He shouldn't have been so cocky, as three years later the Christian rebels had Wau surrounded.

"Does the Army have any petrol?" I asked.

"My friend, I have no petrol for two years now." He laughed at this great joke, so we felt we had to laugh too. But he gave me a letter requesting any army trucks going to Juba give me a lift. "Try the black market," he said, but I already had, and had offered five times the regular price, but even the scoundrels had no petrol.

I started every day searching, full of optimism, but by lunchtime, the heat had exhausted me, physically and emotionally, and I would lie down on my bunk depressed.

I had a premonition of abandoning the bike in Wau, the way you see old cars on bricks. People would come from miles and laugh at the plonker who brought a 'Le Mans' to Sudan.

It would be another "Wau folly" along with the bridge and the wooden piston generator.

I was as trapped as the thousands of refugees in the streets.

In the centre of town was the market area, with wooden stalls and palm fronds. Old women sold small bags of charcoal or bars of soap for pennies. A butcher brought live goats to his stall, then cut their throat on the street, and children fought to catch the blood in plastic mugs. The customers wanted to know the meat was fresh.

A blacksmith was forging arrowheads from scrap springs from an old truck. The Africans waste nothing; they don't recycle to save the world, they do it to save themselves.

Some hunters with spears and clubs arrived in dugout canoes. They had some huge ugly fish, and small dead monkeys to sell. The hunters looked strong and fit, without the haunted look of the destitute townsfolk.

There were beggars with deformities that turned my stomach, and they competed for attention.

"It's like a bad taste contest," Michel said. "Who has had the worst abnormality."

I could give away every penny to them, and tomorrow, more would be waiting. And while there was some food available, if you were broke, you would starve, and no one gave a damn.

The lepers had their stumps of putrid flesh where hands and feet should be. Sometimes even their faces were deformed with lumps and calluses. Leprosy had been cured everywhere in the world apart from Sudan.

I had seen the poverty, driving past on the bike, when it was easier to ignore like seeing it on TV, but now I walked the streets and recognized real people. If I gave them a few pennies the day before, they would follow me wanting more today, so I stopped giving anything.

Was I supposed to feed the whole of fucking Africa? My wallet would be empty if I did, and my conscience fucked if I didn't. It's not my problem, I told myself. Why should I feed any of them? If I gave to one, I'd have to give to all of the starving outside the hostel.

I was fairly poor myself with a rapidly diminishing money belt, but I could afford basic food and lodgings. But I knew I could give someone fifty quid and that would feed them for a year, so why didn't I?

Was my trip more crucial than the life of another human, or a whole family?

My conscience was doing somersaults.

One evening, I was in a street cafe eating beans when an African girl came over. She had a clubfoot and wore a hessian sack as a skirt, and her bare scrawny breasts stuck out over her rib cage.

Her fuzzy hair was matted with mud and so full of bugs I could see them moving.

"Give me money, white man," she said.

"Go away!" I knew if I gave her a penny, I would only attract the rest of the beggars.

"Give me money," she shouted in desperation. Most beggars were quiet and subservient, but I still ignored her.

"Give me food, and you can fuck me, white man!" she shouted, lifting her skirt up to show her dusty muff.

"I am starving! Fuck me!" she screamed.

This girl wanted me to fuck her for the leftovers on my plate. I sat, disgusted with myself, as my sad excuse that this poverty was not my problem detonated in front of my eyes like a nuclear bomb.

The Arab owner punched her and knocked her onto the floor. His only concern was that she would upset the customers in his dingy cafe, and he gave her another kick. The jeering crowd that had built up did the same, as she crawled away in the dirt.

"Wait!" I shouted, and pushed past the mob, giving her my plate and enough money to feed her for a week, then I ran off to hide my shame. I thought Africa had hardened me, but evidently not enough. I promised myself that I would never again walk past a beggar without giving them a coin.

But that was a promise I wouldn't be able to keep. There were just too many.

That night, I discussed it with Michel. We talked about the political situation, and why no one tried to help.

"The Arabs are trying to starve the blacks into submission," he said

"It is working!"

"And this stew is horrible," Michel said as he took another spoonful. It was a thick meat stew with some spices. I had already eaten half of it, but when he said that I took a sniff and instantly recognised the smell of decomposing putrefying roadkill. Arghhh! It was rotten!

We stormed to the counter to complain, but the cook just shrugged his shoulders and scraped the rest of our bowls back into the pot.

We staggered away, trying to vomit but unable too. My stomach wanted the food as much as my brain tried to expel it. But I could smell rotten meat every time I belched for a week.

I had to get out of Wau! This tormented town itself was strangling the very life out of me.

Michel found a truck going west and left the next day for the Central African Republic. I was down and on my own, but the next morning, walking down the street, I bumped into an English engineer called John. Well-fed white people stood out; you just had to say hello. John was about 25 and had been working for an oil exploration company for a year. He told me there were billions of barrels of oil under Sudan!

"I only need 15 gallons of 4 star," I said.

He invited me to his compound that evening.

A British charity had sent two new Toyota vans a year ago;

they had lasted six months before the suspension collapsed.

We syphoned their remaining petrol into my tank and two old plastic cooking oil canisters, and I jubilantly tied them on my back seat.

We chatted over a joint.

John loved Sudan, as it gave him work experience he would only get after years in the UK.

"The social life is crap, though; most of the charity workers are clean-living and wouldn't have a beer, let alone smoke a joint."

'Sex is a disaster, I've gone out with a few local girls but I keep getting the clap, and it's impossible to get condoms," he said.

"I told my foreman the problem. He's the chief of the local village. He brought me his 16-year-old niece and promised she was a virgin. Virgin my arse – she just gave me a dose of the pox too! What was I to say to him at work?"

"Sorry, I'm breaking up with your niece; she gave me Venereal Disease!" I suggested, laughing.

John explained that in Sudan, the girl had to prove she was fertile before she got married, so lots of sex. If the man is infertile, he has a great time screwing around, claiming it's the girl's fault when they don't get pregnant!

"Then when they do get pregnant, the father's already away off fucking someone else, so you end up with loads of kids with no breadwinner. It's nuts!"

"How do they survive?" I asked.

"The charities give them food, and that's easier than farming, then in another thirteen years, that daughter is pregnant."

John was on a roll…

"The Catholic charities have brought medicine and free food, but no family planning. It's totally fucked, but don't ask me, I'm only an engineer!"

I decided to abstain from the pleasures of the flesh for some time, and went back to the hostel, wondering if he was right. On the way, I passed the refugee camp and sitting begging were groups of pregnant mothers with a baby wrapped in a sling and a brood of malnourished children at their feet. But it didn't make it easier to walk past them.

7th February 1980

I tied the two 5-gallon drums on the pillion, along with 3 gallons of water. But with a full tank and all my gear, when I pushed the bike off the centre stand, the suspension compressed to the stops.

Jesus Christ, I thought, I can hardly hold the bike up, let alone ride it! The smooth tarmac on the Italian bridge was like the heaven before the hell on the other side. There was a five-foot drop at the end where the dirt track had eroded away. At the police checkpoint, the cops helped me down the slope, and I signed myself out of this dubious version of civilisation.

"Do you check with the other posts to make sure I don't get lost?" I asked the sergeant.

"Yes," he said, "at the start of every month we check the books!"

"That's reassuring, I have to survive three weeks in the jungle before you come looking!" I said, my sarcasm lost.

This was it; six hundred miles to the next petrol station. I rode off, wobbling like a newborn puppy.

The road was worse than my wildest nightmare, and they had been really wild. The potholes were like bomb craters, all joined up in a continuous line that made up the road.

"Fuck, Fuck, Fuck!" I thought, as no other adjective completely covered the situation. "What madness is this?!"

I disappeared from one crater into another, the bike's suspension bottoming out, and the rear tyre crunching on the mudguard at every hump. By the end of the first hour, I had covered five miles. I had to stop to rest my aching arms every fifteen minutes. It was hard physical work hauling on the handlebars to stay upright. I hadn't got out of 1st gear yet and could have walked faster. My petrol would never last at this rate.

After another five miles, my back tyre burst. I had a repair kit, so it wasn't a big deal, but I had lost my pump somewhere along the way. The local trucks had a compressor, but the police log showed two vehicles passed a day and two trucks had passed already.

It was getting dark, and I didn't relish a night in the jungle. All I had to defend myself from wild animals was a knife and fork. I decided to buy a spear or bow and arrow at the next Sudanese Argos.

Out of the dusk, an old guy of about seventy suddenly appeared on a bicycle. I was embarrassed at being scared on my own. Anyway, I could always steal his bike and cycle off at first sight of a carnivore.

He smiled with his yellow and black teeth and told me to wait, and 10 minutes later a pickup truck appeared with a load of guys in the back.

The driver insisted on fixing the puncture and pumped up the tyre.

"I will follow to make sure it's okay," he said and sure enough, after another couple miles, the tyre blew again as my last inner tube gave up. He fixed it again, and this time it held.

I pulled into the first village, Tonj, after travelling a whole fifteen miles, and set my tent up beside the police checkpoint. The village was a cluster of mud and straw huts and didn't have much to offer, but the cops were friendly and shared their beans before I crawled exhausted and depressed into my tent. The day had been a disaster.

Sleep would be a welcome escape from this nightmare. The track was now smooth hard clay, dried hard in waves after the rains, and coming out of one huge hole, the bike slid sideways down another. I couldn't hold it upright and slipped to the bottom of a ditch, then the bike fell over on me, with the exhaust landing right on the burn on my ankle again. I screamed in agony!

Then petrol poured out of the plastic cans and hissed on the hot exhaust. Panicking, I ripped the containers free and heaved it upright before it exploded.

The sweat dripped off me, as I swore at the continent of Africa in general. I sat down to catch my breath then heard a noise in the jungle behind me. Shit!

I looked around slowly.

Eight African hunters were standing watching me silently from the bushes. They were armed with the best bows and arrows that money couldn't buy. They were black as night, and their biceps bulged between ivory arm bangles. After the fat Arabs and starving Africans in Wau, these guys looked like Olympic athletes, but much more frightening than Tom Daley and his speedos.

They just stood and stared at me. The silence was deafening.

I didn't know what to say, so I waved. It was supposed to be a macho, sort of 'All right, mate' wave. But it came out as one of those girly, waggle the fingers ones! Embarrassing!

They gave me that, 'it's a spaceman' expression, which was fair enough. I mean, a big red motorcycle falls into the hole, a white guy jumps up screaming, throws all his stuff off, then lies down in the middle of the road. Just what you expect to see on your morning monkey hunt!

I felt ridiculous, like when someone spots you scratching your balls in a lift. I took their photograph then re-packed the bike, but when I turned around again, they had disappeared.

The "Bush" was deserted, but occasionally I could glimpse a group of round huts with thatched roofs. A group of men sat under a large tree while the women did all the work. Naked children ran chasing chickens and pushing home-made wooden toys. There were few indications of the current millennium apart from a few metal pots.

After a while, I noticed my luggage top box was at a funny angle, and sure enough, the frame had broken from the pounding. The plastic mudguard was the only thing holding it on. I needed a welder, quick.

I had passed a Leprosy Mission a few miles back; not the first choice of a place to stop, but I needed a welder, even if he only had one arm!

A man with a face like a busted banjo met me at the gate. It was calloused and contorted. He took me to meet Brother Anthony, an Italian monk who ran the mission.

He said he wasn't keen on strangers calling, but as I was on an Italian motorcycle and was obviously a good Irish Catholic, he would make an exception.

"No worries," I said. "I don't hang around leper colonies either, but I will also make an exception."

Brother Anthony had been in Africa for 31 years and dedicated his life to his calling. A wiry man about 60 years old, he was the sort of guy who did everything in a hurry, and I had to run to keep up as he showed me around the camp.

Leprosy was not contagious and all his patients were cured, he assured me every time I asked, which was every 10 minutes. He explained the disease killed the nerve endings, and then the tissues got damaged and infected, then the wounds led to amputations and disfigurement. He still got a few new cases, but they were easily treated with drugs.

"When the disease is cured, the people cannot go back to the community," he said. "They live in the Colony, not because they are contagious. It's just ignorance."

"Some people here look healthy," I said.

"They shun the whole family, so they all stay here, such is the stigma of the disease."

Anthony came to Africa as a young man to spread the word of God and convert the natives to Christianity. But now he looked after physical needs more than religious beliefs.

"The Church's attitude to Africa is disappointing. It is more interested in converting souls than saving lives," he said. "But now they leave me alone. I'm too much trouble for them!" He laughed. "And no one wants to take over."

But he had to be careful, as the Muslim government didn't want him to spread the Christian gospel either.

"I see young men coming out to 'help the suffering' but it's a lie, they come to make themselves look good."

"When I came, I had an old Norton," he said. "I could travel to Wau or Juba in a few hours – the streets were paved in clay bricks," he said, to my amazement.

"But the biggest car then was a Land Rover. Now the giant Chinese trucks tear up the roads."

"The British were dictators, but at least there was law and order. Now, Africans rip off their own people. The whole place is corrupt."

Anthony was a dysfunctional missionary, but he was still a Christian, and I didn't want to insult him by asking him if he still believed in God.

I got up at dawn and limped over to the workshop. The infected burn on my ankle was throbbing and seeping pus. I couldn't complain as more camp inmates appeared with hands and feet missing, and horrible growths on their faces. But Anthony got his orderly to clean and dress my feeble wound.

Then a small boy of about 12 appeared and offered me his hand to shake, and I couldn't help hesitating before I shook it.

"You are a welder?"

"Oh yes, I am very good; I have both hands to work with," he replied, teasing me. He welded the cracks in the tubing and reinforced it so it wouldn't break again.

Things were bad with the Guzzi. The front forks were squirting oil out the top again. The back shocks couldn't take the load and crunched down as the wheel banged against the mudguard with the weight of petrol on the back. Meanwhile, the front wheel crunched with an ominous crack of metal on metal.

I had been driving a suspension system, designed for Italian autostradas, over ploughed fields and moon craters for a month now. It was only a matter of time before it gave up. With the nearest Moto Guzzi shop two thousand miles in either direction, there wasn't much I could do. The front wheel was not even round, it was just a continuation of dents.

My tyres were low-profile Avon Roadrunners, and clearly not designed for deserts, and the wooden splints I had placed in the side walls didn't stop the two enormous black septic boils breaking out again.

Brother Anthony looked at the problem and cut off a 20 cm chunk from an old Land Rover tyre and placed it between my inner tube and outer casing.

This man was a miracle, and his "old Africa Expat" trick worked, the boil disappeared as the old rubber behind took the pressure.

But the wheel was now hopelessly out of balance with the extra weight, so I glued some heavy brake pads to the opposite side of the wheel rim. The glue couldn't hold very well, and the pads would occasionally fly off toward the nearest pedestrian.

Africa teaches the art of creative mechanics, as you learn to fix an old part when you can't get a new one. It made me realise no one actually 'fixes' anything in the West anymore. If something breaks you just replace it, and the broken part gets dumped.

Now, mechanics are people who plug the machine up to a computer, then replace the faulty bit. Nothing here gets thrown away; they will find a use for it, eventually.

In 1980, if your telephone broke, you could take it apart and find a loose wire and fix it. Now if your iPhone breaks, it's cheaper to throw it away and buy a new one, because it's impossible to see how it works.

Machines now are solid-state or factory-sealed and not made for amateurs to repair them.

For the first time in 10,000 years of human evolution, we don't understand how anything works. We just buy it, use it then throw it away.

Bike engineering has come a long way, with strong lightweight materials, and computer-aided design. Ever since man invented the wheel, he has improved it. By 1980, it had evolved into perfection the; Moto Guzzi Le Mans, which I was busy demolishing!

I could finally shake Anthony's hand without wiping mine afterwards. I thanked him profusely for his advice on Africa, life, and welding.

I had huge respect for this man, not just for the work he did, but like me, he had left his home for the wilds of Africa. He had run away from something… as had I. The whole camp came out to wave and cheer as I left. I wondered what fate had in store for me around the next corner.

The sun in Sudan is twice the size of anywhere else I had been and twice as hot, and it rose slowly through the smoky morning haze, casting a pale-yellow glow over the thatched huts. African mornings are serene and give little sign of the terrible intensity that will quickly radiate from the sky.

By mid-morning, the heat was unbearable. Everyone moved like a zombie until late afternoon, when it cooled enough to work without self-combusting. That's unless you are trying to cross Africa on a motorcycle. This mad dog motorcyclist had to go on. The roads were so bad, I travelled for 10 hours just to cover 50 miles a day.

I was an hour out of Rumbec when I realized I was on the wrong road. "You dickhead," I shouted to myself, there were only two routes out of town, and I took the wrong one. It's best to ask directions from as many people as possible and go with the majority, as everyone has a different opinion.

But today democracy was wrong.

This one had potholes deep enough to pop your ears. On the map, both roads joined up, so I plodded on, heaving the bike up and down the trail, in and out of the dips and hollows. I expected my overheating engine to implode into a molten mass of aluminium. It was working as hard as if doing 70 mph but was only going at 10 mph, as there was no airflow past the cylinders.

But today it was the front tyre, which gave way with a puncture. The back wheel of the Guzzi comes off quickly. Take the axle nut off, loosen the clamp, the shaft pulls out, and the wheel is off. The front is a bit more involved as I have to remove the brake calliper, so it's a 30-minute job. I take the tyre off the rim and fix the puncture in the inner tube, then reassemble.

I would wait for a truck with a pump; no point in getting annoyed. I lay back in the shade for a doze, while the flies crawled over my face searching for a nice damp spot in my beard to lay their eggs.

I awoke to find some giggling girls watching me from the coarse yellow grass. Each one had a baby held to their bare breasts, and they wore nothing but a bone necklace and an old rag around their waist. Their feet were bare and as tough as old leather. I smiled, and they burst into nervous laughter and ran off towards a village just through the trees.

They look amiable enough, so I wandered towards the huts, thinking I could be here for the night by the time a truck came. The village had eight or nine circular mud huts with thatched roofs. The surrounding earth was bare and hard- packed to keep the snakes away. In the middle of the clearing there was a fire and a tree trunk bench with a blacksmith hammering away at an old truck spring, shaping the metal into a spear tip.

Two young African hunters suddenly jumped out in front of me. They had ivory bands on their arms and a necklace made from somebody's teeth. They looked ferocious, with their faces cut in scar lines. They cut the skin then rub charcoal in to stop the wounds from healing, so they form raised scars.

These guys lived by hunting and they looked at me as if I had been chasing their daughters.

"I'm not a pervert," I wanted to say. I looked for a big cooking pot, but there was only a kettle. One guy reached out to shake my hand.

"Jambo," he said. "Jambo," I replied.

The village Chief came over, wearing an elaborate ivory chain, like a Lord Mayor. We shook hands, then one woman gave me the ceremonial metal mug of black tea.

They sat at the fire, which I thought was a bit unwarranted in 40-degree heat, while the women stood behind, with the kids behind them. The same scene could have occurred five thousand years ago, minus the Moto Guzzi, obviously. They looked pleased to see me, but no one spoke a word of English. I spent an hour trying to explain I needed an air compressor, not an easy task with a man who has never owned a pair of shoes.

I started to relax, as it looked like they would not make a necklace out of my testicles. Someone dug a burnt sweet potato out of the fire and gave it to me with a nice mug of warm, muddy water. I have had better snacks, but it's rude to refuse. So, I ate and drank, feeling the grit swill between my teeth, and wondering what worms and parasites I had just swallowed. Good roughage anyway. My poo will come out like a cement block!

We chatted by using pictures and sign language. Someone had heard of London, which was a start. More people arrived from the surrounding district; there must have been a hundred now. I was the biggest news in town and it was turning into a party. The women stood gossiping, pointing and laughing, while the children ran to and from the Guzzi but were too respectful to touch it.

They put all questions to the Chief as if he could speak English, and he pretended to be an expert in communications. The other men were free to help translate with actions and drawings on the earth. Occasionally, someone would say something funny, at my expense, and everyone would burst into hysterical laughter. I felt like blushing.

I found that they hunted small animals like monkeys and pigs, then I made a roaring noise like a lion, and they all laughed and shook their heads.

The men talked as if discussing Einstein's laws of physics, but nobody had heard of Uganda, although it was a few hundred miles away. Their world stopped at Juba.

They made the huts of mud, plastered to a frame of branches, with a hole in the roof for the smoke. I had a look inside one. Along one wall was the kitchen, with a rough table with a few pots and pans. Another wall had some straw bales against it, which I presumed was the sitting room. The third wall was the bedroom with straw lying on the floor.

I pointed at the fire to ask why they needed it in the house when it was so hot, and the wife waved her arms about as if swatting flies, while her bare breasts jiggled around like yo-yos. I got the message, the smoke kept the flies out, and she had never worn a bra.

Their only concession to civilisation was a beat-up aluminium cooking pot and a communal plastic toothbrush.

The magic was broken when I heard the roar of a truck struggling down crater alley. It was 1980 again; instantly relieved at the prospect of fixing the bike, I was disappointed, and I knew that the moment was gone forever. We all ran over to the track like it was the second coming of the Lord, and a hundred Africans with spears surrounded the truck.

I stepped out of the jungle, like Henry Morton Stanley himself.

"Mr Lorry Driver, I presume; do you have a pump?" He did.

With my tyre pumped up, I shook hands with everyone.

"Give me arrows," I said, pointing at a hunters' quiver.

The chief smiled and motioned over at my bags. A swap was afoot; I opened my top box and he shuffled through my clothes.

He picked out two pairs of well skid-marked Marks and Spencer Y-fronts, to exchange for a bow and three arrows. The chief was as happy as a bunny at Easter and ripped off his hessian loincloth and put his Y-fronts on, then did a little dance down the road to raucous laughter. Another happy M and S customer!

It was my turn to do a show, and I sat on the bike and pretended to shoot arrows as I rode along, no hands, to more laughter and a round of applause.

It was time to go, and I rode off, tooting the horn while the women made an ear-splitting high-pitched hollering "La, La, La" noise, and the kids ran alongside.

Meanwhile, the worms burrowed into my stomach lining, but it was days like this that made it all worthwhile.

The next problem was swarms of tsetse flies, nasty bastards, who flew beside me like Messerschmitt fighters preparing to attack a lumbering Lancaster bomber. They would bite me right through my rugby shirt, nearly making me fall. Their stings would hurt like hell. The tsetse fly is the primary carrier of sleeping sickness in Africa.

I camped in Akot village, about 30 miles further on. It was a cosmopolitan spot with shops and cafés on the dusty street. Everyone wore flared bell-bottom jeans and early 1970s platform shoes. I sat down at a street café.

Some girls in hessian skirts stopped to giggle and flirt until zealous boyfriends chased them away. They needn't have worried; they smelled of musty old donkeys.

Across the road, men were drinking beer scooped from a plastic bucket, and two of them kept screaming abuse at me. I knew they would soon get enough beer courage to come over, so I retreated to the safety of my tent, pitched beside the police post.

The sun was shining as I started off, and soon I was kicking up and down through the gears, taking the bends fast and jostling for position at the front of the other bikes.

We raced up the coast road with the girls on the pillion. I lined up for the next bend…but I hear flies buzzing! I opened my eyes - back in my tent, the heat was stifling already although the sun was just above the horizon.

I tried closing my eyes again, but it was too late, the dream was gone. I was here, stuck in fucking Africa, miles from anywhere.

JESUS CHRIST!

I floundered in despair at the task ahead and suffered from intense claustrophobia as the heat pounded on my head. It gripped my body like a giant hand and squeezed me until my brains were about to explode out my ears.

Why am I here, and what am I trying to prove? I wondered as I packed up my tent. It would be another arm-wrenching, spine-busting, kidney-crunching, bum-breaking day at the office.

"I won't fall off today," I told myself, as I had every day for the last five weeks. And hell, it was working fairly well - only two small tumbles and halfway down Africa!

I was riding southeast, into the rising sun. The track looked like a great earthquake that had torn a chasm through the jungle, leaving a tortuous fissure in the red earth. But it was just the trucks in the rainy season that had torn the ground into waves like an angry ocean, before it dried hard in the sun.

I rounded a corner and rode straight into a troop of baboons warming themselves on the track. They squealed and ran off into the bush, and a few stopped to point their red bottoms at me in contempt. I was going to 'moon' back, as my raw ass was redder!

My first wildlife! I grabbed my camera and ran off after them. The baboons stopped, then ran off again before I got a shot.

The trees were tall and stringy with dry coarse yellow grass and thorn bushes in between. Every time I tried to get a photo, they ducked behind a bush, then one turned and roared in contempt. Suddenly, I realised what a prick I was, chasing a troop of wild baboons with nothing but a poor- quality East German camera to defend myself; These guys could rip my head off. I retreated towards the road.

But with the excitement, I hadn't paid attention to which direction I had come from, so not finding the road, I tried another direction. Suddenly, I realized I had no idea which way to go. The forest looked exactly the same in every direction.

I climbed a tall tree, but there were only more trees everywhere. The branch broke with a crack and I went tumbling ten feet to the ground, twisting my ankle.

I tried limping in one direction for 5 minutes, then turned right 90 degrees and walked for another 5 minutes, in a sort of square search pattern, but still no sign of the track. I was completely lost!

This was lion country, and those baboons looked frightening too!

Why does my world go like this? One minute I'm riding down a track in the jungle, as happy as a pigmy, then the next I'm in danger for my life! The sun was high, and with no water or hat, I was frying.

I could lie down and die here and by the time they found me, I would just be a shrivelled skeleton with a camera! Something moved. Shit! I sprinted up another tree and got six feet off the ground before it started to bend. Fuck, I had found the smallest tree in Africa! But it was only an impala, and he bounded away.

I found a rotten mango, scraped off the bugs crawling through it and sucked at the moisture. It was disgusting, but it wet my mouth.

I had been walking for hours and realised I was going round in circles when I found my rotten mango remains. My brain was frazzled; everywhere looked the same, and I could only see ten feet ahead. I sat down, and the jungle closed in.

My tongue dried first, then the back of my throat, as I ran out of saliva. Dying of thirst wouldn't be quick, I realized; it would happen gradually and painfully. I staggered on, my pace slowing. I was going to die from stupidity. That annoyed me, as if dying for a 'good' reason would be okay.

I checked the time and it was after 2 pm. It was well over 0 degrees with not a breath of wind. My watch! Suddenly, I remembered an old scouting trick!

If I pointed the hour hand at the sun, then South is halfway between the hour hand and noon.

Or is it north? Hell! Which is it? And the sun was high as I was near the Equator, so it was hard to get a fix. Think, for God's sake, think! I had followed the baboons to the left, or north, so I needed to go south to find the road! I started south, as straight as I could.

My tongue was now as dry as an Egyptian mummy's scrotum. The dryness had spread down my throat, and my ankle was aching. I had to stop to rest every few minutes.

My body was closing down. My eyesight blurred as my eyeballs dried up, and my blood, thick as treacle, thumped in my ears with the exertion. I stopped every few metres, and each time it got harder to get up. I resigned myself to my moronic death.

Dumb ass idiot! I could leave a note, but I had no paper. I had my camera, so could take a picture of 'goodbye' on the earth. Now, I just wanted to lie down and dream.

"FUCK THIS! Get up and walk, you stupid bastard!" I thought-shouted to myself. But I wanted to sleep, rather than the pain of walking. "Get up. Get up. Fuck you!"

I got angry, and that kept me going. Get up! Go on! Get up! Wanker! Wanker! You got yourself into this one, now you get the hell out of it!

My throat was dry down my windpipe now and I made a strange rasping sound with the hot air. I heard people faced with death turn to religion. Bollocks! I just got angry.

The mortification of dying like a useless prick is what saved me!

I realised there was red earth under my feet - the track! I had found the bloody track; my boy scout trick had worked! But which way do I go?

I guessed left. I could hardly walk, and collapsed every few yards. It was now evening.

Then I noticed some huts beside the road! I staggered up to a little ten-year-old naked boy. He was playing with a hoop and a stick.

"Water," I tried to say, but nothing came out, as my throat was so parched my vocal cords had withered. But he got the message and produced a mug of muddy water, which I quickly drained.

"More!" This time a Donald Duck squeak came out, as my vocal cords soaked up the moisture, and some of my strength returned. My ankle started to throb, as did the blisters on my feet.

The village was near deserted and the only taxi in town was a bicycle ridden by a wizened old man. I perched on the rack, and we wobbled back up the trail in the dark.

I heard the roar of an engine and saw lights. The truck had about twenty drunken Africans on the back. I paid off my bicycle chauffeur and jumped on. They had no water, just some homemade beer in plastic bottles. The beer tasted of soapy puke but I gulped it, and it went straight to my head.

Some guys started harassing me as we bumped along.

"Why are you here, white man? What the fuck do you want in Africa?" one drunk shouted, poking me in the chest, but I was too tired to answer. I just wanted to find the bike, and my high- pitched voice sounded embarrassingly like a castrated pig.

I didn't know if the bike would still be there, but suddenly it appeared in the headlights, parked in the middle of the road, where I had left it.

I was ecstatic. I hugged Mr Bully, which took him aback a bit, then jumped down. The driver got out for a fag, and I paid him a few piasters. Everyone wanted to examine the bike. I suppose it was a strange thing to come upon, parked in the middle of the jungle.

The key was in the ignition and my passport and money belt were still lying on the open top box. No one had been past all day.

Suddenly, Mr Bully threw me against the truck. He was a big ugly bastard with a huge fat face and beer stains down his Miami Vice T-Shirt. He could see I had something worth stealing now.

"Give me money, or I kill you," he said. His bulging eyes glared in the truck's lights, his face right up to mine now.

'For fuck's sake, what a day I'm having,' I thought, as if from a distance. I shoved him away and raised my fists. This guy wanted to kill me, but I wasn't going down without a fight.

I heard the thump of a fist on flesh, but felt no pain. My ugly bastard was down, squealing like a baby.

"Weird," I thought.

The driver had hit him, and then the passengers all wailed in, kicking him on the ground while I looked on bemused, and pleasantly pleased!

"He is a bad man," said the driver and gave me my fare back.

"Thank you," Donald Duck squeaked back.

"Do you need anything?"

"No, I'm fine," I said, although I was far from it. I was dizzy and so dehydrated that every time I drank, my mouth soaked it up before I had time to swallow.

They threw my attacker in the back of the truck, still moaning, and drove off leaving me standing disoriented, as the jungle night residents came alive. I felt a hundred pairs of eyes looking at me, and a cacophony of squeals and screeches called out. I imagined myself lying out there, dry as a prune, waiting for death.

A wave of exhaustion washed over me as I hit the starter and the V twin burbled, as soothing as a mother's voice, saying "It will be okay."

I was home.

But as my adrenalin evaporated, the pain came. I was burnt and blistered. It was time to go. In the next village, I stopped at a Christian charity compound. I drank gallons of water, my body creaked as it rehydrated, like an old airbed inflating, but I couldn't stop drinking. My eyes started to focus, but my speech was still squeaky.

I had been close to death. If I hadn't been so humiliated by my ineptitude, I would have perished!

"That was the worst day of my life!"

"You're lucky it wasn't your last," the charity guys told me. "There are lions out there!"

The next morning, I was still weak as a dry fart but determined to make up for the lost time. But a few miles on, the front shocks seized solid.

"When is this going to end?" I shouted to a tree, as I stopped under it to dismantle the suspension.

The front brakes, wheel, mudguard, then the bottom tubes and the inner springs and shocks all came off. I poured the precious oil into my mess tins. The shock absorber pistons had pulled apart, and the tubes were smashed and bent.

In fact, technically speaking, they were buggered. The only thing that stopped the front wheel falling off was the rubber brake hose.

I sat down and stared at the busted bits while the flies buzzed around me. What now?! There was only one answer - put it all together again. I jammed the plungers in, with nothing restraining the springs, and limped into the next village where they locked again, and I parked beside a mud hut and took it apart again. When I turned to pick up a spanner, ten Africans were sitting behind me in total silence!

Then a guy wandered over with a goat on a rope. Suddenly

I had an idea.

"How much for the rope?" I said.

"The goat?"

"No, just the rope."

"Take it," he said, and he joined the twenty villagers watching what I was up to. He looked proud that he had provided expert help.

I wound the cord between the axle and the handlebars to tie the front axle on to the handlebars. The rope would stop the rebound, so the wheel didn't fly off at every bump. It looked rough, but if it stopped a goat, maybe it would stop my wheel falling off. It worked for a couple of miles then the rope broke and the shocks locked up again, but the plan was good. I had to take it all apart … and find a bigger goat!

I found some stronger nylon rope in the next village. It held but stretched, so I had to tighten it every half hour. I didn't need a mechanic. Just lots of rope!

Three gallons and 120 miles to go. It looked like I would run out of petrol before I got to Juba, but then the track suddenly improved. It was flatter but covered in small corrugations six inches deep. It was like riding over a ploughed field. I could go slow and bounce up and down each furrow or go 30 mph and skip over the top. I chose over the top, but the bike started to vibrate into pieces.

If I were to fall at this speed, it would peel me like a potato, but my fuel economy improved dramatically. I stood on the footpegs, with my thighs burning, trying to act as shock absorbers. In the outskirts of Juba, I rode jubilantly into the first petrol station. An attendant stood beside the pump.

"Fill her up," I said, smiling.

"No petrol," he replied.

"No petrol? Why are you here if there's no bloody petrol!"

"Because I am a petrol pump attendant," he explained. "If I do not come to work, I do not get paid."

"So where can I get petrol?"

"Kenya has lots of petrol," he replied smiling. "No petrol in Juba."

My heart sank. After all my efforts, I was stranded again!

"What the fuck is wrong with this continent?!" I shouted at the bewildered attendant.

War surrounded Juba, and starving refugees poured in. It was, quite literally, Hell on Earth.

In Uganda, Idi Amin had just lost the war and gone into hiding. He had killed over half a million Ugandans. In 1979,

Tanzania gave refuge to 20,000 Ugandans. Amin was pissed off and he invaded, because, "If he took over Tanzania, Uganda will look be very big on the map."

Tanzania was unprepared but quickly mobilized.

They had acquired a few obsolete Soviet rocket launchers, which they fired into the Ugandan jungle. They hit nothing but scared the shit out of the Ugandan soldiers, and they fled into Sudan, chased by the Tanzanian army.

Amin's official title was "His Excellency, President for Life, Field Marshal Al Hadji Doctor Idi Amin Dada, VC, DSO, MC, Lord of All the Beasts of the Earth and Fishes of the Seas and Conqueror of the British Empire in Africa in general and Uganda in Particular".

He was a nutcase, but a dangerous one, and his remaining troops were hiding in the jungle surrounding Juba, so it was a dangerous place to be.

There were two roads to Kenya; the long one bypassed Uganda but was 700 miles of dirt roads. The shorter route went through Uganda and was only 100 miles of dirt, then 250 miles of tarmac. I got a hard-on at the mere thought of a tarmac road.

My front shocks made horrendous scrunching noises and relied on my rope suspension system. The front wheel had eight large dents on the rims and was squashed into an 'S' shape. Ever since I disconnected the oil light, the engine had been going perfectly. But, with no petrol, I wasn't going anywhere.

Lepers, beggars and refugees who had lost everything besieged the campsite in the grounds of the old Greek Hotel.

I put a few pennies into their outstretched arms, trying to avoid looking into the mucus-filled eyes of the children.

"I have no more money," I said. I was broke - for a white man, anyway. But I was still wealthy beyond their dreams, for I had won the lottery of birth, being born with a British passport.

The Greek Hotel was a great place to meet other travellers. The main topic of conversation was corrupt border guards, dangerous war zones and how to get out. There were stories of people disappearing without a trace. Everyone had their own horror experience.

I sat in a street café eating a bowl of stew. When I bit on cartilage and bone and spat it out on the dirt floor, a kid scurried across and popped it in his mouth. His mother had sent him under the tables for scraps like a dog. Horrified, I handed him the rest of my bowl, and he scampered off to his mother to share it.

I knew I could give her enough money to feed her for a week, but what about the next hundred beggars? Should I give all my money away to them too? I couldn't feed the whole of Africa. Or was that just an excuse for giving them just a few pennies, appeasing my Western conscience? Is that what charity is about?

I walked past the church, and wondered if this vile place was as low as life could get, or was there worse out there? And why would any God let this happen? Aid workers looked smart in their crisp khaki shirts and shiny Land Cruisers. But I couldn't work out what they were doing as everyone was starving!

In a continent the size of Africa, it seemed weird to bump into travellers I had met before, but there were only one or two roads open down the whole of East Africa. I shared information with the guys coming from the South and gave them news from the North.

This was the pre-internet age, and knowledge came from books or by word of mouth, and the books were out of date as soon as they were printed. Travellers' tales usually got exaggerated, so I had to learn what I could from old-fashioned gossip and try to sort what was true.

But no one had come through Uganda; they had all taken the northern Kenya route. As far as the jungle telegraph was concerned, Uganda was closed.

Then, an American girl said she had met a trucker who would take us through Uganda in a convoy of four other trucks, so there would be safety in numbers.

The Somali truck drivers seemed to be immune from the local strife. Small wiry men, they kept themselves to themselves.

I had only found two litres of petrol, so my only way out was on a truck. It was disappointing after driving this far, but there was no choice.

There were eight Western travellers - the four Americans, three other Europeans and myself and I had only met them the night before.

There were only two trucks. They were full of sacks of rice, marked "Donated by the Government of the USA". Rather bizarrely, they were taking the grain away from the place where everyone was starving!

But, 'ask no questions' was the best policy, and I wedged the bike between the sacks, and soon we crossed the Nile over a fortified bridge.

We travelled in the dark with the lights off, as we didn't want to run into Amin's Army stragglers. At midnight the truck stopped for something to eat. The Italians had introduced pasta to Somalia, but the recipe had been lost, so we had a squirt of tomato ketchup in a tin bucket of soggy spaghetti.

Dawn broke as we crested the brow of a hill to see tropical rain forests below.

"Uganda," the driver announced grandly through the window, with a majestic wave of his hand. The country looked green and fertile after the dry bush I had been travelling through for weeks.

We had just driven off the edge of my last map.

CHAPTER 9

Uganda & Kenya

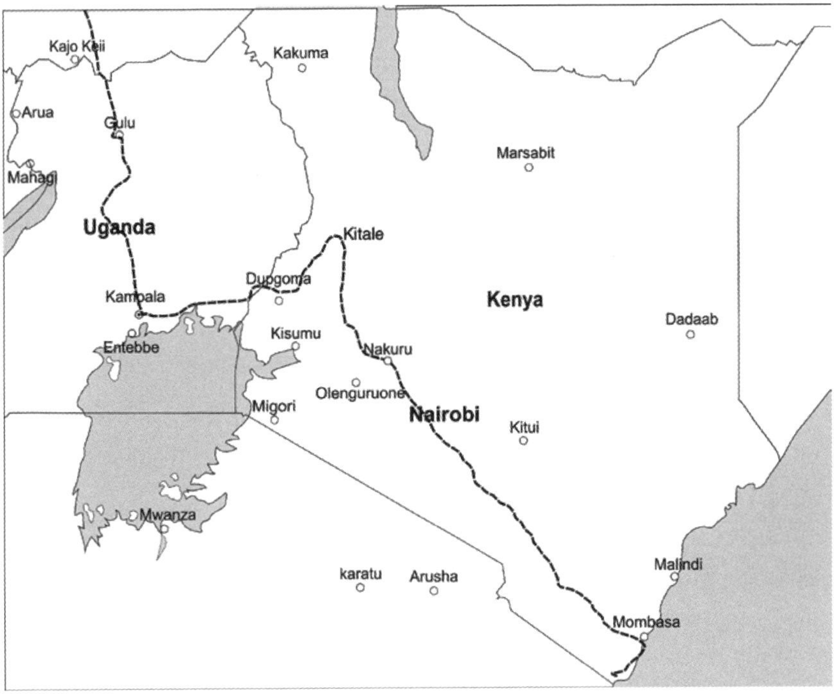

"YOU GO TO UGANDA? YOU ARE A CRAZY MAN!" LAUGHED THE SOLDIER at the Sudan border post in a high-pitched squeak. I looked in the leather-bound registration book; no Western travellers had crossed this year, only a few local farmers.

"Don't worry, it will be okay," our driver assured us. With no petrol to go back, I was committed. Our trucks trundled over the half a mile of no-man's-land to Uganda. The deserted Ugandan Customs buildings had been torched and the scorched rafters still stank of smoke. The next villages we passed were empty too, with only the walls of the burnt-out huts still standing. The countryside was deserted, as the retreating army had stolen or burnt or everything. Our excited chatter turned to a tense silence. Maybe this wasn't such a good idea. Why did I listen to the truck driver? He just wanted our money.

In the villages, the round huts still stood, but the retreating army had burnt the thatched roofs, leaving just the rafters. Furniture and clothes lay scattered. People had left here in a hurry. The hot air had a deathly stillness, without a chicken to be seen anywhere. And there was always a chicken in Africa!

Ten miles later, we stopped in a town that hadn't been torched and a few nervous locals came out of their doorways. We wanted bread, but the shops only had Nestlé's baby milk and boxes of soap powder.

A shopkeeper introduced himself and asked me into the back of the shop, where he lived with his wife and family. They smiled as if I was a liberating soldier and not a tourist passing through. He said the retreating Ugandan soldiers took everything valuable, and the invading Tanzanians took the rest. Liberation was bittersweet, but at least Amin was gone. When I said I was from the UK, they looked pleased.

"All very proper when the British here."

The room had dirt floors, and a thatched roof; it was completely bare. I suppose our arrival was the first sign of normality, law and order after ten years of anarchy. I squirmed with guilt at giving them false hope as the vanguard of a new revival.

"We have nothing but the farm animals we hid in the woods," he said.

They gave me a glass of milk, still warm, straight from the cow. I thanked them and wished him good luck.

Back on the trucks, we moved on again. The road was still a dirt track and lined with banana trees. We entered the next village when suddenly three soldiers jumped out, yelling for us to stop.

They pointed their AK-47s at the driver, and he pulled off the road. I hoped it was the Tanzanian Army, but they had no badges; more soldiers appeared and shouted, "Get off the truck." Some were very young and looked like children holding assault rifles, dressed in an assortment of camouflage fatigues and T-shirts. Most wore mirrored sunglasses with bandoliers of ammunition and rifles cradled in their arms. They appeared to be mercenaries rather than a regular army. One of them was wearing platform shoes, which was a bit random, and he eyed up my motorcycle boots. I wouldn't argue with him if he wanted to swap.

They weren't expecting tourists and looked pissed off at our intrusion in their war.

"Open your bags," a soldier barked. He had stripes on his sleeve and a big Afro like Jimi Hendrix.

We lined up against the truck, facing the soldiers, like in a firing squad. One of the American girls started to weep as a soldier rummaged through her bras with his rifle barrel and started dancing around waving them in the air. His buddies thought this hilarious. Another found perfume and sprayed it on the others, laughing and doing a mock gay dance.

Another American girl was very busty and wore a tight T-shirt and shorts. The soldiers eyed up her curves like dogs on heat.

It was midday; the heat was oppressive, as we had stopped a few degrees north of the Equator. I was sweating, and not just from the sun. An ill-disciplined army of occupation had pulled us over. And apparently, they hadn't been paid for six months.

"What the hell was I thinking of?" I said to myself over and over, as if this would take me somewhere else, perhaps to Kansas like Dorothy in the Wizard of Oz. I could try tapping my boots together 3 times….

I had lost my independence travelling on the truck. I should be on my bike with only myself to worry about. For some reason, I felt safer on my own and I didn't enjoy relying on other people. One of the Americans handed out packets of cigarettes, which annoyed me, as the soldiers would now want freebies from everyone.

"Be careful with my stuff," said another of the Yanks. But the soldier just looked him in the eye and emptied his bag on the dirt track, to rifle through again. They hadn't seen the bike yet, as they were too interested in the contents of the bags.

Kate was getting a hard time; she was African-American, but mixed-race and of much paler skin complexion than the Tanzanians, who were as black as my boots.

"Where did you get that dirty skin? Your mother was a whore and Daddy a white man?"

"I am African-American and proud of it," she said. "You are dirty scum; not pure black African like us." He spat on her arm and rubbed it as if the colour would come off. Kate started crying.

"You want a real black man?"

"Dirty bitch!" they jeered.

Part of me wanted to tell them to leave her alone, but the chicken part said, 'shut up and keep your head down.' The chicken won. I said nothing. The soldiers had all the power and would not appreciate a smart-ass white boy telling them what to do. But I felt like my family's Labrador. At the slightest hint of a threat, she would lie on her back, wag her tail and urinate in a fountain all over herself, as if to beg for mercy.

My bowels heaved and my stomach convulsed in knots. I was close to shitting myself and needed a piss to release the pressure.

"I need to piss," I told a soldier, and he nodded over to the far wall.

As I stood relieving myself, I briefly thought about making a dash for it. Then I saw some officers making four soldiers run round in circles with heavy packs. When they tripped and fell, they battered them with sticks until they got up. Dripping blood and sweat, every time they cried for mercy, they received another boot to the groin.

I shuffled back like a condemned man returning to his executioners. There was nowhere to run. They started on me.

"Why you come to Uganda? To see Idi Amin?"

"No, I'm just going to Kenya."

Then they noticed the bike on the truck. "Who has this?" a teenage soldier demanded.

"It's mine," I said, waiting for him to claim it as a spoil of war.

"Wow, nice bike, Mister."

"Thanks."

Another girl started to cry, which only fuelled their sense of power. The situation was getting out of control. Finally, an officer approached and shouted at the soldiers to clear off back to their posts.

"You have no visa; you must go back to Sudan," he said, looking at my passport.

"The Ugandan Embassy in Khartoum said we would get visas in Kampala," I lied, a little more comfortable with an officer present.

The problem with that was, there was no Ugandan embassy in Khartoum, but he wasn't to know that, I hoped…

"Go to the Immigration Office in Kampala," he said.

"Now, fuck off, my soldiers don't like strangers."

The relief was immense, and we all jumped on the truck. The Army had ignored our Somali drivers who had been drinking tea, clearly enjoying the spectacle. One walked to the back of the truck and threw off a sack of grain for the soldiers, then we drove off.

We sat in silence until out of the town, then someone said, "Well, that wasn't much fun!" and we burst out in nervous laughter. Kate was still crying. We were still in Uganda, after all.

"It's all behind us now," I said, to calm her, as she sat holding hands with her friends.

Twenty miles on, more locals appeared and waved from the roadside, pleased to see foreigners again. We didn't wave back; we wanted to keep our heads down, just to keep moving. But it was too good to be true. Near Gulu, we stopped as steam hissed out of the radiator. The drivers worked on it for an hour, then gave up.

"Water pump broke," our driver said.

"Everyone on the other truck, apart from you and the motorcycle. You stay."

"What? There must be room!" I shouted, as he shrugged and walked away.

'Shit, what a disaster,' I thought, 'my worst nightmare'. My dash across war-torn Uganda had screeched to a halt.

"Tell them you can make room," I said to the others.

"If he says there's no room, there's no room," one of the Americans said, as they climbed up.

"Thanks for nothing, you bunch of wankers," I shouted. The sweat trickled down my back. I offered the driver more money.

"You can go, but no room for the bike," he said.

Should I abandon the bike and get on the truck with the others, or am I going to get myself killed for a stupid motorcycle? But they lifted the bike down and drove off, leaving the broken-down truck, the driver and myself at the side of the track.

"Fuck you too!" I shouted and gave them the finger as they disappeared in the dust. I never heard of them again.

I was in the middle of war-torn Uganda, with 10 miles worth of petrol.

'How did you get yourself in this mess, asshole?' I shouted. The Somali driver looked at me like I was mad, then went to sleep. I sat on the bike, with flies buzzing around me, and wondered what to do. Gulu, the next town, was ten miles up the road. If I drove there, maybe I could find somewhere safe.

In the town, the dilapidated buildings had broken windows and faded paintwork. It had been a prosperous market town, but it was now crumbling in the tropical humidity. The streets had a few people walking around, but the shops were empty. Everyone stopped to look at me as I drove down the street.

Then I saw a rusty 'Esso' sign and pulled up to the pumps;

my tank was nearly dry.

"Petrol?" I said to the attendant and waited for the usual shake of the head.

"Two star or four star?' he asked

"You have petrol!" I was about to kiss him. "How come you have petrol?"

"The Tanzanians stole all the cars, so we have loads of petrol!" he said. Thank god for those thieving bastards, I thought, as I filled up the tank with 93 octane. It smelled like perfume, after the Sudanese turpentine.

And there was a tarmac road! My spirits soared with my fuel level. I could drive straight to Kenya now and bypass Kampala! I should be there tomorrow! I was free! But my euphoria came down to earth at the Army checkpoint on the edge of town.

"You have no visa?" they demanded

"I came from Sudan," I said. "The border was deserted."

"Go to Kampala and get a visa."

"I want to go to Kenya!" I said.

"No, you go Kampala."

Bloody hell! I had no choice; I headed down the Kampala road, my head full of dread again.

The road was empty, but I imagined the rebel soldiers lining up their guns from the tree line. The next town had a burnt-out tank parked in the middle of the road, its turret dead, its gun barrel pointing in my direction but hanging limp, with one track blown right off. Signs of battle lay everywhere, with abandoned trucks and burnt-out vehicles.

When had it happened, last week or ten minutes ago? The next village was empty, as was the next. The closer to Kampala, the fewer people were about in the streets.

I rode on and reached the city before dusk. The modern concrete and glass office buildings looked desolate, but there were parks and grassy banks at the side of the road. It had been a nice town once. Then, I passed shantytowns, with young men loitering. Army lorries full of troops roared past with a purpose.

In the centre of the city, the central police station was a large concrete building painted a surprising gay pastel shade of blue. I strolled in like John Wayne. Everyone had deserted the place; I stood there and rang the desk bell, then a policeman walked in.

"Where is the Immigration Office?" I asked. The policeman laughed.

"Immigration?' he said. "People only leave here! Why would we need an Immigration Office?"

"I have to get a visa."

"A tourist! You will stay here tonight."

"Are you arresting me?" I said, slightly confused.

"No." He was shaking my hand so hard his gun rattled. "There is a curfew, and the Tanzanians soldiers will shoot everything that moves. We have no cats or dogs anymore," he said, laughing out loud.

"You are our guest! I will find you an office."

There was plenty of room in the station, Sergeant Roberts explained. There used to be two hundred officers here. Now twelve brave policemen stayed to keep law and order in the whole of Kampala, a city of over a million people.

When Amin fled, his hated secret police ran off before the citizens lynched them for their crimes, which left the handful of "straight" coppers.

I found the ransacked offices of the Head of Surveillance on the 1st floor; it was a mess, with the big mahogany desk with drawers hanging out. The filing cabinets had been rifled through, and on the floor, there was a smashed picture of the Big Dada, Amin himself.

The filing cabinets were still full of people's details, where they lived and what they did. Some had lines scored through them. I shuddered to think what that meant. Finally safe, the adrenaline drained out of me and I collapsed onto an old brown leather couch into blissful sleep. It had been a hell of a day!

What the hell!! The crack, crack, crack of automatic gunfire made a tremendous alarm clock. Amin's troops are back! Fuck, we are being attacked! I ran downstairs in a panic. Six coppers were playing poker in the reception, their guns hanging over the backs of their chairs.

"What's going on?" I shouted.

"Don't worry, it's drinking-up time; the Tanzanians get a bit crazy and shoot off their guns when they are drunk."

"Mostly in the air, but best stay away from the windows!"

the dealer confirmed, as he shuffled the pack.

I wandered back to my room. Only in Uganda would you feel foolish at being concerned about gunfire outside your bedroom window. Back on my couch, sleep eluded me, as the sporadic gunfire continued through the night.

Next morning, they assured me it was safe to go out, as people walked about in the sunshine in the street. 'Didn't they know there's a war on,' I wondered?

The new President was addressing the nation in the city park today. Army roadblocks stopped the traffic, but with my white face, I talked my way through.

"BBC," I said to the soldiers and flashed my Northern Ireland driving licence. I walked into the press gallery beside the proper Time magazine reporters. I smiled to myself.

"Hi, I'm Sarah, BBC, who are you?" said a face that looked vaguely familiar from the TV at home.

"I'm Chris. I'm just a chancer," I replied.

The BBC reporters stayed in the Hilton Hotel, which had its own generator, and air conditioning. All the other hotels had closed.

"Come and join us for a drink later. Where are you staying?" Sarah said.

"I'm a guest at Police Headquarters. I have my own office!" I said, rather proudly. "What's going on anyway, who is this President guy?"

"Mr Binaisa is the President," she said. "There is a shortage of politicians here. Amin threw them all to the crocodiles!"

Binaisa's timing was perfect as, just when he arrived, the bright sunlight faded to near darkness with a partial eclipse of the sun. The crowd made great oohs and aahs. Nothing like a touch of black magic to start a speech to a superstitious population! A troupe of African dancers gave a party atmosphere, an absurd contrast from the previous night's shooting!

Binaisa's speech ridiculed both Amin and the Tanzanian Army. He promised Uganda would soon be a better place. He pledged money, food, schools and jobs. The same old politician's bullshit. When he asked for contributions to the war widows and orphans, everyone dug into their pockets. Someone walked up to the stage with three cows, and then, after more tribal dancing, everyone went home before the curfew, when the shooting started over again.

Before Amin took over, local Asians ran the economy. But Amin was jealous and threw them out. He gave their properties and businesses to his friends. But within months, the economy collapsed, and Uganda was an economic basket case.

In the Asian's luxury villas, Amin's cronies knocked a hole in the roof, and lit their cooking fire in the middle of the living room. After a while, the houses fell derelict, as all of the floors and timbers had been burnt.

I drove back to the Police HQ before curfew and parked the Guzzi in the 'Chief of Police' parking spot. That evening, the Kampala coppers invited me to the local YMCA for a party. We met up at the reception, and the guys got locked and loaded. Everyone had a gun slung over their shoulders - apart from me.

"Chris, you look nervous," the Sergeant said, as the cops cocked their weapons. "I can't think why!"

"Well, in our town, the cops don't party with sawn-off shotguns!"

We slipped out the back door and through the dark streets in silence, sticking close to the walls and scurrying across crossroads and open spaces. The cops took no chances, and had their guns at the ready, hiding in the shadows as a truck of Tanzanian soldiers drove past.

'Am I fucking nuts?' I said to myself as we slunk through the shadows on our mission. I had fancied a beer, but this was ridiculous. Then, as we dashed across a courtyard, I realised I was quite enjoying the buzz! Only a faint glow from a candle or a charcoal fire could be seen behind the windows.

The cops wore the usual mirrored sunglasses so could see nothing, as everywhere was pitch black. But they would look cool at the party.

The YMCA building was an empty shell as someone's army had looted the furniture. The party had started, with everyone drinking beer made from fermented bananas, served warm and cloudy, straight from the bucket. It was disgusting. The room was lit with candles and paraffin lamps and the horrendous band sang African rock music very loud.

"This is the first time I have smoked grass with a bunch of coppers!" I said, as Sergeant Albert past me a huge joint.

"Enjoy!" He laughed. Uganda makes the worst beer in the world, but it has the best grass, so I guess you can't have everything!

We were a different sort of squad going back, singing and giggling like a bunch of teenagers. Staggering, arm in arm, with the guns slung over their shoulders, we forgot any thought of security; a ten-year-old with a bow and arrow could have taken us out!

Back at the station, the cops had arrested a taxi driver for drunk driving. There were no breathalysers, so he had to walk a chalk line on the floor. When he fell over, he got a couple of kicks and thrown in the cells. Little did he know, the cops who whacked him were stoned!

Next, two teenagers had been caught looting shops. They handcuffed them to the front door and everyone coming in gave them a whack with a truncheon. Instant justice, Kampala style.

Last, some men had beaten up a Tanzanian soldier. The cops laughed with them as they invented some intriguing sentences for the logbook.

"Lock them up for one hundred years!"

"We will make funny faces at you!" said another. Then they sent them home with a slap on the back.

"Don't get caught next time!" How swiftly the liberators became the enemy.

I spent a few days in Kampala, trying to fix my shocks, changing the oil and looking around town. But soon it was time to go, and my friends gathered to see me off. When I had arrived a few days ago the city terrified me. But now I appreciated the unique experience and was quite at home watching tracer bullets in the night sky. Peculiar how we get used to danger.

Uganda had one last surprise, as I approached the bridge at Jinja. I closed behind a bus to overtake. Suddenly, a huge bomb crater appeared between the back wheels of the bus. Someone had tried to blow up the bridge and had left a crater in the middle of the road. Shit!

Too late to swerve, I gunned the engine and dropped the clutch to jump it. The front wheel came up in a wheelie but crashed into the other edge and the bike, my luggage and I took off, diverging in slightly different directions. It was as if I had hit a landmine.

I landed, testicles first, on the petrol tank and skidded to a halt and fell on the ground, my back, kidneys and balls in agony! The crash broke the carrier frame, the handlebars collapsed, and even the headlight had popped out, but worst was a huge buckle in the front wheel. A complete 10-inch section of the wheel rim was bent in, and it had squashed the wheel into a pronounced 'S' shape! I wobbled up the road, aching all over.

I got the usual hard time at the border for still having no visa, then drove through the hundred yards of no-man's-land towards the Kenyan border. I did a double-take, as a big red motorcycle with a GB sticker came towards me.

"Charles Batham, I'm riding up from Cape Town!" said the rider in a crisp English accent.

"Chris Donaldson," I replied, "I'm riding down to Cape Town."

"Would you like a cup of tea?" he said.

"I'd love one!" I said.

We pulled in under a tree, just out of sight of both Customs posts.

Charles had travelled through the USA, South America and Asia for four years and was now on his way to the UK from South Africa. He was on his second motorcycle; the first was stolen in the States.

"Having my bike stolen was bad, but I had five thousand dollars hidden in the frame. Eventually, someone will sell the bike for scrap and find my money hidden in the frame," he laughed.

He rode a 4-cylinder 1000cc Honda Gold Wing, with a huge trailer tent with gas stove, chairs, and airbed. Charles liked his luxuries! He looked at my meagre possessions.

"You enjoy travelling light," he said.

"You won't get that beast over the Sahara Desert," I said, looking at his trailer.

"No, I'll take the boat and train." He had done his homework! "Clever!"

He was about thirty, his blonde hair groomed and his clothes clean and pressed, fresh from civilisation, whereas I hadn't seen a washing machine for months. It was bad timing, as I wanted to spend all day together getting more tips, exchanging routes and contacts, but we shouldn't stop in no-man's-land for long.

Intercontinental motorcycling is a difficult lifestyle. Backpackers fly off when the going gets tough; campervan folk have their home comforts. We had the worst of both worlds. His bike was covered in sponsors' stickers. I had tried to get sponsors before I left, but no one thought I would get far.

"Petrol is the easiest; just go to the BP or the Shell Head Office, and even if they don't sponsor you, they'll give you a fill-up!"

Charles talked to all the radio stations to promote his sponsors, but it backfired in Mombasa when he had announced on the air that he was leaving the next morning. As he rode out the next day, robbers pretended to be police stopped him and stole his cash. They even told him not to be so careless! Charles gave me the address of his friend in Kenya.

"Call in. George's fridge is always full of Tuskers." My mouth watered at the thought.

"Go to the Kampala Police Station; they do a great bed and breakfast!" I said.

We wished each other luck. Feeling weirdly emotional, I watched this total stranger ride away. I imagined I was looking back at myself.

I never saw Charles again, but I hope we meet for another brew to talk about when, as young bikers, the world belonged to us, to wander and explore.

"Why you come back?" the Kenyan border guard said.

"No, that other white guy rode a red Honda!"

Africans probably think we all look the same, but mistaking a Honda Gold Wing for a Le Mans? The insult!

Two hours later, I arrived at George's farm in Kitale.

"I just met Charles Batham. He said you have a fridge full of beer needing sorted."

"Bloody hell, I've only got it restocked!" George said as he invited me in.

"I will get every fucking traveller he meets!"

"No, just the bikers, and there are not many about," I assured him as I took a swig of beer. The taste exploded in the back of my throat. It really was the best beer in the world. I parked the Guzzi in his workshop beside his immaculate Honda 400-4.

"I would have gone with Charles," he said, "You are in the back room. A friend of Charles' is a friend of mine"

George lived in a modest whitewashed bungalow, and out back, he built cottages for the workers and their families. The maid took my filthy clothes for washing, and I had a shower and came out two shades lighter.

George's grandparents emigrated from Portugal fifty years ago and turned the virgin bush into the farmland that he now owned. George was middle-aged, divorced, and married to his farm. He'd lived in Kenya all his life, but now complained the government treated him like a foreigner because he was white. The government had confiscated some of his land to give to black Kenyans, in 'no compensation, land repossessions'.

"Within five years on the land they ruin it," he said. "They cut down the trees, grow crops that the soil couldn't sustain and with very little rain, it soon reverts to desert."

George's social life revolved around the Country Club and after we scrubbed up, we headed there for dinner. It was a relic of British colonial times, with brown leather couches, mahogany tables, and a few balding animal heads on the wall. I had to wear a jacket; my leathers stood out in stark contrast to the blazers and cravats.

The club was full of swarthy white farmers, UN officers, European charity workers and a few Africans. No race barrier now, all you needed was money to join now.

At the bar, two white farmers talked about the new land reform laws.

"It's just a reverse form of racism," said one.

"It will destroy the country. We bring jobs, exports and pay taxes."

"The problem is TMP," said Philip, the town doctor.

"What's TMP?" I asked.

"Too Many People."

The next morning, I ate a big fried breakfast and immediately threw it all up. My stomach wouldn't handle rich food after months on beans.

I didn't recognize myself in the mirror. My face was brown and my body strong, but my eyes looked much older. I had experienced more in two months than in my last two decades. Nothing would intimidate me now.

The blazing sands of the Sahara, and the chaos of Uganda, had stamped their mark on me. It had been challenging, mentally and physically. I endured by concentrating only on today, forgetting the past and not worrying about the future.

In the workshop, I strengthened the front suspension springs, fitted tractor oil seals in the forks and welded the cracks in the Craven carrier. It was made for European highways, and the vibration had pulled the bolts right through the mountings. I needed a few days' rest and George was the perfect host.

"I should come with you," he said, as I got ready to go.

"Why don't you?' I urged. "Take a few weeks off."

Poor George, he had had to turn down the dream twice in one week, first with Charles and now with me. But we both knew he would never leave his beloved farm. The government would have to drag him off his land screaming and kicking.

The road to Nairobi was bumpy and my back and kidneys hurt at every jolt. The stronger springs I put in at George's didn't work well. When you change one part of a machine, it has a knock-on effect on the other parts that work together. Making the front springs firm meant that the dampers were too weak, and the rear springs too soft, and I bounded down the bumpy road like an impala.

At 40 mph, the lumps of rubber in the tyre made the front wheel shake dangerously. Suddenly, the bike would oscillate wildly, faster and faster, while I wrestled with the handlebars.

Then traffic! The first traffic jam since Cairo! The Nairobi skyscrapers appeared like an oasis of civilisation. Then, I passed a KFC and realized I had made it! Battered and unbroken, but more than a bit bent. I knew I could go anywhere now- whenever I decided where!

I found Land Rover John's address in Lower Kibali; I rode up the gravel drive to a thatched cottage set into the hill. It overlooked a valley dotted with colonial mansions and tropical fruit trees. Was this really Africa? Not as I recognized it!

"Bugger me, mate!" John said as he opened the mahogany door. "You made it!"

"Piece of piss!"

We had only spent a week together but hugged like old friends.

John had sold the Land Rover and started a job in his uncle's safari park. Charlie would go back to London, as his adventure was over. In the desert, they seemed like brothers, but now I saw the boys' differences. John was very upper class; Charlie was one of the boys.

"Why don't you go to South Africa?" I said to Charlie.

"I'm done. Time to go back to London; bills to pay."

I thought he should go on, as he had made the break from society, always the hardest part.

The Land Rover survived the trip, but they had adventures too. One night, a roar outside the tent wakened them. They peered outside and saw a pair of eyes shining in the darkness. They sprinted to the Land Rover and spent the rest of the night sitting in their underwear while a lion wandered around the campsite!

"It was probably a pussycat!"

"No, he was huge!" Charlie insisted.

They had news from the other travellers. Margaret and Art's Datsun made it, but the engine had blown up, and the floor pan pushed right in like a banana. They would ship it to Vancouver as a garden ornament, since the thought of scrapping it was unbearable! But they succeeded in driving around the world in a suburban runabout!

Luke and Theresa's VW Kombi had blown the engine and wrecked the suspension. It still drove, but they sold it for scrap and flew home. We decided that the Guzzi and the Land Rover were joint convoy winners!

We went nightclubbing to celebrate, which was a major culture shock. The local girls had enough makeup to paint a Volvo, the biggest eighties hairstyles, and shoes that cost as much as the Ugandan GDP.

Two hundred miles away, a bunch of AK-47-wielding teenagers had held me up in a half-finished war, but today I danced with the sexy ladies of Nairobi. And in the street outside, families begged for their next meal.

At the post office was the 'Poste Restante,' a holding address, where travellers could collect the mail. I had my first contact with home since Cairo. But I read my letters and felt totally removed. The news appeared to belong to a different person, not me. I read about the dog, my cousin Carol, and other inane stuff. It was like a dream, long ago and far away. My family were the same people, but I was different. I had entered a parallel universe of some sort. When I read the letters a few days later, I was homesick and depressed.

Fuck this! Letters from home should make me feel better, not worse, and I decided not to give a forwarding address again. I really didn't want to know! My home was where my bike was, and today it was in Nairobi. Tomorrow it would be somewhere else.

The Nairobi locals behaved more aggressively than the Sudanese and Ugandans, where people smiled at me when I went past. Here, I sensed anger bubbling underneath, and the city made me nervous. People saw what Westerners owned and desired it themselves.

In the shantytowns, raw sewage ran through the streets, in stark contrast to the secure compounds and coiffured gardens where the wealthy Kenyans lived, both black and white.

Maybe poverty is comparative, I thought. If your neighbours are all in the same boat, it's okay, but when you live next door to luxury, your poverty is more extreme.

We think material goods make us happy, but this happiness is short-lived, as it's this need for material things that breeds unhappiness.

And how is happiness measured, anyway? Are we in the West happier than the natives in the jungle, or the Arabs in that Nile village? We are more comfortable, but does that make us happy? It's impossible to be content all the time, as we don't notice you are happy until you are sad again!

In the West, we see happiness as living on a tropical island away from everything that stresses us out. Ironically, the African, living on that tropical island, wants nothing more than to be in London in the rain.

It is an elusive thing, this happiness!

But, on the whole, I was just happy not to be in Wau!

At the British Embassy, I asked for travel advice, but as usual, I didn't learn much; only the British can sound 'expert' in ignorance! The embassy officials looked shocked that I came through Uganda. They said that the Tanzania border was closed and a permit should take two months. I could go back through Uganda, then Rwanda and Zaire around Lake Victoria, but that was a thousand miles of dirt roads. Or I could try my luck at the closed border.

Déjà vu, Israel!

"I want to see the Indian Ocean," I said. "I will try the border or take a boat to India then go to Australia!

The road to Mombasa passed through the Tsavo game reserve, with zebra and antelope off the side of the road. They didn't allow motorbikes in wildlife parks for obvious reasons, but I realized I was fair game here. A leopard can run at 60 mph, while my Guzzi only did 45 mph!

I arrived in Mombasa late. It was dark, and as soon as I turned off the highway into the city, the tropical humidity enveloped me like a wet blanket. I had entered a different climate zone during the day! I usually stopped in daylight, because there could be dangerous animals out there in the darkness, and worse, nasty people.

Mombasa was full of raunchy bars and drunks roaming the streets. I drove past the Islamic University and naively thought I would see if they would give me a room with my student's card. The name 'Islamic' should have been a cautionary flag, but after two months in the Middle East, it didn't worry me.

A dozen students drank beer and milled about the entrance hall as I walked through to ask if they had guest rooms. Some students wore shorts and T-shirts but most were dressed in white Arab galabias.

"What do you want, white man?" said a fat bloke, prodding me with a bottle of beer. Then other students jostled me, obviously enjoying the bait-the-white-guy action.

Shit! The situation just changed from a low amber alert nowhere to stay, to a 'red for danger'; I could get my shit kicked in! I was tired and missed the warning signs.

I looked around, but they blocked my escape route as everyone crowded around. I was this evening's entertainment. "This is black Africa," a big Negro said, rather stating the obvious, I thought. Bullies enjoyed seeing fear, so I tried not to show any.

"I'm just an Irish guy looking to kip in Black Africa," I said.

"Aren't you scared, white boy?" another quipped in.

"No, are you?" I said back. He stood trying to work out what I meant… so did I. I didn't understand why I said it, but it was too late to take it back.

But then he slapped me on the back and laughed, then everyone else joined in, breaking the tension.

"Have a beer, then," he said, thrusting a bottle into my hand.

Most people's aggression is all bluff, so the best response is to bluff back. And for the rest of the time, well, if you're going to get a whack in the gob anyway, what the hell.

The dormitory windows lay open in the vain hope that the Indian Ocean breeze would cool our naked sweating bodies. We drank banana beer, in the dark, well into the night. It's a strange thing that the more you drink alcohol with a foreigner the more you understand each other! And the revolting beer gave us a suffering martyr bond, and the promise of a 'hangover pain partnership' as well!

The guys were Ugandan refugees who hadn't heard any news from home since the war, so they were pleased I could tell them what was going on.

We discussed religion, politics, Africa, and Uganda, laughing and shouting long into the night, as we sorted out all the world's problems, as only the inebriated can do. But as usual, next morning, we had forgotten all of our solutions.

The next morning in Mombasa, I priced a boat to India, to find it was so expensive I wouldn't have enough money to get to Australia. I was going to go to South Africa but I would try the closed border to Tanzania first.

I rode down the coast past colonial beach houses and new tourist hotels and camped for a few days at the Ukunda Beach hotel. But the desert had given me enough sand and sun for a lifetime. I met a couple of Spanish guys who crossed the Sahara on Montesa scramblers a few months back. They didn't believe the Guzzi had made it.

The guards had refused them entry at the Tanzania border and they planned to drive back up the long way, to Lake Victoria through Uganda and Rwanda.

But in Africa, rules are there to break. It would come down to the mood of the border guard on the day. I had to give the border a go.

The Kenyan border guards sat dozing in the shade, with not much to do when a border is closed. I parked outside the ramshackle wooden hut, walked in and looked in the registration book; not one person had crossed for six months.

"The border is closed," the officer confirmed without looking up from his poker game. "You must go back."

"I need to go to Tanzania; my girlfriend in Dar es Salaam is sick. I need to be there," I said to the guys, who looked back as if to say, "Do I give a shit?"

"Come on lads, give me a break?" I smiled.

"It's not us," the Kenyan officer said. "The Tanzanians won't let you in."

"Let me talk to them," I said. "I will pay you an extra visa fee if I have to come back."

That suddenly got them interested.

"OK, on you go," and I paid my visa fee. One down, one to go, I sang as I drove through no-man's-land.

The Tanzanian border guard sat beside the barrier over the road, bored stupid. But the bike always intrigued young men enough to start up a conversation and he let me through to the guard hut. I found that if you act like you have permission, sometimes people assume that you do.

I gave them the same stupid girlfriend story; it was all I could think of. There were three soldiers sitting with their feet up. They looked dishevelled and untidier than the Kenyan soldiers. Since the war, the Tanzanian economy was tanked, and the soldiers weren't getting paid.

"Come on guys, do me a favour; the Kenyans are happy for me to come through," I pleaded.

"Are you going to South Africa?"

"Of course not!"

"What is your business in Tanzania then?"

"I told you, I will see my girlfriend in Dar es Salaam."

"From the UK?"

Shit, I forgot about that part, it's a long way to drive to see a sick girlfriend!

"No, from Kenya."

The guard was flicking through my passport with his fat fingers as he looked at the visa stamps.

"Do you have any Kenyan Shillings?"

"Yes, I have some."

It was dangerous to bribe a guard. If you offer him $50 and it offends him, he will put his price up to $500 or lock you up.

"You know it is illegal to bring Kenyan money into Tanzania," the officer said, staring at me.

"Will you change my Kenyan Shillings into Tanzanian Shillings for me?" I asked.

This was make or break.

"As a favour to you, I will change your shilling for a shilling." We both knew that the Kenyan shilling was worth 10 times more than the Tanzanian ones on the black market, so it was a subtle bribe.

Most African countries used a high exchange rate, to stop people from taking money out of the country. The 'Black Market' showed what the currency was really worth. Kenya had a strong economy and Tanzania was broke.

At border crossings, I would declare what cash I carried, then on leaving, show bank vouchers to show I how much I spent. So, I would hide cash under the battery, wrapped in a plastic bag. But if they found the money, they would confiscate the cash and the bike and put me in jail.

"What is her name?" he said, as he stamped my passport.

"Who?" I said.

"Your girlfriend," he said.

"June," I stammered, "her name is June."

June! What a stupid fucking name, I said to myself, starting to blush!

"OK, have a good trip," he smiled.

I skipped over to the bike, my hand shaking as I turned the ignition, and rode up to the final checkpoint, a simple pole across the road. The soldier was sitting, half asleep, his arms wrapped around an ancient British rifle and he pulled the string to lift the pole.

It was not for another mile down the road that I relaxed, and I screamed into my helmet, "I've made it!" and weaved from side to side on the deserted road. I was in Tanzania!

Cape Town, I'm on my way!

CHAPTER 10

Tanzania & Zambia

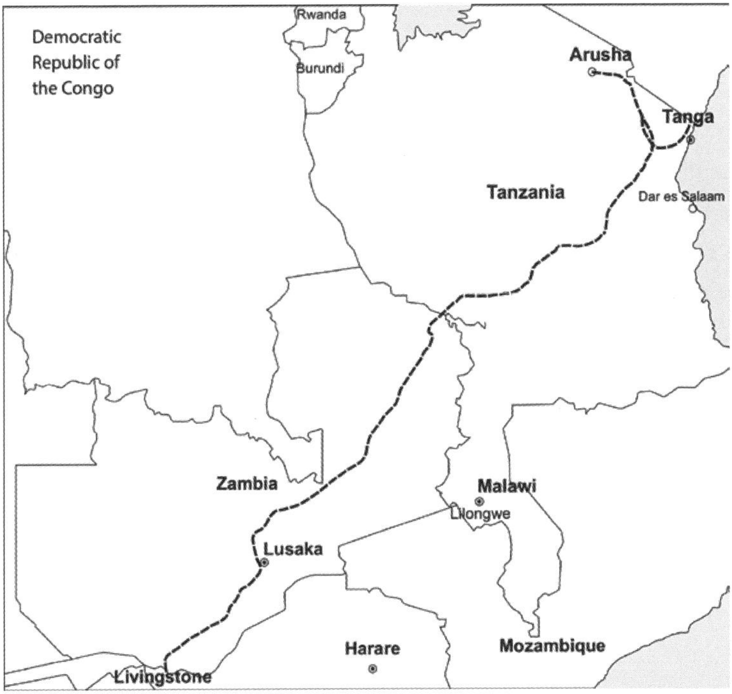

THE TRACK TWISTED THROUGH LUSH TROPICAL FOREST. TOURISM HADN'T reached this part of East Africa. The coastline was beautiful, with palm trees, golden beaches, and luminescent blue waters. In villages, kids played naked in the dirt beside mud huts with thatched roofs.

Everyone waved and shouted, 'Jambo, Jambo', as I rode past. It was only fifty miles to the Kenyan tourist hotels, but a world away. This was the Africa I loved, raw and natural.

But I was alone again, and while this was my choice, the border made me aware of just how vulnerable I was. No one knew I was here and there was a lot of forest in which to hide a body! The stress of facing up to a bunch of soldiers in the bush or the Islamic students in Mombasa was intense.

On top of my security, I had to look after my route, finances, health, mechanics, accommodation, and of course, ride the bike. What was it that drove me on to do this, I wondered, as I started to consider the possibility that I was totally insane? Third-World Africa was a lonely place for a paranoid biker.

My next stop was Tanga, the old German capital of Tanganyika. I stopped beside a couple of blokes on Yamaha XT500 trail bikes.

"Strewth, where did you come from?"

Alex and Kevin were engineers in a hydroelectric plant. They invited me to stay. Again, the bike was my ticket into society.

That evening was the Sailing Club Regatta. It looked like the sun had not quite set on the British Empire. The clubhouse was a relic of the empire, with old leather armchairs and photographs of long-dead commodores. A few old salts in blue blazers held up the bar.

"Why are you guys here?" I asked.

"Been here all our lives, Tanzanian born and bred!" Bill said in perfect 1950s Queen's English.

He was a retired ex-army type. They had spent their working lives in the British East African civil service and hadn't seen the UK for years.

"We can live well here, cheap as chips. I have a small cottage, a couple of servants, a circle of friends and a small pension from the Foreign Office" he explained. "Where else would I go, some council flat in Basildon?"

"Another gin and tonic?" "I don't mind if I do!"

Bruce's Asian neighbours had a Hindu festival the next day and invited us to join in; everyone got soaked with coloured paint, then we stuffed our faces with sweet cakes and fresh fruit juices.

I detoured up to the northern highlands to see the Ngorongoro Crater Wildlife Park and as the road climbed inland, the landscape changed from thick forest to open savannah with baobab trees.

As I arrived in Arusha, lightning lit up the skies and a deluge drenched me, but the inside of my petrol tank was bone dry; all the petrol stations had no go-juice, again! I found the house of my friend of a friend, Denis Pitman and he ushered me in to dry off in front of a roaring wood fire.

Denis was an eccentric English ex-pat who had lived in Uganda with his wife Beth and their five kids. Beth was black, and the first mix-race couple I had met. Generally, the blacks, whites and Asians all lived in separate societies.

When Amin expelled the Asians, Denis had to get out, but the UK wouldn't take Beth because she was not Asian. He had been applying for UK residence, but they didn't believe that he married a black woman and the children were his own. He managed a small wildlife tour company in Arusha, but business was dead now the rainy season had started.

Denis was like many ex-pats, nonconformist and maverick, and didn't fit in with Western culture. He loved Africa, even with the hardships. But now, with the kids growing up, he didn't see a future. The wildlife parks wouldn't let me drive in, but no one told the animals not to leave, so wild animals ran alongside the main road.

On my way to the crater, I turned the corner to find a giraffe standing in the narrow lane with her young calf. I stopped, each as of us surprised as the other. I tried to push back, but the road was uphill behind me, and Guzzis have no reverse. I had no room to turn. The lane was narrow. It was an African standoff.

I knew she wouldn't eat me, but she could give me a damn good kicking with those long legs! Should I shout, or rev the engine? They just stood and swished their tails. Then, with a snort of contempt, they turned and walked behind a tree, then watched, as I rode away.

Denis said the only tourists in the rainy season came to hunt.

"Tourists don't pay enough to keep the parks running." He explained that the hunters aren't allowed to kill rare or exotic animals, and they have to cull them to keep the populations under control. The hunters pay enormous fees, and they give the meat to the local villages.

"We keep the locals on the right side and the wildlife brings in money and food."

"They even shoot the giraffes?" I said, shocked, "Anyone can shoot a giraffe?"

"Yes, we have too many, if we don't cull them, they will eat all the trees."

"Don't you think it's unethical?"

"Well, if you eat meat, what's the difference if the animals die in an abattoir, or get shot? So, why not charge for it!"

In Africa, morals are fine if you can afford them, otherwise, hunters pay the bills.

On the way south from Arusha, I stayed the night at a Baha'i temple. Denis's friend Peter was a priest, and the temple was a rickety wooden house. We had a vegetarian dinner in the small kitchen.

"The Baha'i religion was a search for truth and unity of all religions," he explained.

"We condemn all forms of prejudice. We want to abolish wealth and poverty," he said as he handed me a bowl of watery soup.

"That all sounds very grand," I smiled and slurped.

"We want to get all the religions to work together under one system," he continued.

"You should come to Belfast and run that past the Prods and Catholics there, and see how far you get," I said sarcastically.

"But why not try?" Peter said. " Black Africa is a great place to start, with all the injustice going on."

I could talk religion all day as long as I got a meal and a bed for the night. I parked inside the temple and unrolled my sleeping bag on the wooden floor.

As the sun reached the wet tarmac, steam rose up and drifted into the forest, and I drove around a corner to find dozens of chimpanzees sitting on the road, warming themselves. They stared at me with complete disdain as I weaved through them in the mist. It looked magical.

"There's that plonker who chased our cousins in Sudan," one said, I'm sure. I didn't stop for a photo.

The bike had become part of me and would take me anywhere. I was more at home in the saddle than I was on my feet. The throttle didn't exist anymore; if I wanted to go faster, I just thought about it. I just looked at the next bend and the bike went around it. If there was danger ahead, a truck pulling out, or a hole in the road, the bike slowed down for it automatically. I had now connected my spinal cord to the frame; we had become one.

I was driving in a dream, a fantasy, released from earthly responsibilities. The travelling was a doddle now, after the rigours of Sudan. I knew I would never fall off, and nothing could stop me.

My journey on a motorcycle was a journey of discovery about myself, and Africa was only the backdrop, like the scenery in a play.

I was looking for something, I didn't understand what it was, but wasn't worried; I would know when I found it. Like the sensation you have when you are going out and you know you have forgotten something but you can't remember what. But I didn't really care anymore.

The forest smelled of decaying vegetation and dead frogs, of damp rotting grass and something wicked. The rainy season was following my tyre treads and chasing me south.

After the desert and dry bush, it felt like God had made some mistake like it's not supposed to rain in Africa. Even the Africans seemed unprepared and made do with plastic bags to keep themselves dry. The red soil immediately soaked up the daily deluge, and the trees seemed to sprout an extra six inches with the first splatters. The clouds and mists on the forests and mountains rolled together like the blankets on an unmade bed.

The hospitality concept in Africa was basic; a restaurant was a wooden shack with three walls, a small counter, and a charcoal stove for flatbread and tea.

A hotel was similar, but with another shack out the back. The rooms would be bare, with a metal bedstead, a straw mattress and a single light bulb, which was only there for decoration as there was rarely electricity.

Camping in the jungle was not recommended for obvious reasons, so I stopped at a petrol station that night. There was a large muddy field where trucks parked up, and a wooden shack with a charcoal fire to brew tea or the luxury of instant coffee. An old woman cooked over the stove and a younger more attractive lady served to entice the truckers in.

The ancient petrol pump was rusty and discoloured, with a little glass bubble and a paddlewheel to see the petrol flowing. It was empty. On all sides of the forecourt was the steaming jungle. There was a small shop, with nothing for sale.

I put the tent up on the concrete forecourt and used the bike as my tent frame and hung the tent off the handlebar and the back indicator. I climbed in, listening to the squawks and screams of the nocturnal beasts in the jungle a few metres away.

Tanzania was a mess, with no food and no petrol. I had to buy a few litres of petrol in the back streets of shantytowns, like doing a drug deal.

After Kerogwee, the next four petrol stations had no petrol, but finally, I found five litres in a shack which had a barrel with an antique hand pump. The food shop's shelves sat empty apart from some bread and the ever-present Tate and Lyle golden syrup. What is it with the syrup, I wondered? That was all I ate for days. Stale bread dipped in golden syrup. Mmm!

In Africa, people appear from nowhere. One morning, I was brewing up after a morning's ride, twenty miles from anywhere. The road was deserted and it was raining. Suddenly, along came an old man on a bicycle with a plastic bag on his head. He slowly weaved through the potholes without a care in the world!

Charles Batham and Denis had given me names of ex-pats along my way and I would call and introduce myself.

"I'm riding to Cape Town, and Charles said you might put me up!"

They always said yes, or found a friend with a spare bed. My mum had given me one random address, the mother of my cousins' friend, and as I rode through Iringa, I passed a gate with the Bartholomew name on it.

Behind the gate was an immaculate English cottage with a thatched roof and a coiffured garden. There was a tennis court and a croquet pitch. I had to stop and check it out. Besides, I had about half a gallon of petrol left and they might spare a pint.

Susan Bartholomew opened the door and invited me in after I explained the strange and distant acquaintance. The house was a mix of Laura Ashley floral curtains and solid mahogany African furniture. We sat down on the chintz sofa and had tea and cakes.

Susan was in her sixties. She was very polite, with an upper-class colonial demeanour. She looked and spoke like the Queen.

"My daughter wrote about you, but I never thought you would make it this far," she admitted. Her husband had worked in the Colonial Service but passed away last year, yet she had no interest in going back to the UK.

"What about South Africa?" I asked.

"It's only a matter of time before it goes black too. Robert Mugabe will take over Rhodesia in a few weeks. He will ruin that country too."

"The war in Rhodesia is over?" I said, suddenly realizing that the road to South Africa could be open now.

"Can I buy any petrol? I'm nearly out," I asked.

"I can spare a gallon; my gardener can push the lawnmower next week!" I felt guilty, as I looked at the size of the lawn. But a gallon of the golden nectar would get me to the border. I thanked Susan for her tea and petrol, and she offered me a bed for the night, but rain clouds formed behind me, so I was keen to keep going.

These ex-pats I met were the last remnants of the British Raj, and lived in the past, while the present whirled around in chaos and corruption. But their children had no future in Africa; there was too much bitterness for the past injustices. They would leave for the UK or Australia.

I was living like an African trucker, camping in trucker stops, under their trailers. Petrol was my only cost now and occasionally, stale bread and that special treat, golden syrup.

As I neared Zaire, one of the wettest countries in the world, the steamy forest was luminescent green. The vegetation teemed with hundreds of types of birds, mammals and amphibians that vied for space with the thousands of species of flowers, trees and grasses. It is one of the most fertile places on the planet, but yet it was impossible to get a chicken curry or anything decent to eat.

I would see a rain cloud in my path, a big cumulus cloud, like a floating island in the sky. I'd put on my waterproofs and find that by the time I reached it, it would have moved on. Other clouds would linger, and I would enter their rain shadow like driving into a waterfall, as the rain dumped the contents of Lake Victoria on me.

As I left the cloud, the rain turned off just as suddenly, and the sun appeared. Sometimes I would just stop and wait, and the cloud would move off my route, but others would go on for miles. The engine seemed to thrive on the damp air, as if it made the fuel burn better! Then the sun would dry my jeans and my boots and the black asphalt would steam in the heat.

It was evening by the time I reached the Zambian border, and it was chaos. The guards shouted at the truck drivers and searched their cabs for contraband. A drunk policeman decided I was a prospective victim and arrested me. He marched me up to the police station.

"Have you ever been in Zambia before?" the captain demanded.

"No."

"What is the capital city?"

"Lusaka," I said.

"Ha! You have been here before. You are a South African spy!"

Then he spotted my cassette radio and decided it was a transmitter. I put on the Clash but that just made him more determined to confiscate it. At least he had some taste.

"What makes you think you will reach Lusaka?" his sidekick shouted with more than a hint of menace. "It is a very hazardous journey for someone on their own."

This guy would have scared the shit out of me a few months ago but now, I shrugged off this sort of experience, as they usually just wanted a bribe which I could ill afford, but these guys were drunk and made me nervous.

Every copper in the station was off their heads; they shouted and swore like a bunch of inebriated school kids on their first-ever bottle of cider. Every few minutes, they dragged in a drunk local, beat them with long sticks, and threw him in a cell full of other drunks. Everyone was shouting and pushing people about. It was alcoholic anarchy.

But after an endless interrogation, they let me go. I knew they just wanted money, but I was in no mood to appease them.

It was dark as I drove into Nakonda, and cvcryone in town was drunk there too. It must have been payday or something. The main street looked like an anarchic version of the Wild West, with rows of tin hut bars full of drunken men staggering about. I stopped at one hotel, to discover it was a whorehouse. A gaudy prostitute called out the window.

"Hi, white boy, do you want some loving?"

I smiled and shook my head. "If you don't mind, I'll give it a miss to-night."

Then some soldiers walked out carrying their Kalashnikovs over their shoulders. Zambia had been at war with Rhodesia for ten years, I was white, as were the Rhodesians, which made me a reasonable victim for their rage. One soldier staggered over and shoved his face right up to mine.

"What do you want here, white man?" He drooled; "You here to fuck our girls??" His spit splattered on my face, as his mates laughed.

I could back away from his 'face' as he wanted me to or stand my ground and pretend not to be intimidated. I chickened out and stepped sideways, politely, as if to let him past. I would let him have his victory in front of his buddies.

"No, I'm just leaving."

But, like the wild dogs in Sudan, he sensed my fear. "You go to South Africa?" he demanded, pushing up to my face again. I could smell stale breath and beer along with his rancid armpits.

"No, I'm not," I stood my ground this time. A jeering crowd built up to watch the fun. He would have to face me or push me away when he realized I wasn't moving. But I didn't want to be aggressive or give him an excuse to punch me. I trod a fine line.

We both stood, nose to nose, for what seemed like a minute, but was probably a few seconds, then he sneered.

"White men are not welcome in Zambia," he said. "Fuck away off, out of Africa." I took that as my exit line and backed away, as he turned to get approval from his mates. He was either too drunk or not drunk enough for a fight, I decided and drove off, with shouts of "Fuck off, white boy," behind me.

It was dark and raining, and I had nowhere to stay. I seemed safe while moving, but now too exhausted to keep going, I needed somewhere safe to sleep.

Just outside town was the truck park, with a brazier burning. 'Maybe I'll get a better reception here,' I thought as I pulled in. Two Zambian drivers appeared from the gloom and invited me to join them at the fire. They seemed sober, so I did.

"Is there a hotel in town?" I asked.

"No, stay out of town, it is a bad place," they said. "Stay here."

They accepted me as a fellow traveller, and I pitched my tent in the mud, under an eighteen-wheel truck trailer.

Next morning, a local kid came over to exchange some dollars for Zambian kwachas. I handed him my ten-dollar note, but suddenly, he turned and ran.

"You wee bastard!" I shouted, and I chased after him. We ran into the nearby shantytown, down a muddy lane, through the front doors of a shack, past a family having breakfast, then out the back. I turned a corner, and he had disappeared.

I stood there, my breath heaving, as a few startled locals looked out of their doorways.

Shit! What the fuck was I doing running through an African shanty-town chasing some kid for ten dollars! I'll go round the next corner and there will be ten guys with knives, waiting for me!

I quickly retraced my tracks, excusing myself as I ran back through the kitchen. But I was furious for being duped, I needed that money for petrol and had nothing smaller than a fifty dollar note which I didn't need to change. But my trucker friends felt so ashamed that they had a whip-round for me to fill my tank.

"We are all on the road together, my friend," said one of the drivers.

The generosity of people with so little never ceased to amaze me.

"We will give that guy a slap and get the money back!"

"Thanks, but I want to slap him myself!"

The Guzzi could do about 50 miles per gallon on a good day, and as it was 250 miles to the next petrol station, so with a slightly less than 5-gallon tank, it would be touch and go to make it. With fifty miles to go, I turned on the reserve, and as I pulled up to the pump, the engine spluttered and stopped, but they had petrol!

That evening it started raining again. I stopped beside a truck at the side of the road. The driver had lit a fire under the trailer and he invited me to share a dinner of boiled wheat kernels with salt, a delicious change from my golden syrup diet.

Alex's truck had broken down four days ago and was waiting for a tow truck, which would take another three days. He had to stay with the truck to guard its load of copper ore.

It was Saturday night. I was in the middle of the African bush, sitting under a truck in the rain, and as we chatted, my mind wandered off to home. What were my mates doing? No doubt at the Rugby Club, drinking and chatting up some girls. But I wouldn't have swapped places for anything; I had my wheels, my freedom and an entire world to find.

There was only room for one in the cab and Alex offered it to me, but I slept under the truck on the tarmac. After a breakfast of boiled wheat, but this time with sugar, I bade Alex goodbye and was off again. It was another magical African moment.

The bumpy two-lane road ran through bushland and copper mines, the surface torn up by the heavy trucks. The heavy skies were full of dark grey clouds, and rain fell continuously while the freezing wind tugged at my wet jacket.

Some days, I would start the day with a sense of foreboding as I packed up my gear. But it would usually clear when I hit the starter, the V twin's burble immediately giving me a sense of security. I blipped the throttle; the engine torque shifted the bike to the right and I would instantly relax. Once moving, the fresh air and ever-changing scenery would concentrate my mind and ease my mood for the day.

The sense of menace would come back to me without warning, but it was no wonder, as I continued my journey through a strange and dangerous countryside always getting further from home, on my personal voyage of discovery. I now resigned myself to having no plan for returning home, but it wasn't a concern any more.

In Lusaka town centre, I stopped to check my map, when suddenly a policeman grabbed my shoulder from behind.

"You look at a map, you are a terrorist!" he shouted.

"Well, actually, I'm lost," I explained.

"Where are you going?"

"Rhodesia."

"How do you know this man?" he shouted as he recognized a name written on my map. "This is a bad man." It was the map Charles Batham gave me, and he had written the name of a black-market dealer who could change my money on it. The guy was important enough for the cop to recognise the name.

"It's not my map, someone gave it to me!" I whimpered, but it sounded like a lame excuse even to me! The cop grabbed my passport and instructed me to follow his car to the Police HQ. At the station, they ordered me to stand in the middle of a large room and wait. Four coppers came in and sat at desks in each corner. They all shouted questions at me, without waiting for an answer.

"Why are you here?"

"How do you know this criminal?" I turned round to reply.

"Don't look round when I'm talking to you," the Chief shouted from the front. The hair on the back of my head stood up as I waited for a blow from behind.

Shit, these guys are scary! They were professional and angry. Give me drunken cops any day.

"You want to blow up our bridges?" another shouted.

"You are going to South Africa?" someone else barked, closer to the mark.

"No, I'm just going to Botswana," I lied.

"Why did you have a map?"

"I was trying to find the fucking road out of town!" Pissed off at being arrested again, this time it was frightening, with all of them shouting from different directions. But I hoped, as long as I kept up my story that I was going to Botswana, I would be okay.

They emptied my bags on the desks and started going through my papers.

"There are bridges marked on this map; you blow them up?" I expected a knock to the head.

"It's a road map! That's what road maps do!"

But I had the name of a known gangster written on my map, with no adequate reason. Fuck!

I thought I was guilty myself!

The Chief talked to me as if I had walked dog shit all over his carpet. I had been standing for an hour and swayed from dehydration.

"Can I sit down?"

"No, you cannot."

The Rhodesian army had been blowing up their bridges. I was white, as were the Rhodesians, so that was enough, I was guilty by association.

Then they all got up and left. The minutes passed, it seemed like days; some big flies buzzed and banged against the window. They wanted out too.

They came back to their desks.

"Fuck off," one guy shouted suddenly.

"What?" I said.

"GO! And don't come back," the Commander said.

"I have no such intentions," I assured them and tried not to actually run out the door. Back on the bike, I made a beeline for the border, as quickly as my bent and buckled wheels would carry me.

I could see why the Rhodesians had pissed them off; they had blown up every concrete bridge between Lusaka and the border. The rivers now had rickety wooden jerry bridges, still guarded by soldiers, and they questioned me several times.

The border was at Livingstone, named after the great explorer. Like him, I was stumbling into the unknown. He had gone where no white man had gone before, but evidently, the natives behaved more friendly to him!

I needed a beer badly and stopped in the bar of the Victoria Falls Hotel. I met the manager, Martin Hutchinson, who insisted I stay for two nights on the house! It was my first proper bath since Kenya. I took my laundry for fumigating, and I went down for a five-course dinner. The hotel was empty, as the war had scared all the tourists away.

The next morning, I drove to Victoria Falls and walked down a narrow path towards a low rumbling sound. A cloud of mist turned to spray and I could only see a few feet in front. Suddenly, the ground fell away in a sheer drop to the swirling waters hundreds of feet below. Just ahead the water slipped silently over a mile-long chasm, to thunder and churn at the bottom. The Africans called it 'Water that Thunders,' which is much more appropriate than Victoria Falls.

I had no money for souvenirs but exchanged a couple of Beach Boys' cassettes for some carved wooden animals. Then back to the hotel for lunch, three plates of sandwiches and a couple of beers.

"You look like you haven't eaten for a week!" the waiter said.

"You're not far wrong!"

I was my own man in Africa, and I felt good. I had reached my final border to southern African 'Civilisation.' Every day I had strived against the chaos of Africa, my destiny decided by my decisions alone. The stakes were high, with no safety net in Africa; pick the wrong fight with the wrong guy and you are dead.

Many people holiday in the same place every year, as they love the sense of security. Others go somewhere different as they enjoy getting out of their comfort zone. Every day, I had faced new challenges and any 'comfort zone' was long forgotten. Every day, I could face a new peril.

In Western culture, not knowing what will happen next should be avoided at all costs. Everything in life should be ordered and structured.

Not in my world!

The war was over, but the border had only been open for a couple of weeks. Rhodesia would change its name to Zimbabwe and hold elections that would finally oust the white government. They would install Robert Mugabe as Prime Minister, where he would stay for the next 35 years. But the whites were still in charge for the next few months and, as Rhodesia was across the bridge over the Zambezi River, I thought I was home and dry. They would welcome me like a long-lost explorer.

"Mr Donaldson, I presume; we worried about you with all those naughty black boys," the Police Commander would say.

I hated borders on bridges and felt very exposed. I've watched too many war movies where the guy gets shot halfway across.

At the other end, the white Rhodesian guard stood with his rifle across his chest, blocking the road. He was the whitest man I had ever seen, crisp khaki uniform, long socks, pink knees, and freckles. The white folk I had met in Africa were swarthy characters. This guy was so white he gleamed.

Authority figures in black Africa enjoyed looking slovenly, which had its own menace, as if he doesn't fasten his top button and follow rules, he could be dangerous!

The white man's culture was more meticulous, but they follow the regulations to the letter.

"Welcome to Rhodesia. Go to the Immigration Office,"

he said, pointing to an equally white bungalow.

"Good morning. How much money have you?" the officer inside demanded. He had never been in the sun either. My face and arms looked as brown as his African secretary, after days riding with no helmet.

I showed him £370 in traveller's cheques, which didn't impress him.

"Sorry, the minimum legal requirement is £1,000, so you must go back to Zambia."

I stood and stared in utter disbelief.

'No, no! You can't send me back there!' I screamed, inside my head! I thought how pleased the police in Zambia, Sudan and Egypt would be to see me back!

After all the aggravation from the African countries, now the "white guys" won't have me because I'm too poor, even though an African could live for a year on the contents of my money belt!

"And you need another £1000 to import the bike!"

"Listen, I have a British passport; you're a British colony now, so what's the problem?" I said, about to get down on my knees, and wanting to say, 'under this sunburn, I'm as white as you are, matey!'

"It's the regulations," he smiled.

That is the trouble with white folk: sticklers for rules!

As the border had been closed for years, they didn't know what to do! I was the first vehicle to cross for years.

"Listen, I've bloody driven here from Ireland, you have to let me in," I protested.

"You have ridden down through Africa?"

"Yes, check the stamps on my passport!" and I shoved it across the desk. He thumbed through it and raised his eyebrows. For ten years, no Rhodesian had set foot in black Africa without a tank and a platoon of commandos; and I had crossed the whole continent alone!

He picked up the phone. "Put me through to HQ," he demanded.

"Yes, he says he has ridden here from Ireland… Yes…hang on."

"What sort of bike is it?" he asked.

"Moto Guzzi Le Mans," he repeated down the phone. HQ didn't believe him.

"No, really, it's parked outside," he said.

"They want to know how did you know our border was open if you left Ireland three months ago?"

"I didn't; I was going to Australia…"

He looked at me as if I was nuts, but repeated it down the line.

"The Captain wants to know if you would like a cup of tea?"

We sat and chatted over English tea in china cups, while they stamped my passport and gave me a 5-day visa.

The next issue was insurance; I couldn't drive in Rhodesia without it. They were shocked I hadn't had any the whole way down Africa! That sort of risk did not compute in the white man's culture!

"There's an insurance company a mile up the road."

"I'll ride straight there," I said.

"No, you're not insured to drive."

"Jesus, guys, I've driven 10,000 miles without it; I can do another mile!" I laughed.

"No, the Corporal will give you a lift!"

With the insurance and paperwork sorted, the policemen all shook my hand.

"Be careful, Chris, the rebels are out in the bush! Make sure you stick to the convoys," he told me on the way.

"Convoys? I thought the war was over!"

"There are rogue terrorists; it's not safe to travel alone."

And I thought this was civilization.

The family furniture shop after a bombing.
My Mother talks to the staff while my Dad looks on dejected, to the left of the door. The 'Business as usal signs' are up already.

1977 riding round Belfast City Hall in my underwear for a student prank.

Stuck in the snow.
Austria.

Jeff and Alex put their balls on the line.
Pissing on a Syrian minefield, **Golan Heights**.

Parked up at our Kibbutz,
Israel.

Picking up hitchhikers,
The Dead Sea, **Israel**.

Deserted Palestinian village, cleared for resettlement.

Camping by the Pyramids.
Cairo.

Gearbox out, cleaning the clutch and talking to Japanese tourists.

The most exclusive campsite in the world.

Farmers, working the fields. The same way for thousands of years.

Irish Camel Jockey, Pyramids, **Egypt**.

Desert road,
Egypt.

Temple of Karnak, **Egypt**.

Roll on Roll off, car ferry,
Wadi Halfa, **Sudan**.

Lined up and ready to begin the desert crossing,
Sudan.

The Combi's last stand, Nubian Desert,
Sudan.

Stuck in the sand.
Sudan.

Rebuilding my front suspension, Michel and friend look on.
Khartoum.

Standing room only.
The train to Wau.
Sudan.

Overloaded Le Mans .Not much room for me, with the extra petrol. **South Sudan**.

Moto Guzzi fans, **South Sudan**.

Fork sliders tied on with rope and a black brake pad glued onto the wheel rim for balance. Look closely and you will see the rim is buckled.

Roadside Moto Guzzi workshop, South **Sudan**.

Burnt out Russian tank.
Kampala, **Uganda**.

Cheeky monkey, **Zimbabwe**.

Petrol station campsite,
Tanzania.

Unlucky bus conductor.
Army checkpoint, **Rhodesia**.

Home made armoured cars, Rhodesian Army base.

Convoy assembly point, Bulawayo. Motorists are advised against traveling after 2.30pm. By the look of the shadows, it is well after!

Victoria Falls, **Zimbabwe**.

Leaving Capetown,
First over the starting line.

Changing the sails, **South Atlantic**.

Phil and Frazier playing chess in the lounge, or Sail store.

Retrieving the broken rudder,
North Atlantic.

The crew, from left. Kat, Frazier, Self, Mike, Ton, Cam, Tas, and Phil.

Making an emergency rudder from the spinnaker pole.

Hanging out with the Kids,
Cape Verde.

Hells Angels,
New York state.

Mum and Dad call by. N.C.

Cape Canaveral, **Florida**.

Miami, **Florida**.

Richard Turnage helps me check the cylinder wear,
St Petersburg.

Earthquake zone, **Mexico**.

The Sandanistas have arrived,
Nicaragua.

Nicaragua active volcano.

U.S. Army base Canal Zone.
Panama.

Jorge, waiting by the nose wheel for our pilot to sober up.
Panama.

Turning finals to land, Medellin, **Columbia**.

Christmas day. Note the vodoo doll the guy is holding, **Ecuador**.

Breakfast with Jorge,
Peru.

Jorge cooking magic mushrooms,
Ecuador.

Back street petrol station,
Peru.

Aquas Calientes, Main Street.
The drop off for **Machu Pichu**.

Putting the Guzzi to Bed. I always insisted on a ground floor room.

Alcohol induced Motocross crash,
Chan Chan. **Peru**.

NASA Space station.

Bolivian farmers take a shine to the Guzzi.

Stuck in the mud, **Bolivia**.

Fording a river, **Bolivia**.

The Uros reed islands, **Lake Titicaca**.

A very green, Lake Titicaca, the highest navigable lake in the world.

Skinny in Rio.
The end of the road

Arriving home in 1981 and 40 years later, sitting on my same Moto Guzzi, Le Mans, I finally publish my story.

CHAPTER 11

Zimbabwe/Rhodesia

When I arrived, the country had just started the transition between white-ruled Rhodesia to the new Zimbabwe, and for those three months, it was the last British colony in Africa. Rhodesia had declared a Unilateral Declaration of Independence (UDI) in 1965 and had been isolated from the world, and at war with the rest of Africa, for the last 15 years.

But although the war was over, I was told that rebels had gunned down three motorcyclists recently. I would have to travel between towns in an armed convoy.

The convoy vehicles assembled at the edge of town with armoured pickup trucks placed at the front, middle and back. They had a heavy machine gun mounted in a turret on the back. It had armour plates welded on the sides and they looked like they expected trouble.

The tarmac roads in Rhodesia were pothole-free. It would be shock-absorber heaven. I looked forward to the drive to the curiously named town of Wankie. (The new government would sensibly rename it Hwange.)

I started at the front of the convoy, but soon they were driving at 70 mph, which was too fast on my wobbly wheels, and the cars began passing me. Before long, I was at the back and the last tail gunner pulled alongside, the driver gesturing me to hurry.

I shook my head, pointing at the bike, shouting I couldn't go any faster. He smiled and ran his hand across his throat, as if with a knife, and sped off. I got the drift: fall back at your peril.

My dilemma was that if I went faster, I would crash, but if I got left behind, I was at the mercy of the terrorists. I watched the taillights disappear into the twilight. Like the old buffalo that can't keep up with the herd, he falls behind to be picked off by the lions.

Soon it was dark, and a breeze blew on the long grass verge, making it sway like machine gun barrels were moving it aside. What would I do if there was a roadblock? Do I stop, or blast through in a hail of gunfire? I had heard gruesome tales of torture by rebels; it had been a very dirty war.

I turned my lights off so the bad guys wouldn't see me, but nearly drove off the road! Bugger it! If anyone tries to stop me, I'll blast through, I decided. I would rather be shot in the back than get my balls stuffed down my throat.

I had never felt so alone!

I was so late arriving; the army camp Commander stood waiting at the gates. He thought I had been ambushed. I parked up beside their home-made 'Leopard' armoured cars.

The Rhodesians couldn't import any weapons for 15 years, so they made their own, including some weird contraptions designed for the peculiarities of their war. The armoured car parked beside me was called a 'mine-resistant vehicle'. With a VW1600cc Beetle engine, a raised passenger section in the middle and the front wheels extended for 10 feet, so only the wheel would be damaged if they hit an IED. They even filled the tyres with water to dissipate the explosion.

It cost a fraction of what the West spent on their armoured cars but was more effective.

I joined some soldiers at the bar and they complained about the British helping Robert Mugabe become Prime Minister. "The British wouldn't allow the IRA in government, but they let Mugabe run our country?"

(But, 20 years later they did just that in N Ireland, with Martin McGuinness made Deputy First Minister.)

It had been a dirty war, with intimidation and horrific murders. The rebels burnt alive any tribes who didn't support them. And they knew that for every white family they murdered, twenty more would emigrate.

On the roads and fields around farms, landmines killed blacks and whites, and the rebels even shot down a civil airliner, then hacked the survivors to pieces while they awaited rescue.

Mr Mugabe had promised a peaceful future for the whites, but no one trusted him; most whites wanted to wait and see what would happen. They all said they loved the country and didn't want to leave.

East Africa was an economic basket case after years of corruption, while Zimbabwe/ Rhodesia was prosperous, so why would he want to wreck it by throwing out the Europeans?

History would prove their fears to be justified and as the economy was soon destroyed, the country would go from the most prosperous country in Africa to the poorest in a couple of decades. Nearly all the 300,000 whites would leave and Mugabe would stay in power for thirty-seven years.

The whites' attitude was racist to the core, but so was the blacks', or I should say 'tribal.' Everyone just voted for his or her own 'Chief', leading to a permanent one-party dictatorship. Very few voted for the other tribe.

Democracy doesn't work in Africa as, once a politician is in charge, their "tribe" will support them, as they fear any other "tribe" taking over.

The two tribes in Northern Ireland behaved no differently; people voted for their own tribe, Protestant or Catholic, with no interest in what their policies or views were.

I decided to travel without a convoy and take my chances with the rebels, as going faster than 50 mph meant certain death due to my buggered wheels, as the bike would go into a 'tank slapper'. I stopped at Bulawayo with a biker called Brian, who ran a small engineering company. His wife and children had left for South Africa two years ago after burglars murdered a whole family in their house next door. She had taken up with another man so they would soon get divorced.

"I couldn't afford to see them with the war, and we lost touch," he explained. "My business was here, and I couldn't move it. Now I'm on my own, and the business is collapsing anyway. I've lost everything." He was ready to go if he had to.

Brian had a pristine 'Le Mans' in the kitchen; he also collected snakes and spiders in cages and glass-fronted boxes in the house. Every evening, he would let the snakes out for exercise.

"How many do you have?" I asked.

"I'm not sure at the moment. I lost a couple last week, so give me a shout if you see one in your room."

"Jesus Christ," I said. "Why do you keep them?"

"Well, I never worry about burglaries!"

"Would you not get a guard dog?"

"No use, the bastards kill them with a piece of poisoned meat."

A six-foot python sat in the corner, staring at me with a 'don't fuck with me, mate' look on his face.

I was well-used to various African flying insects, with the multitude of flies and winged beetles that exploded on my windscreen. But the huge hairy spiders gave me shivers and the snakes slithering on the floor were the stuff of nightmares.

"Most of them are harmless," Brian laughed.

"The trick is knowing which ones aren't!" I said.

"Stay as long as you want."

"Just the one night will be fine!"

That night, I dreamt I was in the 'A-Team' in the old TV programme. Every day I got a new task to carry out.

"Your mission, Chris, which you have to accept, (because you are the silly bugger who got himself here in the first place) will be to stay alive today!"

"Your head will self-destruct during the next 5 hours!" Every morning, I would do a double-take of where I was, since I was hardly ever in the same place for more than a few nights. I would open my eyes, look around, and be glad I wasn't in Sudan.

I stopped at the Zimbabwe ruins, from the mysterious civilisation that gave the new country its name. The ruins are the biggest stone structures south of the Sahara.

As I lit my stove for a brew-up in the deserted car park, a small monkey jumped on the bike. I thought how cute, a monkey on a bike, and took a photograph of him, but the next thing the little bastard ran off with my ignition key! He swung through the trees, shrieking, as if laughing at me and kept coming back as if to play, like a puppy with a stick. Only I was the puppy.

He knew I needed the key! I gave up chasing him and hot- wired the ignition. But as I pulled the wires out, he dropped the key on the seat, squealed as if to say, 'Thanks for the game,' and ran off.

Apparently, monkeys are genetically 2% different from humans; the people that are a pain in the ass, that is.

The ex-pats in Africa were a strange breed, like Brother Anthony, the old boys' club in Tanga, George in Kenya, and the Rhodesians I had just met.

All had one thing in common: they all loved Africa, the savage beauty of the land, and the friendliness of the peoples. And they had turned down the safety of Europe and had Africa in their blood. But Africa didn't love them back, and their day had gone. They were the misfits of black Africa and the last white tribe of Africa.

The Chinese are the new colonialists now.

CHAPTER 12

South Africa

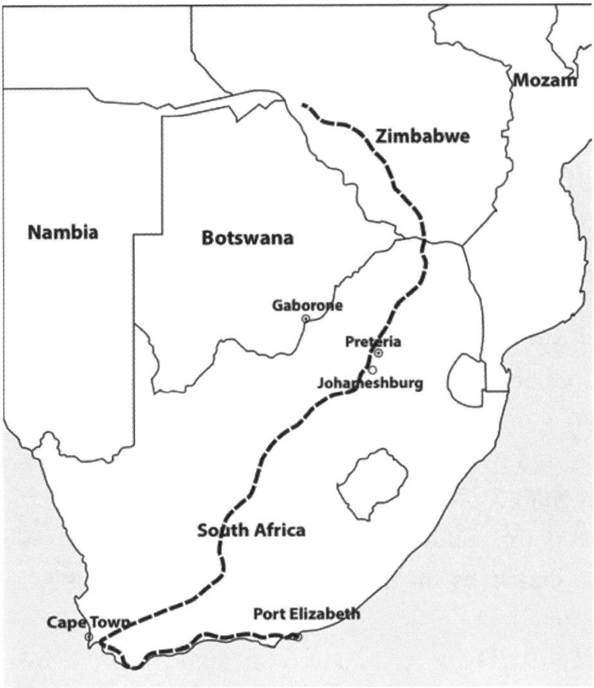

EVERYTHING HUNG ON MY FINAL BORDER CROSSING TO SOUTH AFRICA. IF they didn't let me in, the Rhodesians wouldn't let me back so I would be stuck on Beit Bridge for eternity.

The South African immigration initially refused my entrance. "You don't have enough money to get out again," they said. But they changed their minds when I showed them the countries on my passport.

It was impossible for a South African to travel further north with their passport. They would have been strung up. Suddenly, finally, I was getting treated with respect, like a conquering hero.

"You wouldn't catch me up north with those bastards. Jolly well done!" the milky-white Captain said.

He gave me my petrol ration book and my visa stamp.

"Where are you going next?"

"No idea," I said, smiling like a crazy chimpanzee. I had dreamt of this moment for months.

But it soon rained, so I pulled into the next town of Louis Trichardt. It was Sunday night, the town was deserted, and the banks shut. No one wanted my Rhodesian dollars, and I had no South African Rand for a guesthouse. So as usual, my emotions flew up and down like a barmaid's knickers.

One minute I was ecstatic at getting over the border, and the next I was cold and wet with nowhere to sleep.

I found a public toilet, parked the bike in the gents, then crawled into my sleeping bag on the slimy tiled floor. I woke to the smell of urine and thought I'd pissed myself. But the sun was shining outside, and I was as happy as any man could be, after sleeping in a public toilet.

At the next petrol station, I chatted to some bikers who called up their mates. I soon had an escort of big Hondas and Kawasakis, as I wobbled down to Johannesburg.

The Guzzi looked battered and bruised beside the shiny bikes, my forks tied up with rope, and brake pads glued to the wheel rims. But with two wheels on my wagon, I was still rolling along, singing a happy song. With a big grin frozen to my face.

Stan, the owner of the Moto Guzzi dealers, gave me new tyres, a front wheel and shock absorbers and serviced the bike. He called the newspapers and motorcycle magazines who all wanted to write my story. I was a minor celebrity; people even asked for my autograph! South Africa was the leper of the Western World, cut off by sanctions and travel bans. I had broken through the "black" cordon and unwittingly became a folk hero of the white elite.

"Why don't you write a book?" one journalist suggested. "Hell, I can hardly write my name!" I laughed.

It surprised me that news of the fighting in Belfast had reached this far. I believed South Africa to be a dangerous place. But the newspaper headlined my story. "Tail Gunner on a Belfast milk float rides to South Africa."

I stayed a few nights with a family friend from Ireland who was a vicar. They lived in one of the posh white areas of Johannesburg.

Reverend Fletcher explained how Apartheid law worked. The suburbs in Johannesburg were all colour-coded, with the small white population surrounded by a large, Third World, black population.

"The law classifies everyone as Blacks, Whites, Coloured, and Indian," he said. "Mixed marriages or interracial sex is illegal."

They segregated the beaches, cinemas and graveyards. Even trains and buses. 'White' restaurants only admitted blacks as staff. 'Blacks' could only live in white areas if employed as servants.

The Fletcher kids were shocked when I told them about Northern Ireland.

"Protestants and Catholics?" they asked, "Which ones are the Blacks?"

"They are all white."

"How do you tell the good guys from the bad?"

"Easy; you just ask them what school they go to," I said, as the schools were all segregated. The Reverend was surprised when I expressed my disgust at the apartheid system.

"You don't understand Africa," he said.

I wondered did God-fearing men say the same thing in Nazi Germany?

That evening, my friend in London, Alistair, was playing rugby for Ireland against England and the match was on TV. It was surreal to watch after five months of travel and struggle. But I suddenly felt lonely as I tried to spot Angela in the crowd.

Soon, I left on my last leg down to Cape Town, at the end of my fantasy rainbow. It was now only a couple of days ride across through the Karoo, a desolate semi-desert in the middle of South Africa. Halfway across, the engine coughed and spluttered. My heart missed a beat too, as it sounded like the engine was about to break down. But I just needed to switch on the reserve tap, with another 40 miles of petrol in it. I put my hand under the tank to turn the valve.

Shit! It was already on reserve; I had forgotten to turn it back at the last fill up and was completely out of juice. There was a town ahead, so I jerked the bike from the side to slop the last drop into the carburettors before the engine died. I freewheeled to a halt, shouting, 'Wanker, wanker, wanker,' to myself. I always found this very therapeutic at times like this.

I was on a small back road, with nothing but scrubland and termite mounds ten feet off the ground. While I waited for something to happen, I wondered why the termites built them so high. On my Hassle scale, 10 out of 10 is a 'disaster.' This was about a 3, a mild annoyance caused by my stupidity. I was hot and bothered but I would not die, and half an hour later I flagged down a Bakkie, as they called pickup trucks here.

An old farmer with ruddy cheeks and patched dungarees drove the truck. Two Africans sat in the back, although no passengers sat in the front seats.

"Have you any petrol?" I asked.

"Geen," he said in Afrikaans, shaking his head.

"Can you tow me into town?" I asked.

He grunted, and I tied some rope to his bumper and wound the other end around my handlebars, so I could release it if I fell.

Bakkie man suddenly took off like a rocket, and the bike catapulted from zero to twenty in an instant.

The rope broke, and I coasted to a halt, and Bakkie man returned.

"Can you go more slowly? You nearly had me off!" I said. He grunted, but this time drove slowly to town.

"Give me five Rand for breaking my rope," he demanded at the petrol station.

"Why are the workers on the back, when there's space in front?" I said to annoy him.

"The kaffirs like the fresh air," he smirked.

The town was two hundred years back in time with the run-down Dutch-style buildings, whitewashed gables and shuttered windows. It had seen better days.

In a café, I was very surprised when a white waiter served me. I chatted with him. Andre said he was working here until he finished school. He explained that all the white Afrikaner farmers were descended from the original Dutch immigrants. As devout Dutch Reform Christians, they loved the earth that they farmed.

God's own country, they called it. Unfortunately, God had been a slight miserly with the rain in this corner of his universe and the farmers scarcely scratched a living from the desert sands. But they would never give up. But the young people headed for a better life in Cape Town.

The next day I drove through the wine lands, over more mountains, then there it was, Table Mountain, covered with a thin layer of mist, like a tablecloth. I had trundled into Johannesburg on a donkey, but now was flying into Cape Town on a winged stallion with my newfangled circular wheels, and fresh tyres. This was the moment I had fantasized about.

My euphoria rose as the smooth tarmac led me through the suburbs and into the city. I breathed the salt air from the ocean now. I was overjoyed, and then there it was, the South Atlantic!

At 5 pm on the 23rd of March, after five months, 15,517 miles, and eighteen countries, I parked on the promenade at Green Point. Behind me lay a microscopic tyre tread, which led all the way back to Belfast. There was no welcoming committee, no brass band, just the mountain glowing in the evening sun and Atlantic surf breaking on the rocks below. I expected to be jubilant, to punch the air and drink Champagne, but suddenly, I was as empty as a Sudanese petrol tank. I abruptly realised I was at another dead end. Dejected, I sat back on the bike with my boots on the handlebars and stared at the rollers, with no idea what to do now, apart from play my harmonica.

I still had a Moto Guzzi and $340 in my pocket, but my reality was that the next stop was the South Pole.

"Is that a Belfast number plate?"

"It is," I replied to a small wiry old man.

"Harry West," he introduced himself. "Can I buy you a beer?"

Harry was from Belfast and had been on his way to Singapore when it fell to the Japanese in 1941. The convoy stopped in Durban, while the Army decided what to do with him. He enjoyed Africa so much he came back after the war. I told him that my father travelled on the convoy and got redirected to Durban too, but he didn't recollect the name. That would have been too weird.

I stayed in his small apartment and relaxed in the warm comfort of the sitting room, and somehow it seemed a fitting end to my trip. The next day I paraded around the town like a Queen with no subjects, as no one waved back.

The bike's vibration had broken my camera, so I found Tony Tavener's camera repair shop. Tony hunched over a camera, his big hands looking ridiculous, holding a tiny screwdriver. He was about six foot six and really looked like he should hold a shovel. He was from London's East End and had a goatee beard, a pigtail, and a 750 Honda, none of which impressed me much.

But we talked motorbikes, and he invited me to stay in his flat for a few days. It was the start of a 40-year friendship.

That evening, I met Tony's girlfriend, Fatima. Tony was white, and as she was mixed race, their relationship was illegal.

"It's my part in the anti-apartheid fight!" he said. "Nelson Mandela would be proud of you."

The previous weekend, they had nearly got arrested when the police called early in the morning with a traffic ticket. Tony said she was his cleaning lady, and the cop winked his approval. Apparently, it was okay to shag your cleaner, but not to have a relationship with a coloured girl.

Cape Town had been a seaport for 500 years and had an ethnic mix of blacks, whites, Malay and Indians. The government classified the mixed races as 'Cape Coloureds.' Apartheid wasn't all black and white; they had all shades in between.

I had a blind date with Fatima's friend, Cathy. She was a 'Cape Coloured' and smelled of fragrance and flowers. Her skin was soft, not dry and calloused like the girls who wanted me in Sudan. And her breasts were firm and pert, unlike the last ones I saw in Wau, which hung down like spaniels' ears. I still needed therapy from that sight. I was far from home, and I hadn't felt the touch of a woman for five months. I immediately fell head over wheels in lust.

Cathy worked as a teacher in a 'coloured' school and, in Apartheid South Africa, earned half what a white teacher would. A 'black' teacher would make a third less again. Her school was a collection of wooden huts and the classroom contained forty desks. The class had 50 kids, so some would sit on the floor. The 'black' school had even worse conditions. The darker you were, the worse off your living standards.

Having a coloured girl on the back of my bike was not too risky, as the helmet and gloves camouflaged the colour of her skin, but the problems started when you got off somewhere.

Not only would "whites only" restaurants refuse to serve her, but we could both get arrested, and I would get deported.

We socialized in the "black" or "coloured" areas. Swarthy from my months in the African sun, I was darker than Cathy, who had Malay blood in her veins. And she wore white gloves and a hat to keep the sun off her skin.

I thought it bizarre, that while coloured girls stayed out of the sun to look white, the white girls spent hours on sunbeds to look brown!

We rode out to the Cape of Good Hope, then to Cape Agulhas, the real southern point of Africa. It was a major anti-climax, with nothing there but a lighthouse and a pub selling bottles of Guinness.

One evening, we took the girls to see the new Michael Caine movie, "Zulu" in a black township cinema. The girls couldn't get into a 'whites-only' movie house. The film is about a British Army platoon in the Zulu War, 100 years ago. No one appeared to notice the two white guys in the packed cinema until the Red Coats started massacring the waves of black warriors.

"Don't shoot until you see the whites of their eyes," said Michael Caine.

It was carnage; the Zulus fell in front of the British soldiers. "This has to be the worst movie to watch a black township!" I hissed at Tony.

I could see the whites of a hundred African eyes staring at me, and I winced at every shot the Redcoats fired!

"How do we get out of here?" I whispered to Tony, as the massacred Zulu warriors piled up, six deep.

"I think we are dead!" he mouthed back.

As the movie ended, we jumped up to get out before the crowd, but it was no good, a sea of black faces swept past and enveloped us.

"You got us that time," one big African said, as we jostled towards the door.

"But we will get you soon!" said another, digging me in the ribs.

It was back-slapping good-natured banter; I guess the Africans knew we weren't racist or we wouldn't have been there.

I was in need of some love and affection after my hardships, but Cathy was emigrating to Australia in two weeks, and a relationship was the last thing she needed. She had worked hard to get an Australian visa and get away from South Africa and didn't need any complications. Like me. And I was the one supposed to love them and leave them!

I promised to follow her to Sydney, but we both knew it was only talk. I couldn't afford the bus fare to Johannesburg, let alone a flight to Australia.

We both knew our affair would be short, so we shed no tears on our last night. But the next day the loneliness hit me like a brick. I felt more alone than ever. Far from home, running out of money, and with no prospect of an exit from this isolated and fucked up place.

And I even felt confused about who I was now. The person I had used to be seemed a distant memory. I was a stranger to myself. Did I want to go back or go somewhere else? Life had been easier when I was moving, as the travelling was all- consuming. Now stopped, my life had no meaning or ambition.

There was a motorcycle rally near Port Elizabeth, 400 miles away. I would ride there, if only to hit the road again. Tony and Fatima came in his campervan but blew up the engine on the way, near the town of George. I had lost all faith in VW Campers by this stage.

The rally was full of bikers and their families in caravans and tents. Not surprisingly, I got an award for coming the furthest distance! With loads of bands, beers, and banter, it was a family affair. The white and black motorcyclists mingled at the bar.

Next day, I sat nursing a hangover from hell, when suddenly I heard shouts and gunshots. A hundred riot police with Alsatian dogs charged through the campsite firing tear gas. Some guys, who were doing a tug-of-war competition on the bikes, got arrested for rioting. The police cautioned the white bikers for having a beer with the blacks and then arrested the black guys for trespassing in a 'whites-only' area.

Luckily, I had pitched my tent away from the main area, and I watched as the riot police ransacked the place. Children screamed, and mothers hid their babies as the tear gas wafted towards us.

Then two cops came running over.

"Is that your bike?" the fatter cop demanded, pointing at the Guzzi with his baton.

"Yes, it is," I said, my eyes streaming from the tear gas now, "SOI 222? Which state is that from?"

"Ireland."

"Whoa, nice bike. I'm a biker myself," he said. "What's going on?"

"Just doing what I'm told," and he shrugged his shoulders. "For fuck's sake, give us a hand, Dave," shouted a policeman, as he frogmarched a bloodied black biker away. "Let's go for a ride out next week," Dave said as he gave me his phone number, before charging back to the fray with his baton swinging.

I stood there in astonishment. A riot cop had just asked me out on a date.

Soon the prison vans left full of blacks, leaving an eerie quiet, broken by the cry of children and mothers. Bikes lay on their sides, tents flattened, and the camp looked like a battlefield. The remaining bikers packed up and rode home.

"I'm sorry you saw that, Chris," said Ron, the hotel owner, "but that's what we have to put up with, it's a police state."

'No worries, mate, the Belfast cops wouldn't be much better, if you lived in West Belfast, that is."

He explained that many of the whites didn't believe in the regime or what it stood for. But the government disliked white dissenters as much as the blacks.

The next day, the Cape Times headlined;

'The hotel manager, Ron Davis, has been charged with ten summonses…including serving alcohol to Blacks… allowing Blacks in a White-only area… and letting women in a male-only bar'.

I was learning what living in a police state was all about. The police could do what they wanted, then blame everyone else afterwards. It sounded like Northern Ireland in 1979.

I wondered whether I should contact Dave, the fat riot cop. I despised what they had done, but was curious to find out what made them tick, so I rang him. The next Saturday, I met a bunch of cop bikers at a bar in Cape Town. Dave was fat, along with most of the coppers, and most of them had big Honda Gold Wings.

I had a blast riding flat out to Cape Point, past the Twelve Apostles Peaks, and back. South Africa had great roads and stunning scenery. We broke every speed limit; no cops would stop us. At the top of one pass, we stopped to take in the dramatic view of the ocean and the mountains.

"God's own country," Dave announced, with a grand sweep of his arm, voice full of emotion. I could see what he meant; it was a magnificent landscape.

Back at a bar in town, I felt a little guilty at socializing with a bunch of apartheid fascist fuckers.

"Why did you attack the bikers last week?" I asked finally. "Headquarters told us to go in hard," Dave said. "The Chief of Police doesn't like fraternization."

The conversation turned to politics, and one Afrikaner was clear that he didn't want blacks in government.

"They are corrupt and will ruin the country if it ever happens!"

But even the 'whites' were segregated! The Afrikaners were descended from the Dutch settlers, and I found them more bigoted than the 'English' South Africans. There had been animosity between them since the Boer war.

"Do you think white rule will end?" I asked.

The whole bar went silent, as they looked at each other. I had mentioned the unmentionable.

"Yes, it will," said Dave, and that started them all shouting. Most of them were concerned more about their job than the race issue. Their police jobs would be given to the Blacks, as a Black government would want a Black police force.

Their only advantage in the world, that of being born white, would go. It was weird; the guys who safeguarded Apartheid, the world's most hated regime, didn't believe in it either. These easy-going guys - when you got to know them out of uniform- and not at the wrong end of a tear gas canister. While they upheld a brutal system that was ending soon, they were only interested in their own well-being.

But I realised that when black rule came, the wealthy whites would still afford extra security, or emigrate, but the poorer whites like Dave would lose their jobs.

The beer and conversation raised emotions, and they all started screaming and swearing at each other.

I slipped out before I got the blame.

The whites hung on to power and knew that black majority rule was coming. I thought they should plan for the eventuality by educating the blacks to run the country and not by radicalizing them.

But their fear was too great, understandably as they watched prosperous countries like Uganda, Kenya, and Tanzania turn into charity cases after independence.

I was enjoying South Africa and loved the 'end of the road' spirit of Cape Town, even though it really was the 'Dead' end of my road. I needed to get out before my money ran out so tried to get a job as a deckhand on a ship that might ship the bike.

My only interview was a disaster.

"I'm looking for a job on a ship," I said.

"Do you have a trade or a seaman ticket?"

"No."

"No job then."

"What about a deckhand?"

"We only use Blacks and Coloureds for that."

"That's discrimination!" (Which perversely, was against the law!)

"No, we are protecting jobs for the Blacks and Coloureds." The apartheid system protected jobs for them okay. All the crappy jobs! It was illegal for whites to do manual labour, and not qualified for an officer's job, I was shafted both ways. Foreign ships had all their crew, so unless someone got sick, I had no chance of a berth. I didn't care where they went, but every enquiry was a dead end.

I took some photographs for the Cape Town Times through Tony's photography business, but my money was still running out fast. It didn't look good, and I would soon have to sell the bike and fly home.

I spent my mornings searching for a ship, but by afternoon, I was tired and depressed. Perhaps it was time to give up. I had the ambition to take on another continent, I just didn't have the money.

CHAPTER 13

Sailing Away

GIVE TWO MEN ONE BOAT, AND YOU HAVE A MEANS OF TRANSPORT. GIVE TWO MEN TWO BOATS...AND YOU HAVE A RACE.

One day, I was reading the Cape Town Times to see if they had used any of my photographs when I read about a yacht race stopping in Cape Town. A gale had caused devastation to boats and crew. One yacht, the Gypsy Moth V, had battled into the wind for five days and had gone backwards a hundred miles.

The Dutch boat, Vetus, nearly sank after the hull cracked open. The Kaleo lost her mast 150 miles offshore and was finally rescued by the Navy. The tow rope had broken, hit one of the crew, and smashed him up badly.

I saw a last-gasp way out of South Africa and rang the Royal Cape Town Yacht Club, and yes, there may be a couple of places going. I knew bugger all about sailing, but I didn't mind filling injured men's bunks. Not quite as bad as dead men's shoes, but the next worst thing.

Sir Francis Chichester's old boat Gypsy Moth V was looking for crew members but my interview didn't go well. The English skipper was unimpressed with my lack of sailing experience and wanted £200 towards food. And I thought he was an upper-class twat.

"I will keep you as a last resort," he said.

I nearly told him to fuck off, but decided not to, in case I needed that "last resort".

I bought a Learn How to Sail Dinghies book, so I could try to spoof my way, but I needed some sailing practise before my next interview. At the Simonstown sailing club, some yachty types sat enjoying a Sundowner at the bar.

"Anyone looking for keelboat crew this weekend?" I asked.

"Can you sail?"

"Eh, no, but I'm entering a race to Rotterdam, so I need some practice."

"You should have started ten years ago."

"Why?"

"Would you learn how to ride a bicycle the weekend before the Tour de France?" They laughed.

But one guy needed crew for the weekend's race, on a tiny 17-foot boat, but it had a keel, so that would have to do!

My interview on Monday morning was in Seltrust Endeavour's cramped cockpit, where Mike Dunham, the skipper, was repairing the storm damage.

"You want a berth on our boat?" he said.

"Yes," I said, nodding.

"Maybe you want to see the living conditions below?" He nodded down to the hatchway.

"It's good enough for you, it will be fine for me," I said, thinking if he knew what shit places I had stayed in, he would have been shocked.

"Do you drink dark rum?" asked Mike. "Yes," I said.

"Do you like sherry?"

"I can drink it if the rum runs out," I said, catching the drift.

"So far so good," said Mike to Cam, who came up from below.

Both of them had Captain Birdseye beards and looked like old sea dogs.

"Have you sailed on a keelboat?"

"Yes. In fact, I was sailing yesterday," I said, very pleased with myself.

"Okay," he said, "you've got the job."

"That was easy; did no one else apply?"

"The other guy asked would we be out of sight of land!"

"That was my next question!" I said… "Joking of course."

"You better look below!"

I ducked into the hatchway. The Seltrust Endeavour was an experimental design, 56 feet long but only 9' 6" wide. Cam explained that the ultra-narrow shape meant she would cut through the water, but she leant over alarmingly in the slightest wind. And the narrow hull left little space for the crew.

It was like a small plywood submarine; it was dark and smelled of ancient blue cheese. The galley was tiny with a bench, a couple of cupboards and a cooker. The skipper's bunk and a chart table sat underneath the cockpit.

In front was a narrow cabin with four bunks, entered through a hole in the plywood bulkhead. The floor was covered with boxes of tinned food, and cases of Australian rum, so we would have to crawl over the boxes. There was no fridge or freezer, so all food was in tins or freeze-dried packets. In the bow, was a cabin with two bunks. The toilet was in the middle, in full view.

It was dark and claustrophobic, with no room to sit. My heart sank; this would be the living space for eight guys over 5 weeks!

I met the injured crewman who had pulled a hamstring playing football. His misfortune was my ticket home. We shook hands and exchanged numbers, as he was heading to Ireland to meet his family.

And I met the rest of the crew; Katrina, the cook, looked like a cabin boy, with her cropped blond hair. She was with Frazier, making their way to Europe. Keen sailors all their lives, as were Phil, and Cam, the other Australians.

Then there was Ton, a tall Dutchman from the near- wrecked Vetus. The skipper, Mike Dunham, was an English Channel ferry skipper off looking for a good time. The last crewman was an English guy called Tas' who was in his late thirties, and the old man of the crew.

I felt a complete conman amid these well-seasoned sailors. They lived their dream of sailing to Europe. For them, it was the trip of a lifetime, but for me, it was a free ride home. I had no idea what to expect, living for four or five weeks in this long garden shed, with seven complete strangers. They seemed like a relaxed bunch but they might turn into a pack of crazies at sea!

The Seltrust had had some damage from the storm, but Mike said she had survived last year's Fastnet Race when a dozen boats sank, drowning fifteen crew. He was trying to reassure me but this had quite the opposite effect! This was clearly a dangerous sport and we would sail the South and North Atlantic, well out of the range of any rescue should anything go wrong. I confessed my lack of experience with Mike.

"No worries, Chris, we will team you up with Cam here, and he will teach you all he knows!"

"I hope you are a good teacher, Cam," I said.

"I hope you are a quick learner," he replied, without looking up.

A Dutch shipping company sponsored the race, so I called

Dirk, their public liaison officer.

"I need to ship my bike home," I said.

"We will ship it anywhere in the world, free of charge!"

"What do you mean?"

"Anywhere that our ships go!" he said, handing me a list of ports.

I couldn't believe my luck. I thought my trip was over and I would spend my last few pounds on shipping the bike home, but this was a chance to continue. But Australia was out of the picture, as the race sailed to Europe.

"What about Los Angeles?" I said, on a whim.

"That's a bit out of the way?"

"It's in the Northern Hemisphere!" I said.

"Okay, whatever you say!"

I had made my decision, based on a flight of fantasy.

'Stop; what are you doing?' my sensible head said.

'Shut the fuck up, discover America!' my lunatic head said, and as usual, my 'idiot head' got his way.

Questions like, 'How will you get there? And Where are you going to get the money?' didn't enter my thick skull!

I had overcome many major obstacles in Africa and I had learned that if you believe in yourself, you will prevail. I hadn't quite planned on hitching a ride on some silly boat race, but hell, why not go to America!

I rang my brother at home to tell him I was sailing home, but he didn't seem impressed.

"Call when you get here," he said.

My family really had no interest in my adventures; it was as if to say,

"That's not fair, you going off while I'm stuck here."

I had two days to get the bike ready for shipping. I unclipped the panniers with the stuff I would need, which wasn't much, as motorcycles and boats share little in the way of equipment. We had been inseparable for six months; the Le Mans had been my life, my transport, residence, and entertainment! I actually felt guilty leaving it in the warehouse!

At the press launch, Dirk explained that for generations, slow-moving cargo ships took tea and spices to Europe, before fast Clipper ships raced back to get the best prices.

For instance, in 1866, five Clippers left China the same day. After eighty-four days, three of them reached Dover within ten minutes of each other, charging up the English Channel together at fourteen knots. The fastest Clippers reached Australia in fifty-five days and covered 400 miles in a day. By comparison, in 1980, a fast, modern racing yacht would average ten knots and 240 miles in a day.

The Clipper ships culminated from many years of sailing ship design. But by the time they built the Cutty Sark in 1870, steamships took the shortcut through the Suez Canal and made these thoroughbreds redundant.

The 1980 Spice Race was organised to beat the record of the Kelso, which made it to Dover in sixty-three days, a record that had stood for 119 years!

In 2020, ocean racing is a multi-million-dollar business, and the yachts can do over 30 knots and use professional race crews. They have satellite navigation, live TV camera feeds, all sorts of safety equipment and emergency beacons so, if you fall overboard, rescuers can find you anywhere in the world.

Computers decide their course, with their shore-based team taking the satellite projections for the winds and tides. It's a massive event with 2 billion people worldwide watching on TV.

But back in 1980, our race would be the first from east to west, into the prevailing winds, as we broke new ground. We would navigate by sextants, taking sun readings, as generations of seafarers had done, and would make one daily radio call. Apart from that, and if anything went wrong, we were on our own.

There was an assortment of light offshore cruisers and one-designs like the Seltrust Endeavor. The racer Flying Wilma, that had won the Whitbread Round the World race the year before, was hoping to beat the record. With only a few professional skippers in charge, amateur enthusiasts sailed most of the boats. I felt like a complete fraudster.

The Cape Times did a front-page spread with myself on the bike, parked in front of the boat. In the background, the crew worked to prepare the boat, giving me dirty looks as I posed.

I said my goodbyes to the friends I had made in Cape Town and left to spend my first night on the boat, ready for an early start. The crew was off saying their goodbyes to John Dick, the injured crewman.

I lay worrying about how I would take his place. He was popular and an expert sailor. I was an imposter, a landlubber faking an interest in sailing just to get to Europe and America. They would keel haul me when they found out. I tried to put my worries to sleep but dreamt of huge wild oceans and slimy sea monsters.

The race morning buzzed with final preparations. At the last minute, we painted the name of the sponsors, Seltrust, on the boat! Their sponsorship money had finally come through! Mike invested it in a dozen cases of tins of fruit salad and more rum. I spent my last Rand on five Crunchie bars, one for each week we would be away.

Tony and the guys came down to see me off, and when I saw them it hit me: I was off to sail the Atlantic! I shook with emotion now as the enormity sank in. This was no dinghy race! Never before in the world of ocean racing had anyone, had such a derisory idea of what was going on!

I felt embarrassed again, as the crew only had John Dick to wave them off, while I had all my Cape Town mates shouting and waving. I had taken over before I earned any right to be there.

I sat like a piece of extra baggage as the crew cast off. I was as odd as a boy with three bollocks. Still wearing my leather bike jacket, I couldn't look more 'un-sailor'-like if I'd tried!

A brass band played and a flotilla of spectator boats followed us. Our crew worked like a well-oiled machine, hoisting the sails, pulling ropes, coiling others as our boat caught the breeze.

"Grab that jib sheet, Chris," Cam said, and I looked at the snakes' nest of ropes lying in the cockpit.

"Eh, which one?" I said as he grabbed the one he'd wanted anyway.

The boats jostled on the start line, and the crews shouted over to each other.

"See you in the dirtiest bar in Rotterdam!"

"Not a chance mate, we'll be there first!"

The gun sounded and the six yachts crossed the line. Some boats sailed straight out to sea to look for better wind, and some stayed inshore.

Whichever course they sailed could be vital with the winds and tides. It would be down to the skipper's skill and a huge amount of luck. The spectator boats followed for a half an hour, then finally they turned back with horns blowing. On our own, the boats spread out in the fading light. I watched with dread as Table Mountain shrank and disappeared as darkness fell. It marked the end of one journey and the start of a new one.

We split up into three 'watches' to work four hours on and eight hours off. Mike would come and go as skipper. They paired me with Cam.

Mike sent me to bed early, but I awoke to a horrendous crashing and the shriek of the wind howling through the rigging. The boat was leaning over at a frightening angle and was pounding through the waves. The crew shouted and charged around up top.

'Jesus, we're sinking!' I thought and dashed up on deck! It was pitch black, waves crashing over the cockpit.

"What's wrong?" I shouted.

"Just changing sails; the wind's picked up," someone yelled, and pushed past.

And I thought we would put the sails up in Cape Town and take them down in Rotterdam!

I had swapped my trusty V twin for three sails, which had to be trimmed every time the wind changed.

"Go back to your bunk until your shift," Mike barked. My bunk was now leaning over at 45 degrees, as we charged through the waves, so it was impossible to sleep. One moment I was lying on the sleeping bag, the next, weightless as the boat took off from the crest of a wave, and crashing down as we hit the trough.

When my watch started at 4 am, I felt exhausted already, Cam took the wheel, the boat was heeled over but was holding steady.

"We will change helm every hour; we will steer 310 degrees, but check the wind direction indicator. You need to make sure we get the optimum angle of attack," Cam instructed.

"If the wind veers, we will change the headsail."

I nodded, pretending to understand but thinking what the fuck he was on about!

I could see the fluorescent white of the breaking surf in the darkness. Occasionally, a wave would break over the bow, crash down the deck and over me as I crouched behind the wheel. Cam tweaked the sails, impervious to the water sloshing past. Petrified and totally out of my depth, I clung to the wheel and concentrated on the spinning compass, as if my life depended on it. This would not be the cruise I envisioned!

We talked through all the parts of the boat, what each rope did, and how everything worked.

"That's the theory. Questions?" Cam asked.

"Yes," I said, "can I have a waterproof jacket?" as I shivered in my sodden leathers.

Cam was a wiry character who had worked in a rough Australian mining town to earn the money to be here. They had lived in caves with the nearest policeman a hundred miles away. He would be a good man to have in a drama - or a storm.

Towards the end of the watch, the sky brightened, and the sun rose over the deep blue of the South Atlantic, as the spindrift blew off the top of the waves, catching the light.

"Wow, it's beautiful!" I said to Cam, while two of our competitors' boats appeared on the horizon, and I imagined their crew doing the same thing. At 8 am our replacements appeared, and I crawled down to my bunk, exhausted but fulfilled, my head buzzing with information.

Food takes on huge importance on a boat, as it's a social event. On the 8 am to noon watch, normally everyone was up for breakfast, so there would be plenty of crewmen about to talk to. The noon to 4 pm watch had lunch to break the monotony.

For the 4 pm to 8 pm shift, we looked forward to dinner and rum rations. The Royal Navy did away with the rum ration ten years ago, but Mike thought it was a tradition worth upholding. We would discuss the day, the distance travelled, where the competitors' boats lay, and so on.

The 8 pm to 12 midnight watch was quiet, with a bottle of Australian Sherry to keep the chill out. I would play my harmonica and we would sing sea shanties and Irish songs.

The midnight to 4 am watch was hard, as the brain tried to close down for the night. It was May, so cold in the Southern Hemisphere as it headed into winter for the 4 am to 8 am shift, you forced your body to wake up early. The sun comes up, and you do it all again.

For the next few days, I literally learned the ropes and studied everything. By day four, I had settled in. The sail of the lightweight ocean racer, Lexington, teased us a few miles ahead and the other boats sailed just over the horizon.

Ablutions on the boat became rudimentary. Having a piss is easy; you hold tight to a shroud with one hand and face downwind. Cam told me many drowned sailors are recovered from the sea with their zips down!

Number twos entailed a trip to the pulpit, the steel tubing that goes around the bow. You drop your shorts and heave your bum over the front. It's quite pleasant as you look down and see the bow slicing through the water below. You get a nice fresh breeze around your bollocks. Bombs away, and your load disappears under the boat!

But as the weather deteriorated, it was too wet at the bow so you had to hang your ass over the stern, just behind the helmsman's head. This isn't very pleasant for either party, or anyone else in the cockpit.

The alternative was to strip off, grab the safety line and crawl up through the breaking waves to the pulpit. You need to get your timing right for the drop. Too early and a wave would catch the load and propel it over the deck to land on the helmsman's lap!

As the bow dips for a surge of seawater to wipe your ass, King Neptune performed a complete body wash and a quick colonic irrigation. You can tell that boredom was setting in when dropping your load was the main entertainment of an evening.

We didn't have room for enough fresh water and would start rationing unless it rained to replenish the tanks. We washed with seawater, but the soap didn't lather in it, so you always felt damp and salty.

Our damp clothes stank as nothing dries out when it's covered in salt and they soon rotted and tore apart as we moved about the boat. One evening, while helping Cam tie down the sail, I turned round to see his balls hanging out of a hole in his shorts, just inches from my face. This was no place for modesty, just Australian humour.

"Move your arse, mate; it smells of mothballs back here." Sometimes I had rebellious thoughts of mutiny, but the nearest land was Brazil now. I would read a book every couple of days, and my imagination would take me away with the pages.

A rogue wave over the deck would bring me back to reality!

The narrow wooden interior was squalid smelly living for eight people, and as we entered the tropics, the heat rose to 40 degrees. It was worse when the wind was up, as we had to close the hatches to stop the spray coming in.

My only personal space was my coffin-like six by two- by-two-foot bunk. I lay in the darkness in the claustrophobic cabin; we couldn't use the lights as we had to run the engine to recharge the batteries.

I said to Cam one day, "It would be nice for some excitement sometime."

"Don't say that! Excitement means something has gone wrong!"

He was right; everything would be the same old boring routine, then, bang, a fitting breaks, or a sail blows out, and it's all hands on deck for twenty minutes. And back to normal again.

We continually raced hard, and the crew steered the best course and kept the fastest sails up. Then the next watch did the same thing. It was relentless.

The wind had been from the South since leaving Cape Town, but increased and moved to the North. So, we now beat into it, with the boat leaning over at 45 degrees again.

Every time the wind changed, it affected the sail trim. On some watches, we would change the sail four or five times. We knew our competitors were doing the same thing.

A gale came in and there would be loud thumps, as rogue waves slammed against the hull. But the boat bounded on; she knew this was what they had built her for. But down below, it was impossible to sleep.

Occasionally, a pod of dolphins danced across our bow, as if to say, "We're bored, can we join in?" I heard their squeaks through the hull as they talked to each other.

Another day, we spotted the T shape of the tail of a sperm whale as it lifted high before it dived.

One night, I saw sinister ghostly shadows beside the boat, then realised it was the dolphins. Flashes of phosphorescence sparkled like diamonds as they jumped through the waves.

Some guys complained the food was monotonous, but they hadn't lived on beans, bread and golden syrup for three months! There was porridge for breakfast, freeze-dried stew for lunch and spaghetti for dinner, followed by a treat of tinned fruit and custard, with the rum toddy after.

Sometimes we saved our rum toddy for a couple of nights, so we had a triple measure the next evening. Mike didn't approve but turned a blind eye if we had finished our watch.

Mike was a superb skipper, easy-going and knowledgeable, and everyone had the utmost confidence in him. He was patient with my lack of sailing skills.

"Did my lack of experience concern you?" I asked him later.

"No, I knew you would pick it up," he said. "I was more concerned that as a lone biker you would not fit in with the crew."

I could understand, as it was vital for everyone to get on in the close confinement. It was a psychological challenge and a physical one.

Cam was a great watch-mate to have, too, if I was up on the foredeck for a sail change. He knew exactly which ropes to pull and which to let fly when I needed them. I spent time with Phil, another easy-going Australian, who enjoyed his books, and rum toddies as much as me.

Tas was the only one who didn't get on; a very average sailor, he was having some kind of mid-life crisis. But I wasn't interested, as my own would come soon enough. He would be fifteen minutes late every watch, and on a cold night, every minute was like an hour. But this was no place for a row, and I kept well out of Tas's space.

Ton, the Dutchman, was the strong, silent type and didn't have great English at the start. But he was a steady hand on the boat and soon became everyone's friend. Frazier and Kat kept to themselves in the forepeak, the most uncomfortable place in heavy weather, as the bows banged continually through the waves.

On the ninth day, the wind increased from the South. The boat corkscrewed down the swells, making cooking a struggle with the boat at 45 degrees. The cooker was on gimbals and swung with the wild motion.

With the work surfaces at a 45-degree angle, Katrina strapped in with a harness, so she could use both hands, as the boiling pots swung with the waves. Once the food was cooked, eating it required three hands; I would wedge myself into a corner of the cockpit. One hand to hold the plate, one hand for the fork, and one imaginary hand to hold on to the boat. I shoved it down as quickly as possible before a wave dumped a pint of saltwater onto my plate, or the wind snatched the food away to give to the fish.

To change the foresail in heavy weather meant inching up to the bow with the new sail under your arm. Then I would lie on it to prevent the wind from snatching it overboard, and clip it on to the forestay. I would fasten the new halyard, and sheets, and crawl back to the mast to hoist it.

Then back to the bow and pull the old sail down. All against the gale-force wind and mountainous waves crashing over me. Once unclipped, it became a wild canvas liability, and I crawled back trying to stop the wind catching the loose sail and whipping us both overboard.

We would be reluctant to drag the crew from their bunks at night and would make the sail changes on our own. But it was dangerous; if you fell overboard in the dead of night, the chance of finding you would be minuscule.

Close to the Equator, the seas warmed, and we stripped off to our underwear to do the sail changes. It was easier to move on the foredeck half-naked. We would end up as clean as a cat's arse in the breaking waves. The stronger winds made for more speed, and we finally topped 200 miles a day, but it made for a wild ride. I wedged myself in my bunk with my bags, but it was useless.

We would fish to supplement our food. One afternoon, the line twanged tight and screeched out of the spool. We had hooked something big, and Cam reeled it in, foot by foot. The fish fought like a tiger, but after twenty minutes, it tired and we dragged it up alongside. It was a magnificent 30lb tuna, and we stuffed our faces for two days until it smelled rancid in the heat.

After two weeks, Prodent and Gypsy Moth raced only a hundred miles to our beam, sailing unseen and over the horizon.

On May 13th, I came on watch, everyone sang 'Happy Birthday,' and suddenly a pod of twenty enormous pilot whales jumped our bow wake as if to join the party. In the front cabin, we heard their squeaks through the hull, as if they sang for me too. After about 20 minutes, they got bored and swam off. But such occasions caused great excitement before we would return to the regular pattern of life.

Sometimes I sat deep in my own thoughts, wondering about what a mad year it had been, from leaving Ireland. And now here I was in a yacht in mid-Atlantic, with this bunch of blokes, now my best mates, and on whom my life depended.

I smiled to myself, proud of what I had achieved. I enjoyed the camaraderie but sometimes missed the solitude of my biking days. Some people could find the close confinement on the boat a nightmare; others would hate being on their own in the middle of Africa.

Like some kind of weirdo, I seemed to enjoy both.

On day eighteen, we crossed the Equator, and it was another excuse for a party. The Australians had not been in the Northern Hemisphere before. We threw a bucket of water from King Neptune over them in the time-honoured tradition… and another excuse for an extra rum toddy!

On day 20, as we wallowed in the doldrums, we hooked another fish and it fought hard. Smoke came off the winch handle as the line spun out, and Cam wound it in as it swam under the boat.

"Strewth, it's a monster!" he shouted as he struggled to prevent the line breaking.

"Keep steering the ship!" Mike shouted as the helmsman got distracted.

"Jesus Christ, it's pulling us backwards!" someone laughed.

"Take it up to the bow, and we'll get a tow!"

Suddenly, the line lay slack. We all stopped talking and looked at Cam.

"Is the line broke?" I asked.

"Don't think so; he's come in close," Cam said, furiously reeling in.

I looked back over the stern and suddenly, a huge shark breached the surface thirty metres back with a tremendous leap and it disappeared into the water.

"FUCK, did you see that?" we all shouted together. "It must have been four metres!"

"He looked pissed off!" said a random Australian voice. Suddenly, the line tightened and spun out with a screech, smoke rising from the reel, it snapped with a ping, and he was gone.

After a few seconds' silence, the Aussie banter started,

"Maybe you should use smaller bait, like your dick!"

Someone wiggled his little finger at Cam.

"Thank God he got away, mate, I wouldn't want to get the hook out of that bastard's mouth!"

It gave us something to talk about for days!

The Australian crew brought difficult situations down to earth with silly comments, which defused tension. They would put "mate" at the end of every sentence, which was quite addictive, and we all spoke Australian now, even Ton, who sounded ridiculous with his Dutch Australian accent!

The fresh water situation was getting serious, with no rain to fill the tanks. As we sailed into the tropics, the crew got hot and thirsty. But clouds teased us with a splatter of rain, then stopped as soon as we got the buckets out.

We were rationed to three cups of water a day, and we even cooked the pasta in seawater. We washed the dishes in seawater too, the plastic plates always greasy, and our armpits smelly.

At last, a jet-black cloud floated our way, and the wind blew twenty-five knots, and the heavens opened. Rain bounced off the decks and fell from the sails in rivers into the buckets to fill the tanks. We got the soap out to wash the grime off our bodies and our clothes. We danced naked in the deluge as we scrubbed our armpits. For just a few days we would be a sweet-smelling boat again,

Breakfast, lunch, and dinner became major events, and the crew eagerly awaited meals. But as weeks dragged past, the food got more and more tedious. By the first week, our fresh tomatoes and onions had rotted. By week two it was the potatoes, apples and oranges, and other vegetables. The damp turned everything rancid, including my shorts, which had some sort of mushrooms growing on them.

One day, Mike found Katrina and me cutting the last of the cheese into slices.

"What are you up to?" he said.

"Picking out the weevils."

"Let me see," he demanded.

We had discovered black larvae in the cheese, so we sliced it up to poke them out. Mike was not impressed and threw the whole block overboard.

"It's live protein!" I complained.

The boat was down to freeze-dried stew and tins of fruit salad.

Now, we were becalmed in the Doldrums, where the northern and southern hemisphere's different weather systems cancel each other out and yachts could be trapped for weeks. We could jump in to cool off, with a life ring dragged behind, in case we spotted a shark.

We had to keep the sails filled with the slightest breeze. Everyone whispered and crept around the boat as the smallest shake could kill any speed. If we spotted a cloud, we would steer for it, as there would be some wind beneath. As we drifted closer, suddenly, the wind speed shot from three to thirty-three knots in seconds. It was all hands on deck to lower the lightweight sails then get the heavy ones up to catch the wind. We blasted along for thirty minutes before the cloud moved away, leaving us drifting, to do it all over again.

Then on the daily radio check, we heard that Prodent had lost her mast. Like us, she had been hunting for wind, when a squall tore her mast off before they could change the sails. They were floating, out of control, 600 miles from the nearest port in West Africa, without enough fuel to motor to safety.

"We have to help her," said Mike, looking up from the radio.

"What can we do, mate?" I asked, with my newfound Aussie twang.

"We will share our fuel."

It would mean abandoning the race to rendezvous with her. We would go from being third to last, as Lexington and the Gypsy Moth would get past. After three weeks' hard sailing, we had to throw it all away. It was devastating, but we had to find them before a storm did.

"We can re-join the race after," Mike tried to assure us. This was before the invention of GPS navigation, so both ships gave their position from their sextant sun sight. We reached their position the next day, but Prodent was nowhere to be seen. A yacht with no mast is hard to spot, and with low cloud cover, we couldn't take a sun sight to confirm our position.

"Fuck, I can't see the bastard anywhere, mate," said Cam, behind the binoculars. The Australians now added a compulsory 'Bastard' and 'Fuck' to every sentence, and the 'Mate' at the end.

Mike caught a glimpse of the sun, took a position fix, and we found that we had sailed to the right place. But in the next radio check, Prodent announced that they had made up a jury rig, using the spinnaker pole as a mast, and now sat sixty miles away. We had missed them.

Pissed off, we thought they should have stayed where they had been, and now we had lost two days for nothing.

If cursing could kill, they would have died a horrible death, but all we could do was resume the race.

They did the right thing to save themselves, but it was frustrating for us.

The next day, a swallow appeared and hitched a ride. He was exhausted and happy to sit on our arms and we gave him water and biscuits. He looked cute on the edge of the book Katrina was reading but shit on her lap before flying off.

"That's another fucking sign! Like those Prodent bastards, mate," Phil said, laughing. "Help them out and they shit on you!"

I wanted to write an old mariner's poem about killing a swallow.

Eventually, the wind filled in, and we moved again. The dis-masting had wasted time and miles, but past the Doldrums the wind was steady, but we sailed closer to America than Europe with a long way to go.

On Day 25, a passing ship radioed a storm warning. "Make for the nearest port," the radio officer suggested.

"No chance, that's 700 miles away!" said Mike "We will sail through it."

Typical; after weeks with no wind we would now get too much, and we lashed everything down.

The Atlantic darkened, and the wind built up to a shriek, a wail and a howl. The tops of the waves broke away in streams of foam and the boat juddered and groaned. The bow crashed headlong through swells before rising for the next one. The noise below was tremendous.

It threw us about as if some giant hand had lifted the boat up and shaken it. Everything was an effort, cooking was chaotic, and even warming a tin of soup was dangerous as the cooker swung violently on its mounting.

Half of me was excited to have stronger winds but the other half was terrified to see the savagery of the ocean. As the boat reached the top of each wave, the bow lifted briefly then careered down the other side. I lay on my bunk, weightless for a second, then thrown back down against the wall with a whack.

We could only eat the tinned fruit, and even that was a struggle as I battled to hold on to something. In the cockpit, the wind whipped the food off your spoon before you could get it near your mouth. Some guys threw up, but being a biker, it didn't bother me!

The wind had arrived, but too bloody much; however, it pushed us homeward bound. We sailed faster than ever with only a puny bit of sail up, and the boat drove through the sea like an express train. As it powered down the side of a swell, the bow would dig into the on-coming wave sending a solid wall of green water back over the deck, where it would explode over us, sheltering in the cockpit, and drip through the hatches onto our bunks below.

The yacht was surfing fast and demanded intense care on the helm when a gust knocked us flat. Get it wrong and she would swing broadside and over on her side until the lead in the keel levered us upright again.

A motorbike would never act like this!

After two days, the storm calmed down to 35 knots, still gale force, but the sky turned blue, and the sun came out. White surf and foam flew across the dramatic seascape of deep blue waters. The Gods were still angry!

Next afternoon, I was dozing exhausted on my bunk, when there was a shout, and the boat lurched over on its side. I knew something was badly wrong. As I rushed on deck, the boat swung on her beam and threw me sideways and I just saved myself from flying overboard.

"Jesus, what's going on?" I shouted above the wind, as a wave heeled us over. The wind caught the mainsail, the boat gybed, and the boom flew over, and just missed my head.

Cam spun the wheel; "The bloody rudder has gone!" he shouted.

"Get the sails down!" ordered Mike.

I grabbed the main halyard and let it loose as the jib and the mizzen sails came down and we floundered in the swells. I looked over the stern; the rudder blade was floating behind us.

"Christ, you wanted some excitement, well here it is," said Cam.

We got a line on the rudder blade and hauled it aboard. It was six-foot-long by two-foot-wide, made of steel, but filled with foam. The steel mounting had broken and twisted.

"Fuck, we need a bastard welder!" Cam shouted.

If it had been a bolt that had broken, we might have repaired it with a swimmer with a mask and a spanner, but without a welder it was impossible. A boat can lose her mast and set up a temporary rig to get to port. But with no rudder, we would sail round in circles forever. Apart from actually sinking, this was the worst thing possible.

The boat swung wildly, completely out of control; Mike threw the sea anchor over the bow. It was a large canvas sock tied to a rope, which kept the bow into the wind and waves. It stabilized the wallowing, but we were still shipwrecked in the middle of the North Atlantic. Mike weighed up our options. "It looks like for us the race is over, lads, but that is the least of our worries."

"Can we get a tow?"

"We are out of the shipping lanes and it's near impossible to tow a boat without a rudder," he said. "If we find a ship, we will abandon the yacht."

The breakage was a disaster, but if it had happened yesterday, the seas would have overwhelmed us.

"The nearest land is 250 miles north," said Mike, looking at the charts. "It's an island called Cape Verde."

"Where the hell is that?"

"It may as well be 5000 miles, with no rudder!"

It was still blowing a stink, 30 knots plus, and we clipped on our safety lines. If someone fell overboard now, we wouldn't be able to manoeuvre back to get them.

"We will make a rudder," announced Mike. The crew looked at him thinking he had lost the plot. A racing yacht had no tools or equipment to make a rudder. I was sure he only said this to keep our minds off the danger.

"Lash a plank of wood onto the spinnaker pole and stick it out the back," he continued.

The spinnaker pole was about 20 feet long and normally held the spinnaker over the bow, but now we put it through the safety rails over the back into the sea.

"Put up the storm jib," Mike ordered. The boat steadied as the wind caught, and started sailing, but in the wrong direction.

"Fuck, we'll be in South America at this rate," said Phil. Try to steer North."

"I'm trying!" Even with three men heaving on it, the makeshift rudder refused to point the bow North; the boat was too heavy to steer with a pole.

We tried hanging a bucket in the water on the side to turn her left, but it ripped off in the first wave. We tried the sea anchor out the side, but that dug in and swung the boat round in circles. We were running out of options!

It would be dark soon and we started talking about abandoning the boat if we spotted a ship. In the recent Fastnet race, 15 crew died after abandoning ship. It was impossible to tow the boat with no steering and a repair at sea was out of the question.

We would have to send out a distress signal soon and hope that a passing ship would divert. They would leave the boat to bob around in the ocean like a ghost ship until she ran aground or sank in a storm.

Mike ordered us to raise the mizzen sail to see if that would help. But then, a huge wave broke the wooden panel off the pole, so we lifted it back in to lash on a plank from one of the bunks. Cam played with the sails while we worked on it. We started sailing northeast, towards land!

"Jesus Christ, that's a result, mate!"

We put the pole back in the water but it was the way Cam set the sails and the wind direction that had got her sailing.

A ketch has three sails; a foresail at the bow, a mainsail in the middle, and a mizzen sail at the stern. We played with the sails, one at a time, and found that by hardening one in and letting the other out, we steered the boat by balancing the wind. So, if we hardened in the jib, she would turn right, if we hardened in the mizzen, she would turn left.

It was trial and error, but eventually, we got her going in the right course, to the North East, towards the Cape Verde Islands.

There was now a glimmer of hope.

In fact, once we mastered the trimming, the boat steered herself, and it was easier than steering with the helm.

"We might go faster without the bastard rudder slowing us down!" Cam said as he sat with his feet up. All the watch did was check the compass course, and we sailed 150 miles closer to land that day!

But we weren't out of trouble yet. In fact, quite the opposite, as we closed on the rocky shore with no harbour. We could float about for months in the open ocean, but as we neared land, there would be rocks and cliffs to sink us.

The next day, the black volcano of Pico do Fogo appeared out of the haze. It was bizarre, a huge peak rising 10,000 feet in the middle of the Atlantic. We had to sail through hundreds of rocks in the archipelagos to reach the safety of a port.

Using the rear mizzen sail like a wind vane to act as a wind "rudder", we pushed the back of the boat in the direction we wanted.

We sailed between the two islands close enough to see the surf crashing on the black cliffs on the shore. The wind was blowing hard against the bow as we got closer to shore and she wouldn't turn. Soon, we could hear the waves smashing on the rocks, but finally, using the sea anchor, we turned away from the shore.

Soon the huge mountains caused the wind to blow in different directions, so we worked the sails nonstop.

Ten islands made up the Cape Verde archipelago. Most of the volcanoes are defunct but I saw black ash beaches on the desolate shoreline. It looked prehistoric. Verde means green in Portuguese, but there was no green anywhere, only black, scorched mountains.

We weaved our way through the islands to get to the port of Mindanao. Between the eight of us, we should just keep control of the sails and reached the harbour entrance.

A few rusty fishing boats lay tied up, and the buildings looked derelict. I half-expected a pirate ship full of zombies to come out. Mike called the harbour master on the radio, but there was no response.

"Fuck it, let's sail in," he decided, as it would be dark soon.

It was one thing sailing the open sea, but parking up in a port full of very hard iron ships?

But Mike knew his boat. He started the engine and used the prop wash to push the boat right. With the spinnaker pole out to the left with the sea anchor, along with backing the sails and a bucket on a rope on another pole acting as a brake, we made a most bizarre entrance. Mike swung around in a long curve and parked up beside a German tugboat as if he had sailed without rudders for years.

We had rescued ourselves in the middle of the Atlantic and sailed over 250 miles into a small harbour. We felt ecstatic; with high fives all round, we danced around the foredeck as if we'd won the race! The Germans on the tug weren't accustomed to this show of emotion and called us onboard for a beer and an explanation.

Their tug was huge, big enough to haul a broken-down oil tanker. It hung around, like a vulture in the middle of the Atlantic, waiting for ships to break down, and to tow them in, claiming half the ship's value as salvage.

There were no cranes big enough to lift our boat out of the water, but the Captain offered to hoist our stern to lift the rudderpost out of the water, to weld the rudder back on. It would be worth a try. Soon the bow was deep in the sea as the crane lifted the stern. Mike, Cam and the German engineer sat in a rubber dinghy with a 10,000-volt welder and sparks lit up the harbour.

"What happens if one of those sparks lands on the rubber dinghy?" Phil said.

It looked like the maritime equivalent of me tying my front forks on with a rope in Sudan!

The crew celebrated our survival with a pub-crawl. "Keep out of trouble," shouted Mike after us. "We're not the ones with 10,000 volts between our legs!" I shouted back.

The Cape Verde Islands had their heyday as a coaling station for steamships but had gone downhill for the last 100 years. There was an air of decay and young men hung around the street corners. There was no food in the shops and hardly any fresh water.

The Portuguese walked away from their colonies in 1975, and by the look of it, they took all the money with them.

Sullen children sat around in rags, and old men hung out in the shabby bars. We drank some local beer, and then tried a bottle of local rum called Grog, which tasted rancid. It even had stones and seaweed in the bottom of the bottle.

A friendly local took us to a bar where a dozen attractive girls chatted in broken English. Music started, and a few of the guys danced. We drank and had a grand old time.

"Which girl do you want?" the barman said to me as I ordered another beer.

"What do you mean?"

"You decide which girl!"

I suddenly realised why they were so friendly! We were in a whorehouse!

"I'll leave it for the minute," I said. "Can we pay for the beers?" He gave me the bill, which was extortionate. We were in trouble; we only had a few dollars left. I called the guys in a huddle.

"We have to go, guys, the girls are hookers, and the beers cost more than we can pay!" I whispered.

"I thought mine loved me!" Phil said, forlornly. "Let's do a runner!"

The two massive bouncers watched as if they knew what we planned. We left some money on the table and casually wandered over to the door.

"Where is the money?" one of the bouncers asked, blocking the way.

"It's over there," I said, and one of them walked over to check, leaving the other guy to block the door.

"Run for it!" I shouted, and we bolted past. The bouncers chased us as we ran through the narrow streets, trying to find our way to the harbour. Luckily, they build bouncers for breaking skulls, not for speed records. We didn't stop until we were inside the harbour gates, then we burst into hysterics!

Mike was unimpressed when he heard of our antics.

"I can't take you guys anywhere. We will need an extra lookout. They know where we live, so keep a winch handle ready."

"You were lucky; all the girls here have the pox!" the German Captain, laughed.

"Even the nuns have syphilis!" His first mate said, "And that bar is notorious; they would stab you for a dollar, so you were lucky to get out alive."

The rudder welding was a success, but there was no way to test it. We would just have to hope it was okay as we had two thousand miles of the North Atlantic to cross. We had lost five days, and would never catch up with the fleet.

On the last night, the Germans gave us a feast of lobster and Champagne. But the atmosphere soured when the normally placid Ton picked a fight with one of the German crew, who claimed that Holland was just a German colony.

Ton's parents had been in the Dutch resistance during the war, and the family had suffered terribly. He didn't want to listen to an arrogant German, so punched him on the nose. The party turned to a riot before the skippers restored order, and we all went to our bunks.

Our rather glum crew put to sea at first light. The wind was gusting strongly, but the rudder held good. I felt seasick, but I put it down to the lobster, but we were back in the race.

Day 49

The Seltrust Endeavour surged toward the finish line in another gale, a toy in the ocean's immensity. There is a tremendous force of energy unleashed with huge waves rising some thirty or forty feet. The winds howled through the rigging, as we attempted to steal just a tiny bit of it to propel our craft. Previously, I had felt safe in our little boat but was now well aware of the dangers of being at sea in a small boat. It's a fine line between life and death on the ocean.

A few days later, there was a massive bang at the bows. Shit! We really had hit something this time.

"What the fuck was that?" I shouted and spotted a half- submerged telegraph pole behind us in the surf. Luckily, we had only hit it a glancing blow. If we had hit the pole end head-on, it could have punched a hole in the thin plywood hull.

On one afternoon, we spotted a large fishing trawler heading straight for us, and when we altered course, it did as well, as if it wanted to hit us. We frantically waved and sounded our air horn. The helm prepared to do a crash tack. Mike opened the emergency flares and was about to let one off, when suddenly the trawler veered off and ran parallel to our course.

"What a wanker!" I said,

"There are antennae all over that boat."

"It's a Russian spy ship," Mike said, "They love to practice intercepting boats."

I could see the crew on the bridge, pointing binoculars and taking notes. They shadowed us for half an hour then sailed away. A dangerous example of seamanship.

They say that during wartime, long periods of boredom follow short periods of extreme excitement. Trans-Atlantic racing is the same.

Imagine sitting in the dark for hours, doing nothing; the boredom becomes so intense that you check your watch repeatedly, as if urging the hands to move forward, as we perceive time itself to go by.

Today's society doesn't accept boredom. Today's kids live on Facebook and Instagram. They are petrified of doing nothing. They need to be entertained by useless information, to check their 'shares', and listen to celebrity gossip.

The mighty ocean cuts you off. And monotony becomes a resource, and time for thought is virtually infinite. We can view the seas as an ever-changing landscape, or just a big wet place. It all depends on your perspective.

Now, as we approached the English Channel, another storm blew in with huge waves and a following wind. We surfed down the fifty-foot high waves. At the bottom of the wave, our bow dug into the trough and the boat practically stopped as the wind died, hidden in the next wave's shadow. Then that wave would lift us, the sails filled up with a crack as the wind caught, and we would surge forwards again, up the next wave, all over again.

If the helmsman didn't keep the boat straight surfing down, the wind would catch the mainsail, and throw the boat sideways. This left us exposed broadside for the next wave to bowl us over and could tumble us upside down, like a washing machine. It was exhausting to helm and terrifying to sit, watching and waiting. We were like a toy boat in a giant epileptic's bathtub.

More than once, Tas lost control, the wind caught us, knocking the mast down horizontal until the sails touched the sea, and the water poured into the cockpit hatch.

All we could do was hold on tight to something as our world turned 90 degrees, and lingered for a moment until the law of physics and the four tons of lead in the keel lifted us upright.

I knew now that another breakage could kill us, and my confidence in the boat had taken a hit with the rudder issue. The storm would find a weakness, as we sailed on the limit of the boat's ability. If the rudder broke now, we would be defenceless in the huge surf.

At least when at the helm myself, I was in control of my own destiny, as if at the handlebars of the bike. I knew I was better than Tas. When I took over, my fear turned into adrenalin, as I was in control of the yacht as it surfed headlong down the back of a wave. Fighting to keep her on course, I wanted to shout out at the wind, 'Bring it on, give me some more!' But that would have been very un-Australian!

My transformation from Motorcycle Bum to Ocean Racing Crew was complete.

One night, I was helming, with a big sea following. Cam went below to make tea and appeared at the hatch with the two mugs. He smiled as if embarrassed, then gave me a nod. He shouted something, but the wind snatched the words from his mouth. Then he stepped back and closed the hatch. Confused at his behaviour, I glanced behind.

A massive wall of water filled the whole sky above me. I had never seen a wave so big. I gripped the wheel and braced myself as I felt the stern rise up, and the wave swept over the deck with a roar. The boat surged forward as if caught in an avalanche. I spun the wheel to keep her from broaching as we charged through the furious surf.

Tons of freezing Atlantic water swept into the cockpit and took forever to empty through the drains. (Cost-cutting during fit-out meant the builders used bath plugs for drainage.) The cold water splashed about my waist, thighs, then feet as I struggled to hold the boat straight down the next wave.

This is not what I signed up for!

Or was it? Did I have some death wish?

I loved the rush of adrenaline and the sensation of euphoria when the danger passed. If I did well, I got a boost of endorphins in reward.

The trouble is, like any drug, you build up a resistance to adrenalin, and you become accustomed to the risk. This means that to get the next rush, you must increase the threat.

Drivers race faster, mountain climbers must go higher, and adventurers must take more extreme risks.

Life is so safe now we need to seek out danger, by putting ourselves in more dangerous situations, by climbing higher mountains, and by jumping off bridges with elastic bands tied onto our feet.

When I entered Uganda, the danger had my heartbeat at a hundred miles an hour. But after I had been there a few days, I thought nothing of going out on patrol with a bunch of drunken armed police after curfew. We get used to anything.

Cam's smiling face popped through the hatch.

"Shit, I wasn't sure if you would still be aboard, mate!"

he said, handing me a coffee.

"No worries, mate, I needed a bath anyway!" We both knew that if he hadn't closed the hatch, the boat would have filled with water as well!

After five weeks, dark rum revolted my taste buds as I forced it down my gullet every night. I suppose I could have refused it, but it was all we had to look forward to. We had no mixers, so had experimented on ways to hide the flavour.

We tried a bunch of alternative cocktails to find the best concoction. We tried tinned fruit juice, coffee, tea, baked bean sauce, brown sauce; we even tried rum and toothpaste. I drew the line at shampoo. I would have given my Moto Guzzi for a case of Pepsi.

Some forty years later, and I still can't bear to be in the same room as a glass of McKibben's Rum.

The English Channel is the busiest shipping lane in the world, with ships of every size, and ferries crossing from side to side. Mike didn't sleep for three days. Sailing boats have the right of way, but big tankers can't manoeuvre, so it was up to us to keep out of their way. This was a challenge during the day and a nightmare after dark, as we studied ships' navigation lights to guess their speed and direction.

Then, as we passed Dover, my journey completed a full circle, crossing the imaginary line from when I left the UK eight months ago.

So much had happened, it seemed a million miles away. I was a different person then. More like someone I had met, or an old school friend.

From the blizzards in Austria, the dead-end in Israel, machine guns in Syria, crossing the desert, the great Sudanese train robbery. All the police and all those bastards trying to stop me. And all the great friends I had made along the way!

Then this crazy boat ride home, the storms, the boredom, then the bloody rudder.

It had been a wild ride!

We passed the finishing line at midnight, and let off our flares, blinding us in the orange glare. We hugged each other, sang and danced around the foredeck. This was the first and last time I ever kissed an Australian man.

Ton's family were on the quayside with Champagne, fresh bread and flowers, and they welcomed us all like long lost kinfolk. His brother ventured below deck, before quickly coming back up.

"Ton, something has died below!"

It was stinking, mouldy and damp, as we hadn't had a proper wash since Cape Verde two weeks ago, but we were used to it! We had a shower in the Yacht Club and I put on the fresh shirt and trousers I had saved for the occasion.

The arrival party was a sharp contrast to my arrival in Cape Town, which was a moment of calm. Then I just wanted to contemplate after the intensity of the journey. Rotterdam was wild, and we wanted to party! For generations, sailors have gone on boozy benders when they get into port, not just to celebrate, but as a release of the stress and dangers of the sea. It's like a scream, a release of emotion. We embarked on a three-day pub crawl.

At one stage, Mike found an open window of a house, climbed in and fell asleep on the sofa. When the occupants found him, rather than calling the police, the ever-empathetic Dutch made him breakfast and ran him down to the docks!

The second day, we took the boat out for a Dutch TV crew. Down below, I couldn't believe how rotten the stink was!

We arrived in Rotterdam 54 days after leaving Cape Town. Only five of the eight boats that started the race finished, and we came in last, but we won the trophy for Outstanding Seamanship.

Lexington made it to Freetown in West Africa, but in the harbour, a barge crushed it and it nearly sank. Then some Africans petrol-bombed the boat. Luckily, it was aluminium and didn't burn. Severely squashed, scorched and mast-less, she was shipped home on the deck of a container ship.

Flying Wilma won the race, but still didn't beat the 119-year-old Clipper record, but it would be only a matter of time before technology caught up.

But it was time for me to get back in the saddle.

The rest of the Seltrust crew had fulfilled their dream of sailing to Europe.

I still had to conquer America. My plan was to travel around the States for a few months, then get a job so I could earn enough cash and finally get to Australia. I bade farewell to my crewmates and took a ferry to the UK and hitchhiked back to Belfast.

It was a mistake to go home. So much had happened to me in ten months it felt like ten years, but back in Belfast, time stood still. The best and worst thing about Ireland is that nothing ever changes.

My family had very little interest in my journey. It was as if they thought I had jumped above my station by doing something spectacular. Mum asked did I get enough to eat, as if I had made a British Airways flight to Cape Town. my dad had fought in Egypt during the war and should have had some respect for my desert crossing. But no.

"At least you didn't have the Germans shooting at you," he said.

"No, but I didn't have the British Eighth Army looking after me either."

My siblings didn't really know what to ask either, and I was in no mood to offer. It was easier to talk about the boring family stuff that I had missed in Belfast.

It was the 'Glorious Twelfth of July,' and the Protestant marching bands were out with the usual demonstrations, and the city was in lockdown. Most people got out of town. I took Janet, my ever-forgiving on-off girlfriend, to the West of Ireland for a few days. Donegal is like the Ireland of old, golden beaches, tiny villages and great pubs. I was trying to park in a narrow one-way street when a car came up the wrong way.

"What a Wally," I shouted out the window, "You're going the wrong way!"

"What's up, Cobber?" the driver shouted. Suddenly, I recognized the guy!

"John- fucking- Dick?" I said.

'Who's asking, mate?'

I'd only met him for ten minutes ten thousand miles away in Cape Town and we shook hands while the traffic built up behind us. We abandoned the cars in the street and escaped to Nancy's bar to talk the whole thing over. What was it that had drawn us together; was it luck, or something more?

As we travel through life and make decisions, pure luck often decides our fate. Be at the right bar and you meet a beautiful girl who you fall in love with, marry and have children. Stand at the wrong street corner and an out-of- control truck flattens you.

Ask an Arab was he not worried about driving through town at 100mph, and he will say no, if God wants me to crash, then I will crash. They call it Inshallah, or God's will. The Irish traffic police generally take a different view.

John had been brought up in Tasmania and was back to find his roots, as his uncle lived in Belfast. He was in Donegal for a few days, so chance and our backgrounds helped bring us together.

We became great friends; he stayed in Ireland after I left for California and even took over as a van driver in my dad's shop. We never met again, but I know we will.

It is our destiny.

CHAPTER 14

Fear & Loving, North America

MY PARENTS' WELCOME HOME SMILES FROZE WHEN I TOLD THEM MY bike was on its way to Los Angeles.

"I'm going to ride around America," I announced as if expecting a round of applause. But the sense of occasion was lost on my parents who expected me to start work in the family business the next week.

"So, you left for Australia, rode to South Africa, and now you're off to America," Dad said with more than a hint of sarcasm.

"Well, yes."

"So, why are you going there?"

"Just because!" That was the question I was afraid they would ask, as I still didn't know the answer.

My parents' relief that the prodigal son had returned unscathed, instantly dissipated and turned to anger.

"I've been worried sick," said my mum. "Africa was bad enough, now America?"

"Well, don't expect me to give you money!" said my dad.

"No chance!" I lied, as my continued world conquest relied on borrowing money from them. Without it, I was stuffed.

"There's a good job waiting in the shop, and all you do is laze about on a motorcycle. I don't understand young people today."

"It's time you settled down!" said my mum. But I was less ready to do that, and after a row, I stormed out of the house.

The job option was a poisoned chalice. In the 1980s, jobs were hard to find, but it put pressure on me to complete my travels and come home before I was ready. I felt guilty about letting them down, but I still believed in this insane drive to discover the world and myself.

The trouble was, I didn't have enough money as I had made my decision to go to America on a whim. But with the bike on its way, I had no way out.

I bumped into Sue, an old friend. She had travelled to Canada with her boyfriend last year, and she wanted to move there permanently. She offered to pay for the petrol if I gave her a lift up the west coast from L.A. to Canada. In my precarious financial situation, I agreed. She was great fun, attractive, and looked great in a pair of thigh-length motorcycle boots. Take a hot blonde up the west coast of America all expenses paid? And Canada, why not?

A few weeks later, I said goodbye again to my frustrated parents, and Sue and I boarded a Jumbo Jet to Los Angeles. I'd never flown before, although I'd travelled halfway around the world and back. As the 350-tonne plane lumbered down the runway, I held the armrests and wondered how it would ever take off. But gradually, the nose lifted, the rumble of the runway stopped and it soared into the sky.

After six months travelling down through Africa, and five weeks to sail back, flying blew me away. I covered the same distance in ten hours, while we ate dinner and watched the movie projected on the front bulkhead; this was travelling, but not as I knew it. And Californian Immigration couldn't be more different from Africa.

"Passports, please," said the dude with long hair and aviator sunglasses, as he winked at Sue.

I was carrying my crash helmet. "Are you scared of flying?" he joked.

"No, I'm picking up my bike," I explained, and dropped my papers on the floor, in a fluster.

"Relax, man, you're in Southern California. What sort of motorcycle have you got?"

"A Moto Guzzi."

"Whoa, that's what LAPD ride! Enjoy!" and he waved us through. Brilliant, he never asked to see my cash - they demanded £1000 or a return ticket, and I had £350!

I felt at home immediately in Los Angeles with its sprawl of grimy suburbs and sleazy bars. But I found it soulless; acres of concrete, every block with a McDonald's, a pawnshop and an adult emporium with promises of heaven within. We booked into a rundown motel complete with the fifties flashing neon sign, the dried-out swimming pool, and a vibrating bed.

I'd seen it all before in the movies and on TV and it was locked in my brain like a distant memory of a holiday. What is memory anyway? Just an electronic signal lodged in your brain, after being sent from your eyeballs. I had been TV 'brainwashed' to believe I had lived here before.

I did a dope deal with a Latino kid for some grass, and even he looked familiar. I wanted to ask, "Do you know Columbo, the cop in the raincoat?"

The American supermarkets disgusted me, with their hundreds of flavours of yoghurt and dozens of milk varieties. Although they still stocked my favourite African snack, Tate and Lyle's golden syrup.

I enjoyed having Sue along; it was a novelty to have someone to talk over the day's events. So many times, in Africa, I would have seen something fantastic and yearned for a companion to turn round to and say simply, "Did you see that?" But there was only me.

Down at LA docks, the Guzzi arrived. I broke open the crate as excited as a kid at Christmas, and hit the starter; with a cough, she fired up on the last amp of the battery.

So, it was confusing, I was importing a UK motorcycle from South Africa, into the USA. The Customs Officer rolled his eyes; I'd spoilt his day.

"So, you want to ride the bike in the USA?"

"Yes," I said.

"You must pay the import tax and meet the safety and emission standards."

"No way! How much is that?"

"About $2,200 plus fees."

"But the bike isn't worth half that."

"Well, you can do a temporary transit," he suggested.

"Ok," I said.

"I must know your exit country, Sir."

"Canada?" I suggested.

"Canada regulations are the same; the only place you can drive to is Mexico."

"Well, I'm going to Mexico then." Another decision made.

"Mexico?" Sue butted in, "that's the wrong way. We are going to Canada!"

"You can still go to Canada, but you must export the bike to Mexico within 4 months," the Customs guy said.

"Do you want to see your attorney before you sign the affidavit?"

"Affidavit? What's an attorney?"

"Where are you going after Mexico?"

"I've no idea!" I said as I signed anyway. The affidavit stated…

'I agree to import the vehicle for my own use for a maximum of four months… for onward export to Mexico… that it does not conform to US

Safety and Emissions. And on failure to export… I will have to pay the penalty of $10,000 plus all duties and taxes…'

Well, the bike would definitely not conform; no indicators, or brake lights.

"What happens if I can't pay the $10,000 fine?"

"You will go to jail," he said. "U.S. Customs don't mess about."

The paperwork was completed, but then the security on the gate refused to let me leave without taking away my crate.

"Where am I going to put that?" I asked.

"OK, pay the $150 fine."

Back in the docks, we stopped a delivery truck and while Sue chatted up the driver, I threw the crate on the back of his truck. Men are so silly!

The security man was pissed off when the crate disappeared. He wanted his $150, but it was on its way to Beverly Hills with some marble statues.

And I rode out the gates into America.

Next door was 'Big Jim Christian Insurance Brokers,' and Big Jim sat behind his desk in the Portakabin and asked for details about the bike and me.

"God must be at your side," he said. "Are you a believer?"

"No, not really," I said.

"Well, believers get a better rate."

"OK, I believe," I said. "I do, I do."

"You sure don't look like a believer," he said and went on explaining about God and religion.

Finally, fed up with this nonsense, I cracked; it had been a long day.

"So, if God looks after believers, why have insurance?" I asked. "Why doesn't God just stop accidents?"

"God moves in mysterious ways," Jim said.

"Well, was he moving mysteriously in Israel with the Arabs and Jews always at war? Or in South Africa, where white Christians treat black Christians like slaves?"

Big Jim made a phone call then shook his head.

"It turns out we can't insure you," he said.

"Is that God on the phone?" I asked.

Big Jim stood up, and I saw why his name was Big Jim, and I left before Big Jim did an unchristian act. What always amazed me about religion was how they think they are always right; there was one opinion, (theirs!) and one religion, (theirs again).

It reminded me of the old joke about the guy who dies and goes up to Heaven and is being shown around by Saint Peter. They pass the school, the pub, the Hindu compound, and the Buddhists; then there is a high walled compound. St Peter says, "We have to be quiet here; that's where the Catholics live, and they believe they are the only ones here." All religions are the same; they all know they are right!

But perhaps someone was looking after me? After many dangerous situations, I had survived unscathed. But why did God look after me, while the true believers got robbed or murdered?

Nope, I put my good luck down to my expert riding, my charm, and a strong Italian motorcycle!

But my next problem was the bike. When I tried to change from neutral to first, the clutch wouldn't work. The clutch plates had rusted solid together from being on the boat for 4 months. I pushed the bike along, then jumped on, and kicked it into 1st gear. To stop, I coasted to a halt in neutral. It was impossible to ride two up.

If I rode up to an old school friend's place near Seattle, I could fix it, but that was 1200 miles away in the wrong direction for Mexico. And I would have to push-start at every set of lights, junction and petrol station the whole way up the West Coast of America.

Back at the motel, Sue was furious when I tried to explain why I wouldn't take her up the west coast as planned.

"What do you mean? You can't just dump me!"

"I'm sorry, I'm not dumping you; the bike can only take one, and I'm it," I explained.

"But you said you would take me to Canada!"

"Even on my own, it will be difficult," I said. "I must ride non-stop."

"Fuck you! I only shagged you to see the West Coast!" She was furious at losing her ride.

"I hope you crash and burn," she shouted out of the airport taxi as she left.

"I probably will," I muttered, as I heaved the bike off its stand.

I pushed the bike to running speed and jumped on. Once moving, the gears kicked up and down without the clutch. But to stop, it was back to neutral and coast to a halt. The California sun broiled me alive as I pushed and jumped on. My dream of riding up the great Pacific Highway would be a nightmare of five hundred miles of push-starts and crunching gears.

When I stopped at traffic lights with an uphill slope, I wheeled the bike across the pedestrian crossing, then started it up downhill in the wrong direction. Then I did a U-turn and hoped by the time I got back to the lights, they would be green. Sometimes I did this four times before I hit the green.

I rode through the Santa Monica Hills, and bypassed San Francisco, and the whole West Coast; it was devastating to miss it all. When you travel with someone, it makes you lazy, you never talk to anyone else. Now on my own, I met some locals.

But I worried I had turned into a weirdo. Last night I was in a motel with a sexy blonde living the American Dream.

Now, I camped on the hard ground in a giant redwood forest, content watching the sun go down.

I was on my Guzzi, with four months to discover America, but even having to ride 1,250 miles with no clutch didn't worry me. Most people would call the AA if this happened a mile from home. For me, it was all in a day's work. I had no qualms about driving up the whole West Coast of the USA, just to get to my mate's apartment. It was ridiculous and shows how casual I had become to overcoming major issues. After conquering Africa, I knew I was unstoppable.

Everything in America was so civilised. They cut all the verges and painted the picket fences white. It seemed it only rained after authorization from the Rain Approval Committee. I would miss riding up the Pacific coast road, but hell, I'd been there a hundred times with James Garner's Rockford Files!

Three days later, I pulled into Blessington and found Mickey's apartment. In American cities, the Avenues ran north/south and the Streets east /west. They split into quadrants N, S, E, W, so finding an address was easy. It was lunchtime, but Mickey was still in bed. He worked at a posh French restaurant in the centre of town, run by some distant French relations.

Mickey had worked in my dad's shop part-time. He rode his Honda 550 like a maniac. The Guzzi was faster, but I could hardly keep up. Last summer, we worked together in a delivery van and would end up in his flat, listening to Jim Morrison and the Doors, rolling joints on the album covers.

Mickey came out to learn the restaurant trade and got me a job washing dishes for a few nights at the restaurant. We downed a beer and a joint for breakfast as we caught up on our last year's adventures.

In the seventies, Belfast had restaurants with cooks who warmed frozen ready-made meals, and student waitresses that earned a pittance.

American restaurants had head chefs, sauce chefs, dessert chefs, and apprentice chefs. The waiters were the salesmen, whose job was to up-sell the food and wines. The Maître-d's job was to make sure the city Mayor got the front seats, and the businessman and his secretary got a quiet nook in the corner. In the kitchens, the chef handed me a nasal spray bottle.

"Here you go, Chris, this will give you some energy."

"I'm not ill," I said, confused.

"It's not that sort of medicine," he said as I took a sniff. My nose caught fire and my brain flew into a high- speed wobble. The chef had filled the nasal spray bottles with cocaine mixed with saline solution. Then, he left them randomly around the kitchen, as it was handier than snorting lines of coke off the kitchen dressers, where it might have been mixed up with the icing sugar, which would have been awkward. All the staff worked with permanent runny noses as they served America's rich and famous at a hundred miles per hour. But I wasn't sure which was better, a waiter with a powdered nose, or one that's constantly dripping?

After the customers left, everyone would finish the wine, snort more coke, and hit the nightclubs. It was my first sniff of hard drugs, so my mission was of discovery, where drugs, drink and all-night partying was the name of the game.

Immediately, I was besotted by a sexy Italian waitress with an impossibly pert bottom, barely covered in a black micro mini skirt.

"You're out of your depth, Chris, your beat-up old Guzzi won't crack that one. You need a flashy Corvette for her!" Mickey smiled.

"Where's the car rental?" I laughed.

"Don't touch it if you can't afford it!"

After work one night, Mickey's boss, Dino, came round with his gorgeous girlfriend and a bag of coke. After half an hour, he got up to leave.

"I'm away; she's yours for the night lads!"

I decided Dino was a cool dude, letting us snort coke off his girlfriend's breasts, but letting us have her for the night…

"Isn't she your girlfriend?"

"No! I just rented her for you guys!" he said as he drove off in his Firebird.

Well, this America is a great place! Bosses in Ireland just don't buy hookers for their dishwasher's day off!

"Wait around guys," she said, as we stood dumbfounded, and she pulled out a needle. She injected her arm and her eyes glazed over as she lay half-conscious and half-naked on the sofa, exposing the scars on her arms.

In a few minutes, she had morphed from Playboy bunny to a heroin junkie. Any sexual drive instantly evaporated. This was the other side of the drug scene, the grim result of a destroyed life, and a journey to the gutter for a pretty young girl.

"Come on boys, who's first?" she slurred, then passed out.

We covered her in a blanket to sleep it off, just as our own 'downer' arrived. The next morning, we put her in a taxi and I decided it was time to move on.

On my first day, I had taken the gearbox apart and found a couple of dodgy bearings. The oil had built up on the clutch plates and locked them solid. But I was too stoned every day to put the bike together again. I finally forced myself to stay sober for a day to reassemble the bike.

I tested the bike with a tour around the forests of Mt Rainier. It was a beautiful drive through a wilderness area that the volcano devastated when it blew half the mountain away a few years later.

Mickey and I argued on that night. He was from the Nationalist, Catholic side of Belfast, and the first Catholic friend I'd ever made; I was a Prod from the Unionist side of town. We argued about politics, religion and life.

In Ireland, we never talked about politics, always aware of our different views and backgrounds. Now away from home, we thought we could discuss this sensitive subject. The harsh reality of the junkie incident shook our easy-going relationship to the core. And as immature young men, we didn't know how to handle it, so our shaken morality brought out a fierce row.

After a week, getting high each day became the norm. Luckily, I would ride off into the sunset; but for the guys to break the habit it was impossible.

Some years later, I found out that most of them had died from alcohol, car crashes or overdoses. Dino's nose caved in from cocaine overuse. Mickey survived by signing the pledge. What started as a bit of fun became a monster that ruined their lives! Just like the blonde hooker, they really just worked to feed their habit.

Addiction comes in different guises; my motorcycling obsession started as a way to get to school. Now hooked on this journey, it took over my life. I wasn't interested in anything else. Addicted to life on the road, I lived for today and didn't care about the past or the future.

Every day gave a new buzz from some unexpected happening. I felt sorry for people, stuck in nine-to-five jobs, trapped in a lifestyle they hated but didn't have the courage to confront. What sort of 'cold turkey' would I go through after my journey?

Before I left, Dino gave me a present, a packet of coke, some hash, and a few tabs of acid for my trip.

"Everyone should have 'a Dino' in their lives!" Mickey said. I hesitated… just for an instant… before stuffing them in my top box. Just in case I need another quick break from reality.

I loved being back on the road, with the uncertainty of where I would sleep, or what would happen next. I wanted to see Canada, even if it was the wrong direction. I rode along at 70 mph as the freeway swept through the pine forests. I could make the border in a couple of hours. Suddenly, a cop in front waved me down. Shit! I pulled over.

"You drove over 70 mph back there, Sir."

"Is that too fast?" I said, knowing full well it was.

"The speed limit is 55 mph."

"But how did you see me?"

He pointed up. A helicopter flew down the freeway and radioed to the cops on the ground.

"Wow, that's cool! I said, impressed. "You always do it bigger in America."

The copper started to write the ticket, but looking at my UK licence, let me go with a caution.

I assumed Canada would be like England and Scotland, without a proper border, but found myself in an Immigration Office explaining why I didn't have any insurance documents. I told them I had posted the papers to my address in Vancouver. The Mounties seemed happy, as clearly no one had brought a UK vehicle into Canada from the USA before!

Then, the Captain said, "I want to check out the motorcycle," and called all the other cops in the office to follow him. Suddenly, I remembered Dino's drugs on the bike, just sitting inside the top box. I walked back to the Guzzi, knowing this was to be my last walk of freedom.

"What does she do?"

"Who?" I stammered.

"What's her top speed?" "How far have you ridden?"

"You've been to Africa? That's impressive!" The boys just wanted to talk motorcycles!

"She goes great," I beamed and gave them my travel story, the 30-minute version, anyway. Soon, I was shaking hands with the whole Customs post. I think I will like Canada, I decided.

An old student friend was working as a nanny in Vancouver. It was late evening when I drove up the gravel driveway and rang the bell. The security lights came on, and dogs started barking. The maid opened the door.

"Hi, I'm a friend of Barbara," I said.

"Hi, Barbara!" I shouted as I saw her come down the grand staircase behind.

Barbara had no idea I was coming but introduced me to the family. By the look on their faces, I could tell that a hairy biker turning up at the door late at night didn't impress them.

"Sorry I'm so late, I got pulled by the police!" I said, digging my hole deeper.

Barbara fixed me up in a friend's apartment, who turned out to be another cokehead called Dino.

'How do I attract these Dino guys?' I wondered as I took a drag of a joint. 'Do junkies follow me around or do I seek them out somehow?'

I'll think about it tomorrow… Or the next day…

But really, it was true. One time, I stopped for petrol, and a guy came over for a chat, as they do in the USA. Next thing he gave me a big bag of grass, "To help smooth your way."

I would have preferred cash, but I gratefully received all donations!

What to do!

Vancouver nestled between the mountains and the sea with Victoria Island just off the coast. I wanted to stay longer to explore, but I had lost time in America and needed to move on.

The day I left it was sweltering, so I left my jacket open, then stopped a few miles out of town to zip up. Suddenly, I realised my passport and traveller's cheques had vanished. I drove back twenty miles in a panic, scouring the side of the road for the bag. To a traveller, losing your passport is worse than losing your money, but losing both was a disaster. The British Embassy in Ottawa said they would get a replacement, but they were 3500 miles away, as was American Express. I would have to get them.

I only had $50 cash, but I had a Visa card, so I could buy petrol with the card and live on the cash. There were no ATMs in those days. But I would have to ride 600 miles a day for five days to get there before the weekend.

At 7800km, the Trans-Canada Highway is the longest road in the world; I pointed the front wheel east and put my head down.

The road wound its way up through the Rocky Mountains, with magnificent lakes and impossible gorges. It looked raw compared to the Alps, which looked so well-manicured, like they had been there for millions of years. In contrast, the Rockies looked thrown together yesterday by some frantic God driving a JCB. He'd worked in a rush, leaving rockfalls and landslides along the roadside.

I camped under the trees beside a cascading river, the roar of the water drowning straining truck engines that laboured up the steep gradient. I put my feet up like a proper cowboy beside my real wood fire and mess tin beans, watching the sun go down. 'Don't keep your food in your tent,' the signposts warned, or the grizzly bears would come in to get it.

The next day I was over the mountains, down into Alberta and onto the prairies of Saskatchewan where the huge skies went on forever.

What sort of name is Saskatchewan? And its name was the most exciting thing about it. With roads as straight as a line of coke, never-ending cornfields, occasional oilrigs and the occasional excitement of a Massey Ferguson tractor.

I would break camp at 6 am, ride for a couple of hours, stop for some breakfast, and then do another 150 miles before lunch. By 3 pm, I was up to 400 miles but exhausted. Every half hour I stopped to stretch, and the milometer crept round slower and slower. I would stop for a sniff of Dino's magic powder to keep me awake.

In Medicine Hat, I asked some cops for directions.

"Follow me," they said and escorted me through the city at 80 mph, with sirens blaring. They stopped at the city limits for a chat and to say goodbye. I had to stop myself offering them a joint as a thank you.

Canada gets a hard time for stupid place names. I mean, they probably called the town Medicine Hat after a doctor who lost his hat. Other Canadian names include 'Dildo Harbour', 'Big Beaver', and 'Climax'. I'm sure if I looked hard enough, I would find a 'Used Durex Bay' and they probably named a street 'Stoned Biker Boulevard' after me.

Ireland has its share of strange place names, including

'Ring Rash Road,' and 'Lower Balix', and in County Donegal, there is a town called 'Muff.' You can get a haircut at the Muff Barber's, and the corner shop sells Muff chutney. In the town cemetery, they can even bury you in Muff.

And if you are a good swimmer, you can join the Muff Diving Club!

I camped in lay-bys and barbecued with the truckers and slept under truck trailers if I was too tired to put the tent up. The Canadian drivers chatted and shared their dinner, but were a bit dull, which wasn't surprising after driving up and down this bloody road all year. Their huge rigs had hand-painted mural panels and lots of chrome everywhere. But I always parked the bike in front so they wouldn't drive off early!

By driving a foot behind the trucks, I closed the throttle and got sucked along, saving petrol but keeping a careful eye on their brake lights.

To ease my boredom, sometimes I would sit side-saddle or put my feet on the cylinders or handlebars. My favourite pose was the Superman position, my legs on the top box behind, as I lay flat and balanced my straight arms on the handlebars. When I passed cars lying on top of the bike, I gave the passengers a nod and a smile. The kids loved it, and probably still talk about it 40 years later.

"Do you remember that time in 1980 when the guy passed us on the motorcycle like Superman, Bobby Joe?" they will still ask every Christmas dinner in Manitoba.

I spent long days trying to decide where to go after Mexico. South America seemed like a plan. I drove down Africa, so why not the Americas? Other than it was 'South" and obviously 'America', I knew nothing about it. I would do some homework and reckoned the only thing to stop me would be my lack of dollars. It wouldn't be as difficult as Africa anyway, could it?

I wouldn't go round the world, just up and down! Once I got to Ottawa, I would point south and keep going until I got to the bottom! Simple!

On day four, I hit Ontario where the scenery improved and the odd corner reminded me that handlebars are not just for leaning on.

At a gas station that overlooked another perfect lakeside scene, I got chatting to a guy from Northern Ireland. He was the cousin of Tommy Herron, a motorcycle racer who had been killed at the North West 200 races the previous year. I talked about the madness of road racing, but he said what I was doing was just as crazy.

I drove the 3000 miles in five days without any mechanical problems. Remarkable, considering the thrashing the bike had just received in Africa. It had been an epic drive, but the sort that would put you off motorcycling for life! The British Embassy had my passport ready, and American Express replaced my traveller's cheques.

Michel, my old Sudan travelling companion, had said he would study Law at Ottawa University. I had no contact details for him, but the Law faculty gave me his address. Not much data protection in those days. He thought he was hallucinating when he saw me waiting outside his apartment. The last time we met was in Wau, deep in the Sudan.

Michel had an incredible story to tell. After he got a lift to the Central African Republic, civil war broke out again, and the driver refused to go any further. He walked 100 miles over 5 days to the capital Bangui, where the French Foreign Legion machine-gunned anything that moved.

He caught malaria and ran out of money, but got lucky and was airlifted to the UK. But the British refused him admission because he was so ill, and he flew straight to Canada. He had enough tropical diseases to fill a whole medical journal.

Mentally, he was a mess too and didn't speak to anyone for months. He said three different species of worms lived in his stomach and he could shit through a straw. He even offered to show me.

We walked to a trendy Ottawa wine bar to celebrate our survival and talked like a couple of old soldiers. The few days of hardship had created a unique bond between two people.

We talked philosophically about life being like a journey and a journey being like life. My adolescence was Europe, teenage years the Middle East, and in Africa, I became a man. Would I last through middle and old age, or would my life be cut short, as Michel's had been on his journey? My journey could end at any time with a road accident. Even if I didn't die, it would be a disaster as I had no medical or motorcycle insurance still.

None of our friends understood what we experienced, so it was the first time that we could discuss what we'd been through. When I left, we hugged like old friends. It's strange; you can be friends with someone for years and never really know them, or travel for two weeks and bond forever.

Finally, I started my journey south. I stopped to compare Niagara with their African counterpart, Victoria Falls, but decided it was a damp squib. The Americans were all about health and safety, the falls fenced off with viewing platforms; at Victoria Falls you watched at the top of a cliff, with the water cascading inches in front of you.

In Buffalo, New York State, I found a bar with a bunch of motorcycles outside and walked in hoping to meet up with some friendly bikers. As I pushed through the swing doors, everyone stopped talking and stared at me. I wondered if I'd wet my pants, and then nearly did when I realized it was a Hells Angels bar. 'SHIT, do I apologize profusely, say I'm lost and leave, or go in?'

I walked up to the bar, put my helmet on the counter and at once regretted it. It made me look like a pansy, as no one else owned crash helmets. The barman wore a swastika tattoo on his arms, and said, "You're not from around these parts, stranger?" I nearly laughed out loud as I couldn't believe someone actually said that.

"I'm from Ireland; I'm riding around the world. I've ridden here from Africa," I told him.

"Aff… Ree… Kaa," he said as if he'd never heard of such a place.

"What are you riding, son?" asked an old guy with a grey goatee and a ponytail behind his bald forehead, but with arms big enough to crush a small Chevrolet.

"A Moto Guzzi."

Well, that stopped the conversation dead. My interrogator raised his eyebrows… as if to say give me further details… before we kill you.

"It's Italian," but that clearly wasn't a good thing either. "It's a V Twin, like an Italian Harley Davidson."

"Let's have a look at this, eh, 'Italian Harley'," the bald one scoffed, and strolled out front, followed by the whole bar.

I stood there for a few seconds, before realizing they expected me to follow. Well, either they're interested in seeing the Guzzi, or they will kick the shit out of me. Luckily, it was the former, and after a few questions and a bit of tyre-kicking, we all wandered back to the bar for lots of guffaws, beers and backslapping.

I crashed at their campsite out the back and teamed up with two of the "good ole boys" that rode south for the winter. True nomads, the guys lived in Florida in winter and New York State in the summer, working casual jobs, selling dope and staying with their network of Hells Angels clubs.

Horace was about 6ft 8ins with a big bushy beard and a booming voice. He looked ugly enough to pull your head off at the slightest provocation.

His sidekick, 'Tiny', was small but clearly the boss, but calling a Hell's Angel 'Tiny,' seemed preposterous, so I called him his real name, Gregg.

"It's Tiny; only my mother calls me Gregg," he said, "and you're not my mother."

Their 'Hard Tail' and 'Shovel Heads' Harleys had old pushrod engines, and no rear suspension, as suspension was not cool. They never drove over 50 mph and stopped every half hour. A journey that should take a day, took three. But it was great to be part of the gang.

Every time we stopped at a gas station, it was the same routine; petrol, fag, tighten nuts and bolts, fag, all the time chatting to everyone.

"Don't you have to check your bike out?" Horace shouted over as I sat writing some notes in my journal.

"No, I did that in Vancouver."

"Hell, that's 4000 miles away," he said, shaking his head in disbelief. His Harley would need two engine rebuilds by then!

They laughed when I read out a list of Harley Bikers characteristics I'd put together while waiting.

Harley Riders always;

1. Are dirty from working on the bikes.
2. Travelled in gangs to carry all the tools and spare parts.
3. Stopped every thirty minutes, they are so uncomfortable.
4. Used tiny petrol tanks, as they break down before they run out of gas.

Eventually, after a few beers, Tiny agreed that the Italians made a reasonably good V twin.

Praise indeed!

With a chest-crushing bear hug from Horace, we parted company in New York City. They would hang out here, but I had a job in North Carolina before my money ran out.

First, I made an obligatory tour of The Big Apple, past the Empire State Building and World Trade Centre. I drove around Manhattan, got lost in Harlem, then noticed burnt-out cars, derelict buildings and black teenagers hanging around the street corners. Harlem was not a good place in 1980. Sitting at a red light, a siren whooped, and a police cruiser with wire grills over the windows, and dents all over it pulled up.

"What are you doing?" a loudspeaker barked.

"I'm lost," I shouted back.

"Take the second left and keep going. Don't stop at the lights. This is East Harlem, and they don't like white boys here!" He sped off through a red; I took his advice and got back to Manhattan, pronto.

Back in Ireland, a friend had introduced me to the legendary Stanley Woods. He was a ten times Isle of Man TT winner, and in 1935, won it on a Moto Guzzi. His friend, Nico, another retired racer, owned a shabby bar in NYC. It was dark and full of depressed middle-aged men staring into their whiskeys.

Nico introduced me to the Moto Guzzi dealers. They let me do some work in their workshop, but charged me for the parts. But they had no interest in publicity from my journey. They said Americans didn't care where Africa was.

Americans don't know about anywhere outside their borders. A New Yorker asked me where Ireland was!

"Is it west of Manhattan?"

I felt a bad vibe in New York City, with unfriendly people, potholed streets and aggressive drivers, and headed south the next day. After two days' ride, I arrived late evening in Hickory, North Carolina.

It was foggy, so I set up a tent in a field off the road. With a job interview early next morning, I needed to make a good impression. They expected a well-dressed young man, not a dirty biker; I kept a clean shirt and jeans for the occasion. In the morning a police siren nearly blasted me out of my sleeping bag. I opened the zip to see a pair of police boots.

"Get out of the tent and keep your hands in view, Sir," said the boots' occupant in a slow southern drawl.

I looked outside to find the fog had cleared. But I had camped on the front lawn of a mansion belonging to some local dignitary, who was watching from his front door.

"We're arresting you for vagrancy," he said.

"You can't do that, Officer," I pleaded, "I'm starting a job this morning!"

"Who with?"

"A guy called Ed Arditti," I replied. The cop spoke on the car radio.

"You're lucky; the house owner doesn't want to press charges, now get going."

He returned to the cruiser, and the younger officer pulled me aside.

"Hey Chris, give me a ring when you're in town. I have a Harley myself; I'm Hank," and he gave me his number. With a whoop of the siren and a wave, they left me standing on the lawn in my boxers, while the neighbours watched from behind their net curtains.

Ed Arditti exported American furniture, and my dad had done business with him.

"I was expecting you," he said from behind his desk.

"Really," I smiled.

"Yes, the Police rang me." "Oops," I blushed.

"I hear you camped in the Mayor's front garden last night!"

Not the best start to a job interview!

Ed was a larger than life ex-New Yorker. He took me shopping to get some clothes and then sorted me with lodging at a house in town; by the afternoon, I had a job making upholstery.

Hickory only had two bars, and about twenty churches. But it had a speedway track, and everyone knew everyone. I'd seen the wild side of America and was ready for some deep Southern hospitality.

Ed's daughter, Joyce, was at the University of Georgia, in Athens, and he suggested I go down to see her for the weekend. I jumped at the chance, although 250 miles was a long way on a blind date!

"Remember, Chris," Ed said to me, "Joyce is my daughter and I'm your boss, so no hanky-panky!"

"Of course not," I assured him, as sincerely as any 21-year-old male could.

I appreciated it's not every Dad who would send a biker on a weekend with his daughter after an introduction by the police.

Joyce met me at the door of the student house she shared with three girls.

"I'm Chris; your dad sent me."

"Yes, he sends us boys all the time!" she laughed, inviting me in.

The girls welcomed me as only Americans can do, with complete openness. Some say the Irish are friendly, but in my opinion, Americans are the most hospitable.

It was Halloween, so we gate-crashed a fancy-dress party at a Frat house. Georgia University had over 25,000 students, and it was the final of the University football league. It was a big, brash, fantastic razzamatazz for a Belfast boy. And when the Georgia Bulldogs won, everyone partied all night, dancing on the tables and downing shots of Jack Daniels. The Ulster Polytechnic would never seem the same.

The next day, I started work in a furniture factory. I put pieces of wood into a hole-drilling machine all day. After five minutes it bored me stupid. I couldn't believe people spent their lives doing this.

This was the Deep South and I couldn't understand a word anyone said, nor them me. Someone started taking the piss out of my accent, so for a laugh, I started to copy the southern accent, putting "Y'all," at the end of every sentence. Suddenly I could communicate, and within a few days, I had perfected the slow Carolina drawl.

On the factory floor, the guys were all friendly, until I started talking to the black workers on the other side of the workshop. My white friends made it known that it was "us", and "them", and you don't mix.

The government made laws to protect ethnic minorities. So, if someone had a Cherokee grandmother, they had minority status. So, they would be offered a job before a 'black' or 'white person', as the company looked good by increasing its allocation of ethnic minorities!

Apartheid was government policy in South Africa, but in North Carolina, while they had equality laws, the white and black societies didn't socialize together. There was no aggression towards the blacks or vice versa, but they obeyed the rules of separation. Whites and blacks mingled in the streets and shops but socially, they were as different as chalk and cheese.

They would not accept me into the black community either, so I would go with the flow and stick with my own; I would not rock the boat. Segregation, 1880's style, was alive and well in 1980's Hickory.

On weekends I worked at Ed's country cottage or rode over the Blue Ridge Mountains' winding roads. Birch, maple and hickory trees covered the mountains, and people came from miles around to see the colours change in Fall.

I took Ed's 16-year-old son, Jeff, out for a few illicit beers in town. American kids smoke grass at 13, learn to drive a car when they're 16, join the army or buy a gun at 18. But they can't buy a beer until they are 21.

In the factory, I enjoyed being part of the team. I enjoyed doing something tangible after living in transit for so long. We started at 6.30 am and finished at 3 pm. Some workers would go straight to another job; Americans liked their big cars and fancy houses and worked hard to pay for them.

My workmate, Sterling, raced Speedway. His car ran an enormous turbocharged V8 engine, stripped and strengthened, to take smashing into the concrete barriers. The cars could get around the oval track in 17 seconds, and when Sterling wasn't driving, he was working overtime to pay his expenses.

Another guy, Bud, owned a 200-year-old frontier log cabin in his back garden and a range of ancient muskets. He taught me how to fire, clean and reload with black gunpowder and ball. It would take me about a minute to complete the cycle. But if it had been 150 years ago with some Cherokees coming after my scalp, I'm sure I would have been quicker. Its effective range was only about 50 yards, so you would need to make the first shot count.

My favourite hangout was 'The Company' motorcycle shop, where I would work on the bike, and then a few old boys would pick up their banjos while we drank moonshine. It was the first time I heard Bluegrass and I didn't believe how similar it sounded to Irish music. By the time the duelling banjos started, we danced like idiots around the Harleys.

Yeehaw! Squeal like a pig!

Terry was one of the band members and had flown Phantoms in Vietnam. He wouldn't talk about it much and preferred telling me about flying an old WW2 Flying Fortress. The government tried to stop wild Mexican mice from invading America, so they bombed the desert with sacks of insecticide. The mice survived, but he reckoned he hit a few cows.

The Company was more a club than a shop, with a mixed bunch of businessmen and factory workers. Americans cross the class barrier the way the British can't, but they didn't cross the racial divide, and the bikers were all white.

I realized that the Hells Angels back in New York were all white too. While they were rebels and anarchists, they didn't accept blacks, while ironically, the white bikers in South Africa had got arrested for drinking with the blacks.

I loved hanging with the lads, doing work on the bike it didn't really need, just being part of normal society, after the pressure of my constant moving.

In Ireland, if someone moves ten miles away, it's traumatic, like they have emigrated. Americans think nothing of moving to the far side of the country. And because of this transience, they are hospitable to strangers. Within a few weeks, I loved being at home in the normality of small-town America. It couldn't have been more different from my West Coast, fast-living, drug-fuelled experience!

I was riding home one evening, after a few moonshines, when a cop car pulled me over. I was driving with no insurance, and under the influence and past the date I should have left for Mexico.

"Can I see your licence, Sir?" I handed him my UK licence.

"Is there a problem?" I said, panicking, jail bitch, here I come.

"Yes, you have no wing mirrors," he replied.

No wing mirrors were the least of my worries, but in America, a bike has to have mirrors. Someone nicked mine in Egypt. They are probably still mounted on their bathroom sink.

"Hey, you're Hank's buddy! I remember you!' he said.

"I hope you're enjoying your stay in Hickory. Drive carefully!"

My girlfriend Dana was a real Southern gal, laid back and a student in the local college. She owned her own car, a blue 1970 Chevrolet Impala, huge in every direction—five metres long, with a 6.7-litre V8 engine burbling under the bonnet. But best of all, it had bench seats across the front, great for that fantastic American invention, the Drive-in movie!

The Drive-in was a large parking lot with a giant concrete screen and an enormous projector. The cars parked beside a pole with a speaker on a cable. The 'Blues Brothers' film was just out and we packed the place. As the movie started, I understood why the population explosion of the 1950s coincided with drive-in movies. By the time Jake and Elwood drove away from prison, most occupants were snogging away in the back seats.

The movie is about two brothers who played in a blues band and seek redemption on 'a mission from God' to save an orphanage. Great music, the biggest ever car chase and a crazy script. As the credits rolled, everyone was revving their engines and racing for the exit in their own 'Blues Mobile' cars!

On the way out, Dana said, "You're on your own Mission from Gawd, Chris!"

"I guess I am," I said, drumming on the dashboard, "Rolling, rolling, rolling, … rawhide!"

"I wonder, will you have a happy ending?"

I hadn't reached that part of the screenplay.

Ronald Reagan was running for President, and Lucy, my landlady, asked me to a Republican Party meeting, which was more like a church gathering. The candidate talked more about religion than politics.

God was clearly a Republican, so obviously, the Democrats ran with the devil. That the Democrat candidate was a divorcee was clearly further proof. This was Bible Belt America with a church at every corner and to get elected you must appeal to the masses.

Like politics in Northern Ireland, it saves having to think for yourself when you just do what your church leader says. I got the impression that if this guy was a convicted paedophile, he would still get elected because he sang in church, twice on a Sunday.

Lucy was about 60 and recently widowed. She drank a bottle of vodka every day and was neurotic. Her only redeeming feature was her double garage. At first, she gave me the freedom of the house and I brought girlfriends back, but when I started dating Dana, she changed her mind. It soon became clear she wanted some 'Donaldson action' herself. I knew she was hitting the bottle, but one night she walked into my room and offered me $100 for me to fuck her.

A hundred dollars was a heap of money, but Lucy, she was old and crinkly and easy to refuse. But it was a decision I would have some regrets about when I was sick and broke in South America! That $100 would have got me a doctor's appointment!

Morals are great when you can afford them!

I started locking my bedroom door, but then the key disappeared, so I moved the wardrobe against the door every night. One night, I snuck Dana in the window but Lucy heard us and started screaming.

"I know your parents, Dana Mathews. I'll spread it all around Hickory you're a slut," she shouted, banging her fists on the door.

"Lucy, you're not my mother!" I shouted back.

"You can get out of my house too, you dirty Irish bastard!"

"I've paid rent to the end of the month!"

She started throwing things at the door, smashing the furniture, screaming and shouting, half-wrecking the house. When I got home from work, the house was perfect, and Lucy was smiling as if nothing happened.

I told Ed, as her husband had been his friend, and he needed to know she was ill. A few days later they took Lucy to hospital with a mental breakdown.

"I hear you've been driving all the ladies in Hickory mad," Ed remarked.

"Give me a break!" I squirmed in embarrassment!

"Never mind, you can stay with us."

I moved into Ed and Shirley's spare room, but it was on the second floor, so I had to persuade Dana to climb the drainpipe.

My parents arrived to buy some furniture from Ed. We sat down for a steak dinner and Dad announced that he would make room on the container for the bike. He wanted me to fly home to start work. When I told them that I was going to South America, they nearly choked.

"Do you have some sort of death wish?" Dad said, "What are you trying to prove?" Both questions I'd been asking myself, so finding it difficult to argue, I changed the subject.

"I will drive to Tierra del Fuego," I said.

"It's in Argentina or Chile… I think."

"Well, you will get no help from me!" my dad said and stormed out.

I'd still hoped to borrow some money from him, and without it, I knew I would struggle. But after driving Lucy mad, I realised I needed to get driving south. I had been getting too comfortable and forgot about my mission! The four-month limit Customs Affidavit had run out and if I got stopped, I would get fined $10,000, or go to jail.

I enjoyed life in Hickory, but the extended stopover made it harder for me to take to the hardships of the road again. I wasn't looking forward to travelling again, after months in a comfy bed. I was reaching travel burnout, physically and mentally. I had lived in the USA for so long I thought it my home, but my yellow UK number plate stuck out like a Mexican in the White House. It was only a matter of time before the cops pulled me again.

My departure was emotional; Ed had taken me in and treated me like a son. I thanked the family for everything and said my goodbyes to all my friends that accepted me in so unreservedly in this small backwater town. Dana was cool. We had got fond of each other but we knew that our time together would end. She had her studies, and I had my 'Mission from Gawd!"

The final Sunday, when we took the Chevy for a final drive, we parked up to watch the sun go down.

"Good luck, Chris, and I hope you find what you are looking for," she said, as we sat looking over the mountains from the big back seat.

The leaves of the trees turned golden brown in the autumn sunlight. Winter was coming.

I was no closer to that answer.

On a damp drizzly morning, I left. I didn't want a big send-off with people waving, I just wanted to slip off down the road unnoticed, in case I changed my mind and came back. I crossed through South Carolina in the rain, and then passed Athens, Georgia. I was going to call to scc Joycc, but I knew I needed to put some miles behind me as every mile would make it harder to change my mind and go back.

I camped in a lay-by off the interstate and I was freezing, so wore all my clothes in the sleeping bag, remembering the Blue Grass band would just be starting a session. Dana would go to the movies with her friends, and I would miss Shirley's pot roast tomorrow. I listened to the trucks roar down the interstate, a few yards from my soggy tent.

I had Don McLean on my tape deck and sang myself to sleep.

"So, bye, bye, Miss American Pie,
Drove my Chevy to the levee, but the levee was dry,
And them good ole boys were drinking whiskey and
rye,
Singin' this'll be the day that I die, This'll be the day that I die!"
What was I doing, and what the fuck does that song
mean, anyway?!

Before, every time I stopped for a few days, I wanted to move on. And this was the first time I hadn't wanted to. Next morning, I forced myself onto the bike again, but even the Guzzi sounded sad. I put it down to riding for months without luggage weighing me down.

Sitting on the saddle had been my home and my comfort zone, and now it seemed awkward and alien. Where had my Mojo gone? Everyone warned me about Mexico.

"Hell no," the lads at the factory said, "they'll steal the fillings from your teeth!"

"Don't trust them an inch!"

I said I had been worse places, like West Belfast, but the warnings stuck in my mind.

My mates, Kenny and JC from Belfast, had moved to Miami, so I made it my next mission to see them, if only to put off Mexico for a while.

I stopped at Cape Canaveral, that mystical place for kids my age, which brought back memories of long nights watching the Apollo launches on TV, as the huge Saturn rockets took off, and looking into the sky as Neil Armstrong and Buzz Aldrin landed on the moon, the bravest men ever. I was only exploring the Earth; they explored the universe. The mechanics of the lunar module looked basic, not the hi-tech mechanics that I imagined.

My mates had already gone back home with their girlfriends, but their flatmate, Theresa, said I could stay for a few days. That night, her friend called in. Jeanette was a nurse. We had an instant attraction and talked on long into the night after everyone had gone to bed. The next day she dumped her boyfriend, and we spent a few magical days getting to know each other.

Shit! I knew romance was not what I needed at the moment; I was trying to cut ties with Uncle Sam, and just when I need to harden up, I meet a girl! I seemed to have a similar effect on her too, as she snuggled up on the back of the bike.

Like a possessive Irish mother, the home of the brave and land of the free was doing everything it could to keep me. Jeanette had long dark hair and was petite, with a cheeky smile. She was bored with her life, her job and Miami, and obviously, her now-ex-boyfriend.

In ordinary life, when a relationship starts, you build up feelings over time as you go about your daily life. It's very different when you have a time restriction; everything was on fast forward and was so much more intense. We knew I would move on, so it was as if we tried to get years into a few days.

With wartime romances, the danger and risk make the relationship more passionate, and I suppose my journey had a similar effect. I did not understand the effect that I had on people I met. My wandering lifestyle was inspiring or unsettling to people. I could look upon it as a romantic notion of freedom or anarchy to their ordered society.

"Take me with you," she said to me when I talked of moving on.

I told her she was crazy.

"I have nothing to offer but long days in the saddle and a sore arse," I said.

'Sounds like fun," she laughed.

"No, really, it will be dangerous too, Mexican bandits, road accidents, God knows what."

"Sounds like Miami on a Saturday night!"

"We will ride for twelve hours a day, in the rain and cold, over dirt roads."

I told her we could meet bad guys with guns; we'd be sleeping in the tent or flea-bitten hotels, but she would not be put off.

Tired of travelling alone, I was persuaded. Maybe it was time for a change of direction in my adventure? I agreed she could come but with the proviso that, if it didn't work out, she would have to go home alone. She accepted and told her boss and flatmates she was leaving. Understandably, I was as popular as a leper in a whorehouse.

We both knew it was madness, but I wasn't in the 'let's- be-sensible' business, and neither was Jeanette. I dumped some luggage to make some room for her cute ass, and Jeanette bade farewell to her shell-shocked friends, her well-paid job, and her secure life, to go off with some fucked-up, wandering biker from Belfast.

Who could blame her? It was a perfectly rational decision! Not! When her friends gathered that morning, it wasn't to see us off, it was to talk her out of going. They pulled Jeanette aside to tell her what a mistake she was making. Theresa was furious, and I thought I might get lynched.

"What sort of bastard are you? I give you a bed for a couple of nights, you eat my food, drink my drink, then fuck off with my best friend!"

"I'm sorry," I said, although, if I was honest, I could sort of see her point!

"It's not his fault; it's my choice," Jeanette replied.

I assured Theresa that this was not my normal practice. I had stayed with lots of people, but this was the first woman I had stolen.

"This is not rational behaviour!" Theresa shouted at me. She was right again, but I hadn't been rational for a long time, and it was only to be expected that some of it would rub off on other people.

"You two need to grow up!" yelled Theresa.

"We don't, but you do! All you want is to return to Ireland and get fucking married," said Jeanette. "It's you who needs to get a life!"

Eventually, they all calmed down, and the girls wished us well, so with Jeanette holding on behind me, we sped up the Gulf coast towards Mexico. I put my Steppenwolf tape full blast on the stereo! We laughed and sang into the slipstream and Jeanette drummed the beat of the song on my back.

'Get your motor runnin', Head out on the highway, Lookin' for adventure, and whatever comes our way. Yeah, darlin' go make it happen, Take the world in a love embrace, Fire all your guns at once and explode into space!'

They made rock-and-roll for driving in America. We were young, in love… or lust… carefree, and the warm Florida breeze swept past us as we flew up the freeway.

As I read my journal now forty years later, I think what madness! What were we thinking of? That crazy impetuousness of youth! But brilliant! As we get older, what takes away that fun, that recklessness of life, the 'anything is possible' outlook that we had when we were young? It is old guys who are crazy.

I stopped in St Petersburg to see my old Scoutmaster, Richard Turnage, as it was Richard's fault that I was here in the first place! The scouts filled my impressionable years. If not for Richard, I wouldn't have had my extreme sense of adventure!

If not for the sea treks in dinghies, I would never have got onto an Atlantic racing yacht.

If not for the Venture Scouts, my love of bikes would never have sparked.

If I blamed it on one person, it would be Richard; it was his fault I was here!

Richard had his own adventures. He sailed to America on the replica of Sir Francis Drake's ship the Golden Hind for the five-hundredth centenary. Then, in swashbuckling style, he married the Captain's daughter. He settled in Florida, where he now worked as an engineer.

It was after 10 pm when we found the small bungalow set back from the road. In these days of Facebook, it's hard to imagine turning up unannounced, after we hadn't seen each other for five years. Richard was gob-smacked;

"Hi, Dick," I said, as he stood at the door with his mouth hanging open.

"Chris Donaldson!"

"Dick Turnage!"

"OK, but don't call me Dick; no one had called me that for 6 years since I left Belfast!"

"I don't believe it," he kept saying as he opened a bottle of champers!

"The last time I saw you, you were fifteen and rode a scrap BSA Bantam. Now you drive up on a Moto Guzzi with a girl on the back!" He shook his head.

"The last time I saw you, you were a scoutmaster in St John's Parish Church!"

Liz, his wife, wanted to hear all about his previous life. Richard was five years older with similar curly hair and beard. He seemed smaller than before, but 'heroes' always seem larger than life. Those early adventures led to our own exciting enterprises, and it was right our paths should cross in Florida. I caught Richard looking at my SOI 222 number plate. "I never thought I'd see a Belfast plate in Florida," he said.

"Unbelievable," he said for the hundredth time!

I wanted to de-tune the engine for South America, so we took off the cylinder heads and checked the pistons and rings. They looked perfect, and then I added thick gaskets between the cylinders and the engine, to make it run on low-quality petrol.

It was a bonding moment, between Richard and I, sweating over the Guzzi under the orange trees. Afterwards, we nursed a few Budweisers, and talked about old times, and watched the sun go down.

Richard invited us to a barbecue at his boss's house, which had a huge wild garden which we raced around in golf carts.

"Don't crash!" shouted Rob, as I nearly slid the cart into a small lake. "There are alligators in the water!"

But as the days went on, I had a nagging doubt. Something wasn't right about having Jeanette along and I couldn't work it out. Even though it was great having company, for some reason, it felt wrong, like I was cheating on a lover. My lover? It was a bloody road trip!

Half my head said I had to go on alone. But the other half said, what was I thinking of? She was fun and sexy, and we had got very close, and the extra money would be handy – if not essential. But how could I protect her from dangerous situations, and protect her in countries like Nicaragua or Colombia? I would put her in harm's way, with risks I knew lay ahead, but she didn't. Round-the-world motorcycling is a very dangerous occupation.

I could blame the extra weight on the bike as being the problem. It took a year to get the Guzzi set up for one person and my gear. Put a person on the back and she handled like a pig again. Okay, it handled alright on the freeway. But in a few weeks, back on dirt tracks and potholes, it could be too much for the bike carrying two of us.

I made a mess of explaining my decision because I didn't know what my problem was myself. Confused about how I felt, I didn't want to lose her, but I needed to do the journey alone. She wanted to come to the Mexican border, but she would have lost her job by then. She had only been gone a week, so she could go back with her tail between her legs and plead insanity.

I had made it clear at the start that our adventure might not last long, but she presumed we would make it out of Florida. I had to tell her to go; I didn't want to be responsible for her losing her flat, her job, her friends, or her life. And I wasn't ready for the responsibility of her life in my hands.

What are you doing? I said to myself as I said farewell to Richard and drove Jeanette to Tampa Airport; her boss had said that if she was back on Monday, she could have her old job again.

Distraught and confused, I opened the throttle towards New Orleans, all alone again. What had I done? A beautiful girl wants to join me, and I had turned her down? What the hell was I thinking of? It started to rain; I was miserable, but I deserved it as I was an idiot. I camped up in a lay-by and crawled into my tent feeling sorry for myself.

What had I done? But I had this job to do, and needed to be on my own to do it, for some stupid reason! In the morning, I felt no better; I was done in, the bike felt done in.

I had gone soft in the USA. It had been fun. Sex and drugs and rock and roll. The great American adventure.

I set myself this next task; to discover the world or discover myself. Surely there must be an easier way. Like a $9.99 self- help book or something? Maybe some sleazy psychotherapist? It would be expensive, but less dangerous!

I found a poem in my sleeping bag.

My, Mr Moto Guzzi Man
You rode in on the back but of your red machine, On the way from wandering
From where you have been to where you go, The way wanderers do,
In search of the world,
Always two steps ahead of your feet. The black curls
Escaping your helmet That cradles your head Dance on their leather stage
Laughing at the wind
As you ride.
You eat your donated dinner
In exchange
For a second of sharing
In your travels
The fulfilled fantasy
Of escape
From the daily chore of life
Perhaps
The feeling is mutual
Jeanette
Good luck and good wisdom on your travels
I'm not sure which you will need more!

What had I done? But I had this job to do, and needed to be on my own to do it, for some stupid reason! In the morning, I felt no better; I was done in, the bike felt done in.

I had gone soft in the USA. It had been fun. Sex and drugs and rock and roll. The great American adventure.

I set myself this next task; to discover the world or discover myself. Surely there must be an easier way. Like a $9.99 self- help book or something? Maybe some sleazy psychotherapist? It would be expensive, but less dangerous!

I had lost my zeal for travel, and Jeanette drew me back like a magnet. My dream now blurred. And going further than ever from home, with less money, less enthusiasm, with a beat-up motorcycle that had gone way beyond the call of duty. I was on my way to the moon without enough fuel to get back.

The roads in South America looked better than in Africa, but the politics sounded as bad, if not worse. I was pushing the beat-up Guzzi to complete one last journey, to Tierra del Fuego… The Land of Fire and ice.

But the Mardi Gras was in Rio in March; maybe that was a more attractive destination? A great party for the end of a journey, perhaps! According to all Americans, I would get my throat cut in Central America. Nicaragua was in the middle of a revolution, El Salvador was having a Civil War, Guatemala, Costa Rica and Panama were all unstable and drug barons ran Colombia.

I had no idea what was going on further south! I had a Southern drawl, my brain worked in dollars, and I felt at home in the States; what was I trying to prove by going to South America, anyway?

Another one-way trip, with no money to get me home. It's strange how something ridiculous can become acceptable. My only option would be to sell the bike to get home.

I had driven around half the world with no insurance, apart from four days in Rhodesia. What would happen if I wrecked the bike and couldn't sell it? I had no idea what was at the end of the road, and also, I didn't really care. I was back to 'think about today and forget tomorrow' mode. Was this a good thing?

I made my miserable way around the Gulf of Mexico, past miles of farms, oil fields, then the bayou swamps and plantations, and I found it dull and boring. Every day a drudgery, every mile a struggle. In New Orleans, I parked up in the French Quarter for a coffee and listened to a street jazz band and soaked up the atmosphere.

"Would you like to learn about Buddhism today, my friend?" a small bald man said to me.

"Do I look fucking suicidal or something?" I replied. I was not in the mood.

Someone was trying to convert me again. Really America, if it's not drugs, its religion!

"You can have dinner and a bed for tonight."

"Okay, you have talked me into it," I relented.

The precarious state of my wallet meant I was a tart for the price of a bed!

"As long as you're not Catholics," I said. "That would be just too much."

He looked puzzled.

"It was a Belfast joke," I said.

The Temple was an ornate terrace house in the middle of the French Quarter. As I listened to Sam the Monk talk about Buddhism, it seemed to make sense. It was a more liberal religion than most, but then again, when any religion sells their story, they are always so believable. Just car salesmen, making promises that they can't keep.

"Whether you think Buddhism is a religion depends on how you define religion," Sam explained.

"Buddha's mission was all about the suffering, and human misery," he went on.

"It's about being a nice guy because you want to be, rather than doing what some God tells you to do," he said.

I had tried to read 'Zen and the Art of Motorcycle Maintenance,' for the past year. It was about motorcycles and Buddhism, but it took forever to read, which was great as I only had room for one book! (I finally finished it five years later!) But I wasn't quite ready to convert; I reckoned I was a nice guy, anyway. I didn't need someone to tell me what to do at this stage in my life.

Besides, I was on a mission from Gawd already! Intermingled with my Zen, I managed to hit the jazz bars for a bit of music and some 'Soul' of a different kind before lights out at the temple!

Next stop was Houston, where I met up with an English guy called Edward. He was one of those eccentric English gentlemen you meet abroad and he rode an immaculate 1930 Brough Superior.

Brough Superiors were the Rolls-Royces of motorcycles. Lawrence of Arabia had one given to him by George Bernard Shaw. They are a vintage classic which you would never imagine being in modern-day Houston, with a proper English gentleman with a full King George beard and a deerstalker coat.

We cut a strange sight as we went into a cowboy bar for a few beers and some line dancing, swapping our helmets for Stetsons. There, a bunch of Texans gave me more warnings of all the evil things that would happen to me in Mexico.

CHAPTER 15

Paranoid Biker in Central America

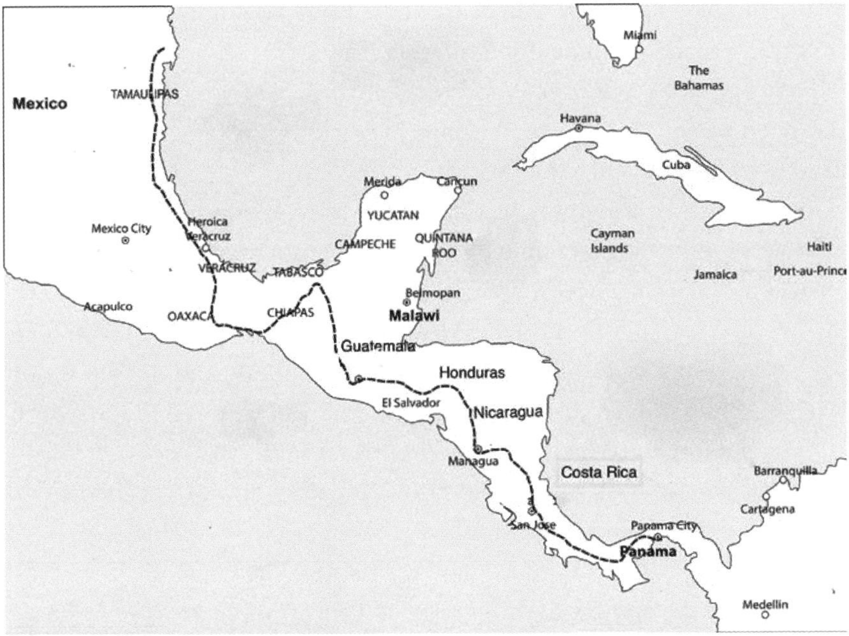

I SLID DOWN THE EDGE OF THE NORTH AMERICAN CONTINENT, LIKE A GRAIN of sand in an egg timer. At Brownsville, Texas, I felt the lawlessness in the air, with groups of Mexicans hanging around outside seedy bars. Over the border, even the streetlights looked dark and foreboding after the bright neon lights of Texas.

The Immigration post stamped my passport and waved me through. The guards knew they stood at the edge of civilisation;

"You'll be back tomorrow, go on, you crazy son of a bitch!" Their looks said to me.

I entered Mexico with my head full of dread. I wanted to U-turn straight back to the land of the free, the home of McDonald's, and where everyone spoke their own curious version of English.

I followed the Mexican Gulf coast and met up with a couple of old hippies at a gas station. Frank and Sherry drove a battered Chevy pick-up truck with a homemade house on the back. It was made of planks nailed together, complete with dormer windows, a pitched roof and a small chimney, like a Gingerbread house, and obviously designed and built with the aid of some mind-altering drugs.

They had never got over Woodstock and travelled south for the winter and good weed. Sherry wore a long cheesecloth skirt and wore a head-band, which said 'peace' on the front.

In need of the company to quell my Mexican psychosis, we agreed to travel together for a couple of days. We camped in a field and Frank rolled a big fat joint while Sherry cooked up some dinner on the open fire. My head relaxed a little, and the Mexican bandit worries drifted off with the smoke. The grass was greener with the marijuana, and the sun shone brighter. My paranoia just needed a spliff, then all was well in the world.

"Thank God and Mexico for good grass," I said.

"Mexicans are cool, man," said Frank, inhaling down to his boots.

"What about the bandits?" I asked.

"Don't worry, they'll think you are the bandit!" he laughed. "Seriously, they are friendly people, man."

Frank finished every sentence with 'man.' It was quite addictive, and I started to do it myself… man.

If only I knew more than "Dos cervezas, por favor, man" in Spanish.

Africa was an English-speaking continent, but I'd forgotten that Latin America spoke Spanish and Portuguese, and I spoke neither. Frank's attitude helped me relax, and my confidence grew. I can do this, I said to myself, I can, I can.

Frank was an anarchist who lived off the grid. Like the Hells Angels, he never owned a house, paid taxes or stayed in one place for long. A modern-day gypsy, he roamed the countryside staying with 'settled' friends who let them camp for a few dollars, while he did odd jobs and sold some grass.

He believed everything to be a conspiracy, and that the U.S. government were trying to find him and track his movements.

I wondered why these rejects from society drew me to them, before I realised that's what I was too. The term 'drop- out' changed from an insult to a compliment in my head. My conservative father didn't agree and scorned my chosen lifestyle. He just couldn't fathom the attraction. I wondered which was the real me, was it the middle-class Belfast boy, or the roving nomad with no fixed abode?

Frank loved Mexico; it was cheap, with few government controls, and he could live for months on his savings. His enthusiasm for the place was infectious and just what I needed to settle my nerves.

But their van drove at a 30mph top speed, with the weight of their log cabin on the back. So, I rode on alone, promising to wait in San Cristobal, but we knew that we wouldn't see each other. At their rate of travel, it would take months to drive that far.

Travelling through Tampico in warm rain and low clouds, past empty golden beaches, the roads deteriorated by the mile. I was back in the Third World. Near Vera Cruz, I stopped where Cortez first landed in 1519. Cortez built the first Spanish town here, and it had changed little since, with cobbled streets and stone cottages, although trees now grew through the dilapidated buildings.

His sailors became so terrified of the Indians that he burnt his ships to stop them sailing home. I wondered if I would have to burn the Guzzi to stop me doing the same thing. At least I wasn't the first paranoid Westerner in Mexico!

Modern Mexicans had different opinions about their history. To some, Cortez was a hero, but to others, a foreign invader. The government ignored these historic buildings instead of protecting them. The ruins of his house, probably the oldest house in the whole of the Americas, now had trees growing through it. An old wooden sign proclaimed, 'Here lived Hernan Cortez, conqueror of Mexico.'

After I walked around the ruins, a well-dressed couple came over to talk.

"My son loves your bike; is it okay if he sat on it?" The father said in perfect English.

"Sure," I said, expecting a young teenager, but it was a man in his twenties. But he smiled with the innocence of a child. He got on the bike and smiled so hard his face could break.

"Last year, Bolo rode his scrambler across a railway bridge and fell on the rocks below," his father explained. He had been in hospital for nine months and while his physical injuries had mended, it left him brain-damaged.

"I am so sorry," I said.

"Yours is the first motorbike he has seen since!"

José invited me to stay, and I parked in the back garden of his cottage that he had restored. Bolo didn't want to leave the Guzzi and sat smiling away at me. I smiled back embarrassed. He had married a few months before the accident, and Julio, his beautiful wife was by his side.

I told them of my trip around Europe and Africa, while we barbecued roast pork and drank beer. I spoke of my crossing of the Sahara Desert and driving over railway bridges.

Suddenly, Bolo jumped on the bike, cried out and gave me a 'thumbs up'. He understood what we were saying!

Julio burst into tears of joy and the family hugged me and thanked me for being there. It was his first communication since the accident and was a wonderful moment to share.

The raw emotion of the situation humbled me at this hugely emotional moment.

I knew that my journey touched many of the people I stayed with but Bolo's reaction was like an electric shock, in its raw appreciation of my presence.

Yesterday's paranoia of all things Mexican evaporated, replaced with the family's love and affection of today.

I told them of the tales of Mexican lawlessness that I had heard in America. "Ah, we make stories up to keep the Yankees out!" José laughed. "I suppose you thought we all wore big moustaches, sombreros and carried knives in our belts!"

I laughed out loud, but actually, I did think that. The conservative North Carolinians filled my head full of such notions about their southern neighbours. I wondered why Americans lived in fear of things foreign. But who was I to talk? Belfast was much worse, where the city has a 'peace' wall through it to keep the two religious factions from killing each other. What is it that gives people such fear of different cultures instead of learning to enjoy their diversity?

José explained that there was a problem with crime, related to the supply of drugs to- where else but the States. So, the Americans caused the crime that they feared, by buying drugs from the Mexican criminals. My fear of all things Mexican had vanished by the next day, as I rode my Guzzi down the street where Cortez once rode his horse before he seized the whole of Mexico.

And as I drove off, I wondered again why I had been so lucky and not fallen on my head. Mentally, I travelled with a positive attitude, and an open mind, which I believed helped make good things happen to me. Negative people attract negative things, as they always see the bad in a situation, and miss out on good opportunities when they arise.

Bolo took a risk by riding over a railway bridge once, and had nearly killed himself; I had taken a thousand more risks and got away with it.

I still started every day saying my mantra, that I would not fall off today, as I had since Sudan, but surely there was more to it than that. I didn't believe in God, superstition or the stars, so who on earth was looking after me? Most importantly, how could I make sure he kept doing it?!

I visited the nearby Mayan ruins of Palenque, a lost city going back a thousand years. They had only cleared 5% of the site, and thick undergrowth covered most of the pyramids, and it was obscured by an eerie mist as I pushed through the vegetation. It smelled rank with the decomposing plants and moss. I could hear parrots calling, and the chatter of small birds and monkeys shrieking. Remembering my baboon day in Africa, I kept well away from the noise. I came across crumbling buildings and climbed pyramids with roots growing through them and imagined I had discovered them. It was mesmerizing and sparked my interest in this forgotten culture, decimated in the name of God by the Spanish 500 years ago.

I left the coast and headed for the mountains. When the conquistadors landed, they forced the Indians into the hills where they remained, with remnants of their old culture and religion, blended in with the Christian church.

The road climbed ever south through the mountains to San Cristobal de las Casas and the Yucatan. I visited tourist sights when I could as it was past the tourist season, and as in Egypt, the sites lay empty, so much more evocative than with hordes of sightseers.

As the road climbed up from the banana plantations into the tropical mountains, I soared through the clouds to the clear sky above. The bike struggled up the steep gradients and the high altitude combined with the poor-quality petrol made the engine 'ping' and the petrol pre-ignite, overheating the cylinders. Then that oil light came on again, so I disconnected the bulb, but the engine was making a horrible knocking noise. It sounded like there was a war going on inside. I held my ear against the cylinder and heard the tormented bearings grinding in the thin, overheated oil.

I stopped in Oaxaca, an old Spanish Colonial town with central squares and courtyards. People lived as they had for centuries. In the evenings, they wandered arm in arm, through the streets, chatting about the day's events.

A huge cathedral dominated the square; an ominous presence, reminding the peasants who was in charge. Nearby were the partially excavated Monte Alban ruins with impressive buildings and staircases leading to religious sacrificial platforms, where the priests ripped out the still- beating hearts of their victims.

The cannibalistic Zapotec Indians loved human sacrifice, and I tried to imagine what the scene would have been like 2500 years ago. There was a games courtyard with lines of stone seats for the audience. After the game, they sacrificed the winning team's captain in celebration! Obviously, a good era to be a fat lazy bastard!

When I returned to the bike, I found three Westerners waiting for me. They worked at the Israeli embassy in Panama and were amazed to see Israel included on the list of countries painted on the panniers. Deborah had stunning Italian features, which made her look like a young Sophia Loren. She was statuesquely beautiful. She worked with security in the Embassy, which made her even more erotic.

I can't remember what David and Levi even looked like. Whatever!

They were touring Mexico in an old Chevrolet car and said that bandits had robbed them at gunpoint a few days ago, which severely dented my new-found Mexican confidence! The Yucatan mountain region was quite wild and murders and robberies were rife. Maybe the Americans talked sense, after all!

"Be careful if anyone flags you down, and pretends to be police," David said

"So, what do I do? Drive on?" I asked.

"No, the police will shoot you for not stopping," they laughed.

said.

"This reminds me of Belfast," I said,

"and Israel!" they laughed.

Independent travellers had cash and things of value. The bandits would get on a train at one station, and walk up through the carriages, taking valuables at gunpoint. Then they would jump off at the next stop and catch the next train back. Government austerity made people desperate.

We agreed to travel south together for security, but I was love-struck and would have followed Deborah anywhere anyway! We camped well off the road and out of sight. At night, the jungle would come alive with fireflies and the noise of crickets, and strange farting noises from a frog or toad. I couldn't imagine what made the other shrieks - monkeys, big cats? I was glad of the company in the other tent.

I checked who Deborah was with romantically, but they seemed all good friends. I was too young and un-Jewish to interest her, but that didn't stop my infatuation. We discussed Northern Ireland, and as ever, I was embarrassed when I tried to explain what the Troubles were all about. They couldn't understand why 2 factions (Protestant and Catholic) of the same religion (Christianity) would hate each other so much. The Israelis thought they had much more right to hate the Arabs.

I, of course, was able to give them my opinion of the Palestine issue, but they insisted that their war was a question of national survival, not just religion. I said that Northern Ireland was more about whether the wankers from London or the wankers from Dublin would tell us what to do. It's funny how much easier it is to give advice on other people's problems than it is to sort out your own.

More importantly, back in Mexico, I wondered if I should turn Jewish, if only to get a snog with Deborah.

The recent earthquake had damaged the roads and parts of it had slid down the steep mountainside, leaving nothing but a narrow pedestrian footpath to cross. It was just a few feet wide and a hundred yards long, but I reckoned I could get the bike over. The cars waited for the bulldozers or turned back to find a different route.

"I'll see you in San Cristobal in a few days," I said, and with my handlebars scraping the mountain wall on my left, and a sheer drop on the right, I drove across the gap.

I worked out that to have any chance of reaching Brazil, after petrol money, I would have to live on two dollars a day. Even if I camped every night, I would have to live like a peasant and survive on bread and water.

The bike hated the high altitude and crap petrol. I wasn't in the right mind for travelling either; what was I doing here, anyway? And why put myself through this ordeal? And, I asked myself again and again, why did I dump Jeanette?

While travelling long distances, you have time to reflect on yourself and your surroundings. It's like a religious meditation from the Church of Moto Guzzi. I was depressed at how little I had changed my personality. In North Carolina, I'd slipped straight back into my old temperament, particularly with the bits about me I didn't like, as if I had learned nothing from my journey.

While I felt more confident and assured while travelling, I reverted to my previous state of being when I stopped. So, what was the point of my travels, anyway? Why go through this shit, if I'm going to return to my old self?

The answer was obvious - nothing.

I'd achieved nothing and lived with some idiotic fantasy that I would gain some astonishing skill by riding around on a bloody motorcycle! In fact, the further I travelled, it seemed the less I knew, and many days I had forgotten what the question was in the first place.

At the top of another mountain, I could see the forest for miles, and the sun was low on the horizon. As I descended, I slowed for the first bend, then disaster, my front brake failed, and the lever came away in my fingers. I scraped around the first hairpin bend, wheels skidding on the gravel, just missing the sheer drop to the valley. I tried the rear brake, then with a crack, it fell off. Someone had sabotaged the bike, and I was now out of control, careering down the steep mountain road.

I scraped around the next corner using the engine braking. The V twin screamed as I changed down gears to slow down but I was still picking up speed, and the next corner had no crash barriers protecting the sheer drop. The handlebars locked solid, and I continued over the edge of the cliff, and into the abyss, spinning and somersaulting and screaming, falling into the dark canyon below. A cock crowed.

I sat up, covered in sweat. I was in my tent in a banana plantation. I had gone to sleep worrying about the futility of the journey but the nightmare resulted from a sick brain. A fever was wracking my body and doing strange things to my head. I got up, suddenly happy not to have crashed and determined to get to Panama, come what may.

First, though, I will check my brakes.

After I empty my bowels, that is.

The further south I drove, I imagined North America squashing me in. In Canada, I had driven 3000 miles to cross it. But now in Central America, the Pacific and the Atlantic oceans converged, until, by Panama, they would be a mere 51 miles apart, joined by the Panama Canal.

I felt like I was spiralling down the funnel, out of control, getting faster and faster, as the walls narrowed, until at the bottom I would fly out, or get stuck in the spout.

I remembered my conversation with Michel about a journey having a life, but it seemed like this journey was terminally ill.

If I cut the trip short and go home, I would be restless there too. The problem was not my journey; it was my head.

I had painted 'paranoid biker' on my panniers, I reckoned tonight, I would have to add 'neurotic.'

Africa challenged me and tested me to the full but gave me immense pleasure when I succeeded. In the Americas, the novelty of the experience wore off, and the challenge lessened. The trials were now a pain in the ass, instead of an opportunity. So, I lost any pleasure in a quagmire of disillusionment.

The lack of money was a constant source of stress, and my body was wracked with fever and every few hours, my bowels blew open to release a flock of very smelly starlings.

Where was home? Hickory, Cape Town, Belfast? I had no idea now. I was a tramp of no fixed abode, a vagabond. I rode further into the unknown and, with every revolution of my wheels, the pressure got more intense. I was on a one-way ticket to the end of the world, Tierra del Fuego, whatever the fuck that was, anyway.

It was hard to find somewhere safe to camp in Mexico. There was so much poverty. I could tell the way the locals looked at me that they were envious of my possessions. Everyone was a potential bandit, as everyone carried a very large knife, a Panga, used for chopping down banana trees …or the heads off tourists…

My next 'Civilisation' would be Panama City, which would have transport back to the States if I wanted to forget about South America. I focussed my sights on that destination.

To get to Panama, I had to travel through Nicaragua, which had just finished a revolution. The rebel Sandinistas had taken over the country, but the old government had retreated to Honduras where the USA supported them with fresh arms and supplies. The Nicaraguan border was closed, and everyone I met was waiting to see if things would settle down before risking it.

After Panama, the road stopped at the Darien Gap, two hundred miles of impenetrable swamps between Panama and Colombia.

Then, if I survived that, there was the small matter of Colombia having a civil war with the drug lords like Pablo Escobar. Eventually, I would have to cross the Andes, some of the highest mountains in the world, and the Guzzi engine had already informed me that on no account did it like heights.

So, apart from the lack of money, the Civil Wars, drug wars, swamps, malaria, and the highest mountain passes in the world, I was home and dry.

My guidebook title was South America on $15 a day. Shit! I had only $2.00 a day to survive on, which was only workable if I lived like a local.

I was one very poor gringo.

Some travellers wanted to go to Tierra del Fuego, but there was nothing there but the road back. So, what was the point? Just to say I had ridden to the southerly point? So what? I've got my bragging rights already.

My other option was to go to Rio for the Carnival, but one step at a time, one day at a time.

On the 24th of November, I made it to San Cristobal de las Casas, a city high in the Central Highlands of Southern Mexico. It differed from the Spanish Mexicans in the North. The city maintained its old colonial layout, with narrow cobblestone streets, red clay tile roofs and ornate balconies. They painted the facades of the buildings in bright colours. Locals still used horses and donkeys for transport. The Indian women all wore multi-layered voluminous black skirts and funny coloured hats. They were short with round faces.

I noticed the wealthy Mexicans had 'Spanish' European features. The Indians were a different race. They were descended from the Aztecs who had escaped from the conquistadors into the mountains. It was a welcome distraction for me to act like a tourist for a couple of days and enjoy the sights and sounds of the city.

GUATEMALA

I was on my own again headed south, to cross into Guatemala, riding through lush green hills and valleys, past stunning volcanoes and beautiful lakes. My schizophrenia improved with the scenery and I tried to enjoy the here and now rather than worrying about the future.

But the beautiful Guatemalan landscape hid a brutal war where the military government asserted their control over the peasant population, under the guise of putting down the communists.

Their civil war continued on from the USA-sponsored coup, which ousted the democratically elected left-wing government. It is estimated that the government murdered over 200,000 people. It seemed outlandish that such a beautiful place should harbour such dreadful happenings.

In Guatemala City, skyscrapers rose beside poverty- stricken shantytowns. Burger King served the rich while the peasants begged outside. I stopped at a KFC, just to feel the air conditioning and eat a chicken leg. I came out refreshed, as the fantasy of pretending I was in North Carolina recharged my mental batteries. Then back into the forty degrees heat to find the address of some friends of friends.

I stayed for a couple of nights in an apartment belonging to Simone and Alphonso, who warned me not to go out after dark; it was too dangerous. If the drug dealers and thieves didn't get me, the corrupt police would kidnap me for ransom. The police would murder about 30 people in the city every night. There is nothing like fear to keep a population oppressed.

Then the government realised that making people disappear was more effective than killing them. You kill someone, they are buried, and life moves on. If they disappear, the loved ones never know if they are dead and live in constant uncertainty.

In the apartment, it was awkward, as my hosts had married recently and spent every evening shagging their brains out in their room, while I watched Guatemalan soap operas on TV in Spanish.

So, I could get fucked over in the streets or stay in listening to Simone getting fucked next door. Either way, the experience was fucking crap, so I left for the prospect of a good night's sleep in Honduras.

I wondered how there could be a land so fertile and the people so destitute; food was so abundant, but yet poverty and despair were everywhere. The problem with humanity is that when 50 people find a piece of fertile land big enough to sustain 100 people, they will breed until 200 people live there. So, again they will go hungry, and this hunger will produce corruption, which then descends into pain and suffering.

The farmers work the fields for a pittance while the profits go to their masters. In the city, the peasants scramble for a job and take whatever they can get to sustain their meagre existence. If they lose their job, someone else will take it.

I could speak reasonably good 'Enganish' by now. Enganish is when you talk in English to a local but throw in whatever Spanish words you have. You must also speak louder than normal as the volume helps Fernando, the foreigner, understand.

So, ordering a beer, I shout out something like;

"Dos beers, por favor" or "Two cervezas, please." This worked okay, just, but a good intake of alcohol helped, as when you are drinking, you speak every language fluently.

Luckily lots of the locals spoke 'Spanglish' or, Spanish with lots of English words added. With a combination, I could get by. And my Spanglish was improving every day. I was quick to learn that adding an 'O' or an 'A' onto every English word worked too.

"Is-A this the Road-A to-a NicaraguA?"

This must be spoken with a heavy emphasis on the 'A' When the local shrugged his shoulders and looked blank, I would repeat it, but this time shouting it at the top of my voice, as the guy obviously didn't hear me. As long as I based most of the discussions on motorcycles, food, drink or travelling, I actually communicated with locals quite well!

I arrived in Tegucigalpa, the Honduras capital, and looked around the museums and cathedrals. But I quickly lost interest when I met a traveller who confirmed that the revolution in Nicaragua had closed the border south. I would have to take a boat to Panama, but with the roads closed, the price was exorbitant; it was another disaster, and I was stuck again. I would have to return to the States, just as I was getting to like being on the road again.

The only way to know if a border was closed, was to try crossing it. I decided to try to talk myself in. After making a small financial contribution to the Honduran border guard's weekend fund, they stamped my passport.

I rode despondently across no-man's-land. The road was deserted. On the other side, the Nicaraguan Soldiers of the Revolution stood waiting for me. Armed with AK-47s they all looked very young, only fourteen or fifteen years old.

"Where are you from?" they demanded, trying to pretend their voices had broken.

I was nervous and scared, with more substance on the 'Scared!' When a border guard is a young teenager, it's extremely intimidating. You know that he might sink to insurmountable depths of depravity just to impress his boss or be one of the 'big boys.' Either way, he will ruin your day.

At first, they swore at me in Spanish, but when I showed them my passport and assured them that I wasn't American, they relaxed.

"You give me dollars," one gun-toting teenager demanded, as I sat on the bike with the engine running. I would not outrun any bullets, but it gave me more confidence.

"No, you give me dollars!"

He looked confused for a second, then they all laughed. Just schoolkids really, but with big guns and battle-hardened faces.

"Ronald Reagan bad. Ortega good," one said, looking at me to judge my reaction.

"Yes, Ronald Reagan shit head. Ortega good," I agreed. "Ian Paisley's a cunt too, if that helps."

The FNSL initials stood for the Sandinista National Liberation Front, but they got the letters mixed up. The rebels had thrown out the Samoza family, whose three generations of presidents had ruled the country for the last fifty years. Nicaragua was an authentic banana republic. I was shocked to learn how the USA had destabilised the entire region. The CIA saw any 'democratic' government as a Marxist take-over, and successive US governments propped up the right-wing puppet dictators.

Managua still felt like a war zone, not just because of shootings, but also the aftermath of the huge 1972 earthquake which had killed 10,000 people. It destroyed 23 acres of the city, which was still lying in ruins. I rode around the city blocks and mounds of concrete with the remains of the buildings now covered in undergrowth, the tombs of the thousands of victims. As darkness fell, I sensed the ghosts of the squashed emerge from the rubble and swirl around the empty streets of the once vibrant neighbourhoods.

The President had kept millions of dollars of aid, which led to the unrest and his eventual fall from power in 1980.

The locals loved the houses that survived the quake, as they believed the decrepit and cracked buildings had some weird earthquake-proof property.

The city was spooky, with fresh bullet holes on many of the buildings. And it didn't look like everyone was thrilled with the changeover; young kids stood menacingly with guns at every street corner.

I stopped in a motorbike shop, and Geraldo, the owner, invited me to stay. Geraldo was an expert on motorcycle mechanics and ancient history. He told me about the many similarities between the Incas and the ancient Egyptian cultures. He gave me a new fascination for the ruins of the Aztecs.

Outside town, the Santiago Volcano, like Nicaragua, was ready for an eruption; I rode right up to the rim of the smoking caldera. It was pretty cool, even with the heat of the magma below, if more than a little unsafe. But hell, this was Nicaragua in 1980!

I crossed into the terribly boring Costa Rica next door. While Nicaragua had its Civil War nightmare, its neighbour had been peaceful since 1948 when the country had a short Civil War. The rebels overthrew the government, disbanded the army, and they have all lived happily ever after. With no army, there is no war.

The biggest problem with Costa Ricans was they would never say, "I don't know," when asked for directions. They would pretend they knew where I wanted to go and point in the wrong direction. For a Latino man, to say 'I didn't know,' would be like admitting they had a small cock.

Physically I was in poor shape and had the shits after drinking dodgy water in Nicaragua. Mentally, one moment I felt euphoric about some small success, then the next I just wanted to lie down and die; I was burnt out and exhausted.

I had left Belfast on a 3-month journey to ride 8000 miles through 8 countries.

One year and 32,000 miles later, I was still rolling along, and had ridden through 26 countries on the bike, and had added another 10,000 miles on the sailing boat. I had been travelling for four times longer and four times further and was still going, the wrong way.

I had every right to be done in, and my lack of money was the main cause. I was going further from home, with no means of return, on a beat-up bike. The slightest road accident or health issue and I was well and truly buggered. I had about USD 350 left and five thousand miles to travel if I went on to South America, and I needed to decide what to do.

As I travelled, with the dangers and the loneliness, something locked in my brain every day. It was that intense. It's weird that the brain remembers some things vividly but forgets others completely. It's probably related to some Darwinian survival of the fittest.

My last 12 months had affected me more than my previous twenty. I knew that something profoundly significant had happened. I just didn't know what the hell it was.

My journey was now like some sort of weird yoga class. A never-ending mind-altering, bike-riding, meditation. I had removed myself from my home, to float in the ether of this surreal experience and take whatever came my way as normality.

I guessed that's why I couldn't bring Jeanette with me: it would have corrupted my experience. The pleasure of the company would have taken away from the pain that I seemingly needed. Like some religious penance, comfort would have taken away from the trials and tribulations that were clearly necessary for me in order to achieve what I wanted. Jesus only did forty days in the wilderness; I had been at it for four hundred days.

Why the Hell am I doing this!

But now something was wrong; I was like the Seltrust Endeavour with no rudder, with the physical challenges and dangers, the mechanics of the bike to fix, the thieves and rogues to avoid, the Rebel Armies to placate. I was going through the motions of learning, but nothing was sinking into my brain. It was like reading a book, but not being able to remember a word.

By getting out of my habits of home, my past association with my family and friends didn't count, so everything is new. When someone meets me on my travels, we do so with no preconceptions, like what religion they are. I found it a huge emotional freedom.

By removing the routine and familiar, everything was sharp. Without the cloud of normality, I should be able to see reality and the truth.

With the old habits gone, my personality and mood could change every morning.

I changed my name from 'Chris' to 'Alex' for a few days, just to see what it felt like!

Every morning, I loaded the bike and started down the road. After a while, I would stop in a café for a breakfast of white rice and a fried egg, with salt and chilli flakes attempting to give it some flavour. I would chat with strangers, try to improve my Spanish, smile at the inquisitive children, and work on the bike. Then, I would search for petrol, look at the sights, and find somewhere stay.

Most days I was quite content working this way; it was only when I stopped somewhere for a few days the questions in my head started. Then the, 'what am I doing' thought reappeared. I travelled freely, with no one to question my motives. Surviving the roads was all so demanding, it left no time for idle thoughts.

Is this what contentment is then? The ability to think of nothing? No wonder dogs look so happy when they are well fed or fucked. Happiness is having a full belly, an empty ball bag, and an IQ of 2.

The more you question, the more you ponder, the unhappier you will be.

Ask any dog.

In Panama, the smart money was on dumping the bike and jumping on a flight Stateside, and back to Miami. It was crunch time. As I approached Panama City, I spotted a Yamaha 1100 with a German sticker on the back. A young German guy called Jorge owned it; he was making his way down from the States to Tierra del Fuego. We chatted over a coffee and agreed to drive into town together and we crossed the Bridge of the Americas and drove into Panama City.

It took ten years and seventy thousand men to build the canal between 1904 and 1914. The huge lock gates raise ocean-going ships eighty-five feet up to the man-made Gatun Lake. The locks are one hundred feet wide, and the ships leave about a foot clearance on each side. They then sail over to the far side where similar locks lower them down to the Atlantic.

The Yanks based the Army there to keep control of it. Its primary purpose was to take American goods from one side of the country to the other. In fact, America treated the whole of Central America like their own colony. Big brother America's CIA controlled the whole of Central America, using money and intimidation. We will pay you if you do what we want, but you might die in a car accident or disappear if you don't.

With Panama's currency linked to the US dollar, it was a centre for every dodgy company in Latin America.

"I got to have a KFC," I said to Jorge, "I've been living on rice and eggs for too long!"

I loved the shiny seats, plastic pictures of chicken legs, and the staff in nylon uniforms. It was just the bit of normality I needed. Well, a room in the Hilton would be better, but KFC was what my pocket could afford. The AC was the best treat, and the two of us nibbled at our chips as the sun scorched the concrete in the car park. Then a couple of gringos on Honda Gold Wings pulled in, the riders checked out our bikes and sat down beside us uninvited.

"Are you guys really from the UK and Germany?" a dude with a crew cut and aviator sunglasses asked.

"Yep, who's asking?"

They were soldiers from the US Army base. We told them about our journeys, and they invited us to stay in the Motorcycle Club in the Canal Zone Army base. Free bed and board in exchange for us giving the bikers at the base a talk about our travels!

"How long have you guys been travelling together?" one of the Yanks asked, as we mounted up.

"Well, about thirty minutes, actually," we laughed.

A few more of their mates arrived on Harley-Davidsons, and with a ten-bike escort, we rode through the gates of the United States' Canal Zone base. The guards saluted us, in and out, for the next week. The base had neat rows of whitewashed barracks, mowed lawns and squads of soldiers marching around chanting silly army songs.

The army had given over one building to their bike club, and we made ourselves at home, our beat-up machines surrounded by the sparkling chrome of the soldier's bikes.

We gave the bikes an oil change and slept on sofas and drank beers in the free bar, all courtesy of Uncle Sam. Two days later, I gave the Army Bike Club the talk about my travels through the Middle East, Africa, North and Central America.

I finished by telling them I was thinking of going back up to North America now.

"Hell, no," a few hecklers shouted up. "Finish the fucking job."

"I'm kind of burnt out from travelling," I said back to the rabble.

"Relax, Irish!"

"Smoke some weed."

"Get laid!"

"Thanks for the helpful suggestions," I said, "I'm open to all advice!"

We all gravitated to the bar after the talk. One senior officer pulled me aside.

"Finish the trip, Chris," he said.

"I've decided to go back," I said, "I'm done in."

"Well, if you don't finish it, you will always regret it."

"South America was never on my wish list; I don't even know why I'm here," I said.

"When you look back in 40 years, you won't regret what you did, only the things you didn't do," he said.

The Yanks on the base treated us like royalty and next night they invited us to a barbecue with a Harley owner, whose garden backed out onto the Canal. We chatted, drank beer and smoked some weed while watching the ocean-going freighters sail past the bottom of the garden.

Another day, we went to Tobago Island on a speedboat and sunbathed. I needed the break. I never got laid, but otherwise, the therapy was working.

In Panama City, the First and Third Worlds survived together, with Indians living in rundown favelas beside the concrete and glass skyscrapers of multinational offices. We rode down to the bay where pirate ships used to shelter.

Driving into the American Canal Zone reminded me of crossing the border into Rhodesia. I left the chaos of the Third World and rode through the painted gates to the pothole-free roads and the North American sense of order.

I rang Deborah at the Israeli Embassy, and she invited me to a reception at the Mira Flores canal lock gates. And the next day, I drank Champagne and watched small trains called Mules dragging the ocean-going ships through the locks.

The celebration was for some Jewish refugees who had fled to Central America after the war. I sat beside an elderly Jewish lady called Joan. She was wearing a sleeveless granny dress, and I spotted the tattooed numbers on her arm. I made her day when I told her I had been to Israel.

"You are a concentration camp survivor?" I asked.

"Yes, I was in Auschwitz," she said.

"My friend in Israel's mother was at Auschwitz; she had the same tattoo."

She looked at me like she had seen a ghost, "What was her name?" she demanded.

"I… well, I can't remember; it was a year ago," I said. "But I have Alex's number, I will give it to you."

Her eyes filled with tears of joy. "I would love to talk to her. When they liberated the camp, it was chaos and everyone just disappeared in different directions."

Deborah, the woman I wanted to bear my children, was walking past and looked disgusted that I had made this old lady cry, but Joan explained the situation. I promised to forward the number the next day, which would give me another reason to talk to Deborah.

After the reception at the docks, they whisked us away to a party at the Hilton Hotel pool. There was a jazz band, and the pool was full of beautiful girls in bikinis. Men in black suits walked around keeping a watchful eye, and the Israeli Ambassador was going around shaking hands.

"Do you think I should tell him what a fuck-up they are making of Palestine?" I said to David.

"Only if you want thrown out of the party," he laughed. David and I had argued about Israeli politics and the Palestinian situation, but he agreed that it was a time bomb waiting to explode.

"You're the guy who toured Israel on a motorcycle," the Ambassador said.

"Yes, it was fascinating," I replied, grabbing another smoked salmon canapé.

"We have an old saying in Ireland," I said to David.

"What's that?"

"You don't bite the hand that pours your Champagne!" I had been living the life of a travelling monk, so the culture shock of sitting drinking Champagne with girls in bikinis was extreme! This culture shock fuddled my brain. One minute, I was eating plain rice and fried eggs, poor as a Mexican maggot, the next and it was the Hilton for Champagne. But after a week in Panama, I had relaxed, and my mental and physical well-being improved enough for me to decide to go on to South America.

The bike was serviced, and my head was slightly sorted. I would finish the job. My main worry was money and how to stretch it out to Brazil.

I decided to go to the Mardi Gras; Jorge suggested I borrow money from my parents but I knew they would just tell me to come home. Besides, I was too proud to ask. I would rather starve.

We started looking at the next stage of our journey, and how to drive to Colombia. The Pan-American Highway stopped just out of town, at the Darien Gap.

I contemplated driving, but found that a British expedition with two Range Rovers, thirty packhorses and lots of the Queen's soldiers, took five months to cover the 250 miles. I thought the better of it!

We looked for a boat to Colombia and then discovered that the local airline could fly the bikes the next day. We packed up and drove to the airport.

"Sorry Señor, the plane was full. Wait until next week,"

the girl in the office said.

"Shit," I said to Jorge, "we can't stay at the base for another week!"

"Have you tried the private airport?" she said, pointing south.

We followed the road as it petered out to a dirt track then through the gates of the old airport. It was like going back fifty years, with old corrugated-iron hangars and run-down buildings and DC3 Dakotas, sat with their noses pointed haughtily into the sky.

We couldn't find an office, just a grubby bar with a few aviator types lounging about.

"Anyone heading south? Colombia?" we asked, as if hitching a lift in a roadside café.

"A plane goes tomorrow," the barman said. "The pilot will be here soon."

We waited as the pilots arrived at the bar; it was like a scene out of the Battle of Britain. Drinking alcohol and flying didn't worry these guys.

When our man came in, the barman introduced us.

"Can you fly us to Colombia with our motorcycles?" I asked.

We chatted, and it turned out he had a Norton Commando in Colombia.

"Sure, I'll fly you to Medellin tomorrow morning," he said.

Captain Maximo was rough and unshaven, wore a wrinkled white shirt and looked more like a dodgy car dealer than a commercial pilot. But he wore a pilot's cap, which was good enough for me.

"Fifty dollars," he said. "Cash."

Another pilot came in and Maximo ordered a beer, then another; they were getting stuck in! Jorge tapped me on the shoulder and whispered;

"Do you think we should get our pilot pissed?"

"Probably not," I said, "but what the hell!"

Unknown to us, we had walked into Pablo Escobar's hub for the planes ferrying cocaine to the USA from Colombia. General Noriega was the President of Panama and allowed the cocaine in, then laundered the money back through his banks.

At first light, we pushed the bikes over to a battered old plane with four massive propellers sitting on the apron. The DC6 would have been scrapped if it was a car, as under each radial engine sat a bucket to catch the stream of oil. Jorge looked at me and shrugged.

"Must be Yamaha engines!" I said.

"At least there's four of them," he laughed, nervously, as they fork-lifted the bikes up through the hatch. They had no passenger stairs, just a metal ladder to the cockpit.

Captain Maximo swore at the engines as one by one they started with clouds of smoke and the roar of a thousand Harley-Davidsons.

The plane had only three seats in the cramped cockpit, two for the pilots and one for the flight engineer who sat looking at a panel of dials and switches that he used to control the engines. Maximo pulled down a folding seat for Jorge, and I stood behind the pilots.

"Give Chris your seat," Captain Maximo shouted to the engineer. "You do bugger all anyway."

The engineer shouted back, "Who keeps these bloody engines running?"

"It's okay, I'll stand," I said as I panicked at the sight of all the switches, red lights and dials with swinging needles.

I had only had one oil light on the bike, and I'd disconnected it!

I stood behind the pilot and held on to the seat as the crescendo of noise grew, and we taxied down the dirt runway carved into the jungle. At the far end, the plane swung around and Maximo shoved the throttle levers forward before the roar of the four engines reached a climax. I expected blood to come out of my ears, as we started our take-off roll, gathering speed as it bounced down the runway. I held on as the nose lifted and we took off over a boneyard of crashed old aeroplanes at the end of the strip.

"We won't join them today!" laughed the pilot.

I arrived in North America, on a shiny Jumbo Jet, with movies, meals and beers. Now I left for South America holding on to the back of the pilot's seat on this flying bucket of bolts. We climbed up above the forests and rivers of the Darien Gap. The jungle looked forbidding. We shout-chatted with the captain over the engine noise.

"Don't hang around in Colombia," he bellowed, as he adjusted the controls. "There's a turf war going on, and you don't want to be in the wrong place."

"What do you mean?" I yelled.

He put his index finger to the side of his head and mouthed a pretend "bang" with a smile. I got the message.

CHAPTER 16

Colombia & Ecuador

THE PLANE BOUNCED DOWN THE MEDELLIN RUNWAY LIKE A MILLION RIVets in a metal bucket. As they unloaded the bikes, I waited under the wing and boiling oil dripped on my scalp and sizzled onto the damp concrete. The mechanics climbed ladders to tighten the nuts and bolts, which were about to fall off.

Three-quarters of all the USA's cocaine came through this airport in 1980. The drug barons made 60 million dollars a day, so our extra fifty bucks probably wouldn't have made much difference. Captain Maximo shouted to the ground crew as they prepared to refuel the plane.

"Fill my friends' bikes first," he said.

We topped-up with 100 octane aviation gasoline, courtesy of Pablo Escobar. The Guzzi purred in appreciation.

The airfield had a wartime-like atmosphere; everyone seemed to have a gun, and we got the distinct notion that we shouldn't linger. They stamped our passports.

"No photographs," was all they said.

"Where is the exit?" I asked.

"No photographs!" "Okay, okay!"

In 1980, Colombia was the most dangerous country in the world. With drug cartels, communist guerrillas and corrupt politicians fighting for power, it created a perfect storm for the breakdown in law and order. The rebels had been at war since the 1960s, and their favourite pastime was kidnapping Westerners!

The drug barons and the two of us were the only people in Colombia with large motorcycles, and everyone eyed us suspiciously when we drove by. Every street corner had a checkpoint, with serious, no shit soldiers. They made the Nicaraguan army look like a bunch of school kids with guns, which was, of course, exactly what they were.

We got lost in the winding streets immediately. One minute we passed exclusive villas with armed guards; next, we rode through shantytowns. The police stopped and searched us, then let us go when they found nothing; we were the only people in town who weren't carrying a kilo of cocaine in our bags. Not for the first time, I got the impression I was intruding on someone's war. We had planned to stay in Medellin for a few days, but we could sense the danger in the air and decided to get the hell out of Dodge as fast as possible.

The road climbed high into the green hills surrounding Medellin. I rode up to a large villa, thinking it was a hotel. But it was a private mansion and the armed guards told us to get lost, just as an armour-plated limo pulled up, and the occupant asked us what we wanted.

"I asked if we could camp in the gardens," I said.

"Where are you from?"

"Ireland and Germany."

"You are most welcome, but you must camp between the security fences," he said.

"Thank you!"

"You will join us for dinner at seven," he said, as he drove past.

"That sounded like an order," I said to Jorge.

The house had two lines of barbed wire fencing surrounding it, and a tall outer fence that the gate was on.

Fifty metres back was another fence, so if someone got through the first fence, it would trap them between the two. Heavy security for a house, I thought. The owncr didn't mind having us for dinner but he didn't trust us in his inner sanctum for the night.

"We will be trapped, right in no-man's-land, if someone attacks," I said, as we put up our tents.

"Better than being with the wild animals outside," Jorge said with Germanic logic.

We walked up the sweeping drive to the red-tiled hacienda and the butler showed us to the infinity pool where we watched the sunset over a beer. We couldn't believe our luck.

"What does he do for a living? Drugs?" I whispered to Jorge.

"Just don't ask, whatever you do," he hissed.

"As if I would be so bold," I said.

Alphonso welcomed us like old friends. The house had marble floors and a huge curved staircase, with old statues and original oil paintings on the walls.

"I collect Colombian art," he said. I sat down on a velvet sofa while the butler handed me another cold beer.

Alphonso spoke English with an American accent, then his wife, Ella, appeared in a slinky evening dress. Their two small children wouldn't leave us alone, excited to have strangers to talk to.

"We don't get many foreigners in Colombia," Ella said, rather stating the obvious.

"Colombia is not safe; you should be very careful," Alphonso continued, "Do not trust anyone, not the police or soldiers. They are all corrupt."

I couldn't resist it; "So what business are you in?" I asked. "Pharmaceuticals," he said.

Jorge nearly choked.

He explained that the different drug factions fought for market share, but there was also another group in the fray; the communists fighting for their ideals. They wined and dined us, and asked about our travels, then at about ten o'clock, Alphonso got up, and made it clear we should go back to our tents.

"I have to check the guards; they will see you to the gate. Good luck on your journey," he said, shaking our hands warmly. "But get out of Colombia quickly!"

I have always wondered who Alphonso was, and if he survived to see his kids grow up.

The road meandered through fertile hills, spectacular valleys and pretty Spanish colonial villages, but with armed checkpoints everywhere. We camped in a half-finished house near the border. It had no windows or a roof, only four walls, but it seemed safe as we hid the bikes out of sight. We lit a small fire in the living room; it was a cool evening, and so I slept in my sleeping bag without the tent.

I woke, hearing a noise at the front of the house. I froze, not wanting to breathe… there it was again. Someone was moving but trying to be quiet. I couldn't decide whether I should get up and risk making a noise, or lie still. If I woke Jorge, he might get up with a start, but I mustered enough courage to get up. In the half-light, I made my way to the front and peeked outside, expecting to see a band of drug dealers… There was no one there. Then I looked down. Two tough but unarmed chickens pecked at the ground, oblivious to the terror they had caused me. I wanted to stab them! I tried to go back to my sleeping bag but stayed awake the rest of the night. The next morning, I yawned, exhausted.

"What is your problem?" asked Jorge

"A gang of chickens attacked last night," I said and explained.

"Drug-dealing chickens?" He laughed and started clucking and waving his arms about like a demented hen, trying to peck me.

"Oh, pluck off, will you?" I shoved him away. But I never slept well camping out in South America, as I never knew how safe the location was.

The road was climbing high above the clouds, and the mist condensed on my visor. The air was cool and fresh after the tropics below. Then the road would descend again to the valley floor and the blazing heat. To the less neurotic traveller, we rode the most glorious roads in the world, but to a paranoid biker wanting out, it was slow going. It was a huge relief to cross into Ecuador.

Jorge's calm personality restored my faith in Germans. He was a perfect travelling companion. But he had some very Germanic features, like his orderliness. He split all his bags and panniers into sections with foam cavity dividers to hold the tools and parts. He had a hatchet he had never used in its own compartment. Every day when we packed, I would wind him up by asking,

"Did you use the hatchet last night, Jorge?"

"No, I did not," he would reply, not fully grasping the intricacies of Irish sarcasm.

"But someday you will need my hatchet, and you will pay me a lot of money for it!"

The road to Quito rose ever higher through the mountains and we struggled for breath at the altitude. On the plateaus, we would find people wearing the traditional woven and brightly coloured ponchos and floppy black hats. The women busied themselves with their tasks with a baby hung in a sling at their breast. With sparse fields of grass for sheep and goats to graze and the hamlets with small stone and thatch cottages, it could have been Ireland 100 years ago, but without the ponchos. Most peasants would run away from my camera, but some brave souls would stand and smile a toothy grin.

In the middle of the high Sierra was a NASA Space Centre, complete with gigantic satellite receivers, completely out of place in a Third-World country.

"Let's see what's going on," I said and rode up to the gates. They invited us in for lunch, the American scientists delighted to show us the complex. Ed, the boss, explained that the mountains in Ecuador rose higher than Mt Everest, which was news to me.

"The earth is not actually round but is more like a squashed orange which bulges in the middle. This makes the mountains in Ecuador further from the centre of the earth than the Himalayas."

Ed clearly loved telling this story.

"So, while Mount Everest is higher relative to the sea level, Ecuador is as close to outer space as you can get, so perfect for communications with spaceships and satellites."

After a space-age lunch and geography re-education, we rode out the gates, past a donkey and cart. As we camped that night, we laughed at the clash of the worlds of modern science and ancient agriculture.

"Ed will have a drink in the local bar tonight and will discuss the diaphragm on the second stage of his rocket booster for his Moon shuttle."

"And Manuel will say he's worried about the loose spoke on his cartwheel." Jorge laughed.

South America batters your senses by letting you think you know where you are, then hits you with completely conflicting experiences.

The capital, Quito, lies perched 9000 feet above sea level. Stunning Spanish colonial squares sit alongside a hodgepodge of ugly concrete developments, obviously designed by drug- crazed town planners. I spotted a couple of cops sitting on Moto Guzzi Eldorados; I rode alongside one and waved. He did a double-take and pulled me over.

He said, "I'm taking you to the Headquarters."

"You're arresting me?"

"No! I want to show you off to the Chief!"

He switched on the siren and we weaved through the traffic. Jorge followed well behind on his lowly Yamaha. The whole police station came out to see us. The Captain was all smiles; he was a short man with a big moustache, as all the coppers were—short with big moustaches. He told us that the police had ridden Moto Guzzi for years and loved them. They hoped to upgrade to newer models soon.

"We will get Moto Guzzi Californias, the same as the LAPD," he said.

The police workshop was an Aladdin's cave of Moto Guzzi parts. It must have had fifty Eldorados sitting in various stages of repair, and shelves of spare engines and parts.

"Service the Le Mans; give Chris whatever he needs," the Chief ordered the mechanic.

"Sorry, we don't do Yamahas," he said to Jorge.

"I feel like a criminal," Jorge whispered.

They replaced my front wheel bearings and changed the oil, filled our tanks and then invited us to lunch.

"We will escort you out of town," the Chief then insisted, so with sirens blazing and ten Moto Guzzi police outriders, I felt like a Head of State as we blasted through the city streets.

This was not our customary police experience but things went rapidly downhill. As we got closer to Peru, we stopped at more checkpoints. I was tiring of this soldiers-with-guns nonsense and was dangerously blasé about AK-47s being pointed at me by cocky teenagers.

They would try to intimidate us and shout for papers, before searching the luggage. If they thought you looked scared, they would demand bribes. I tried to appear 'self- assured' rather than 'arrogant.' But most importantly, I would emphasize that I wasn't American.

The map of the world I had painted on my screen helped explain where I was going, and sponsors stickers over the bike made me seem like a Formula One car. Unfortunately, actual sponsors didn't exist, and the only thing I got free was the stickers. I found the child soldiers more intimidating than any wrinkly old Sergeant. Young kids would be more unpredictable.

"Americano?"

"Ireland, No Yankee!" I said, smiling like an imbecile. Many of them couldn't read. One time, a soldier was looking at my passport upside down, so I turned it the right way up, then his mates started laughing. I cringed and realised I had made him appear silly, and he started shouting at me. But, grudgingly, he saw the joke but gave me dirty looks from the corner of his eye. I drove on around the next bend and stopped to catch my breath, my heart rate racing.

But generally, the young soldiers would point at the bike,

"Como es de grande?"

"Ocho Cincuenta, Moto Guzzi, Italiano," I would reply. "Bueno, bueno!"

I would give the engine a handful of throttle, blipping the engine, and they would cheer in appreciation. Kids always want a bike engine to rev up, for some reason.

It was always good to have Jorge there with his easy smile and laid-back style to help calm the situation.

At one checkpoint, a cop demanded money to paint his house. Further down the road, another tried to sell me ballot tickets for the Police Christmas raffle.

"I wouldn't be here at Christmas," I said.

"Buy one anyway," he said, smiling.

It was a… 'Buy a ticket, or I will cut your balls off and feed them to the pigs,' smile.

The porkers in the farmyard across the road appeared hungry. I bought two tickets. At another checkpoint, the cop found my sheath knife in the bottom of my pannier,

"Keep it in your jacket pocket, as you will need it," he said with one of those fake smiles. I wasn't sure if it was advice or a threat.

A few wanted their picture taken beside the bike. I promised to send it on. But it was stressful trying to be friends with them always with the sinister threat of their guns. The guy facing you is poor and uneducated, envious of your wealth. And when you stand at the pointy end of an AK-47, you are at a major disadvantage.

At a roadside cafe near Guayaquil, we were drinking a coffee when a fat bloke, with another of those big Mexican bandit mustachios, sat down at our table.

"You mind if I join you?" he asked.

Jorge and I shrugged. It obviously wasn't a question.

"Are you going far?" he asked.

Jorge said Chile at the same time I said Brazil, which sounded like we made it up. We both laughed, but he stared back blankly.

"South," we said to clarify, but it sounded more like a cover-up.

Our new friend considered our reply as if it was of grave importance, leant back on his chair, and winced. He put his hand round behind his back and pulled out a huge black revolver, which he put down on the table. We stopped smiling and glanced across at each other, but he continued chatting as if he had put a packet of cigarettes on the table. After a few minutes, he stuck it back in his belt.

"Adios amigos," he said. "Take care, this is a dangerous country."

"What was all that about?" I said to Jorge when he left.

"No idea, but let's get away to fuck!"

Jorge spoke English with an excellent schoolboy accent. I had taught him all the swear words in a Belfast accent, but this time he wasn't sounding funny at all. We jumped on the bikes and drove off as if leaving a bank robbery.

"He was a cop, and was checking our stories out," Jorge mused as we camped that night.

"But was the big gun being macho or a warning?"

"I was going to put my cock out on the table," I laughed, "You think that's big? Look at this; you show me yours, and I'll show you mine."

Our bravado and laughter weren't merely childish humour; it helped dissipate our fear.

I was down to a couple of hundred dollars, but I had my Visa credit card with £500 of credit. I walked into a bank and handed them the card and asked them for fifty dollars. After checking my signature, they phoned the card number to get an authorization code. The teller came back looking serious.

"Sorry, we cannot give you cash, and we will keep your card," she said.

"What do you mean?"

"Visa have blocked the card and we must keep it."

"That is my card, and I'm not leaving without it," I said through gritted teeth.

"No, we will not return the card."

I refused to leave without it, so the teller went back to the manager's office. Then, after about twenty minutes she came back and handed me the card cut in half.

"Sorry, Visa's instructions," she offered politely.

I went ballistic!

"You bastards cut my card," I shouted. Security was called, and they threw me out of the bank.

"Fuck you," I shouted at the door. But it was me that was fucked. I would have to survive on rice to drive to Rio now.

I later found the problem; my credit card statements had gone to my dad, with the £50 debit that I had spent on petrol in Canada when I had lost my traveller's cheques. He gave it to his secretary to sort it out, but she ignored paying off the £50, thinking there was £450 credit still available. And when she didn't send the minimum payment, Visa blocked the card and instructed the bank to cut it up.

This would be a tight trip with the card, but I could starve without it, and with over half my money needed just to buy petrol.

We rode through three climate systems in one day riding from Ecuador to Peru. We drove from the freezing high- altitude mountain roads down to warm, wet, equatorial forests. We then entered the Atacama Desert, one of the driest places on earth; even drier than the Sahara.

At the side of the road, a guy was working on a motorbike with an Austrian sticker, so I pulled over; Louis, a short, stocky Austrian with a huge bushy beard, was on a Yamaha 500XT Enduro and had been having overheating problems. Louis had been teaching in Lima and wanted to see the country before returning to Europe. He asked to ride with us as he was freaking out with all the police aggravation.

Louis was short, and the Yamaha 500 was a tall bike, so he had to do this little jump to get on before he moved off. I giggled to myself every time. By the time we got to the Peruvian border, it was late, so we rode off the main road to set up camp.

Louis produced a bag of magic mushrooms and made some disgusting soup.

"Anybody feel anything but sick?" I asked as I sipped it.

"They are yuck!" Jorge agreed. "I feel nothing, not even my feet."

When nothing much happened, we finished them. We were sitting around the fire when I heard a sound in the trees.

"There's someone in the bushes," I whispered to the others.

"I can't hear anything," said Jorge. "The mushrooms are making you paranoid."

Then, I heard the unmistakable sound of a rifle being cocked. Shit!

"Alto, Alto!" came a shout; I turned around slowly but could see nothing but trees. We sat, very much "Halted," and not going anywhere already, so we sat and wondered what to do. Suddenly, a dozen soldiers surrounded us, armed to the teeth, shouting and squealing like castrated pigs. They pointed their guns at us in that universal 'put your hands up' sort of way.

We raised our hands, as half of the soldiers were pointing sit down, and the other half were pointing stand up, very much spoiling my mushroom trip. I wanted to say, "Cool it guys," but my tongue had become disconnected from my brain and was floating in mid-air. Thankfully, an officer appeared.

"Why are you camping here? This is a high-security area," he said in perfect English.

Right enough, we could see a high-security electric fence through the trees with a lookout tower.

"Oops!" Jorge said, giggling. The mushrooms had kicked in.

Then I noticed the soldiers surrounded the officer and the three of us, with their guns pointing in like the spokes of a wheel. If one of them fired a shot, they would all open up, killing everyone.

"There's going to be a massacre!" I said casually and nodded to the troops, their guns at the ready. I was quite unconcerned as I thought the bullets would just go through me. The officer barked an order at the soldiers, and they put down their guns, obviously disappointed that they would not shoot us today.

"You must move. This border area is sensitive. We thought you must be Peruvian saboteurs." He said, "Peru and Ecuador have been at war over this land for many years."

We packed up as hastily as half-stoned brains would let us.

"Go back at least five kilometres before you camp," he ordered.

The ride back from the border was totally surreal; at one stage I thought I was going too fast, it seemed like about 100 mph. I checked my speedo and saw I was doing about 20 mph. The magic mushrooms had hit, and I was flying! We found a place to camp and set up our tents again and then lit a fire in silence.

"What was that about?!" I said and we all fell down with the giggles.

The next morning as we packed up, Louis looked worried.

"What's up, mate?" I asked.

"Shit man, I had a terrible trip last night. I dreamt that soldiers were going to shoot us. I'm never doing mushrooms again!"

Peru and Ecuador had been having a border row that started back in the Spanish times. We had camped in the middle of disputed land that both sides claimed. Tension had been building, and less than a month later war broke out, with the Peruvian air force bombing the area we camped in.

CHAPTER 17

Peru & Bolivia

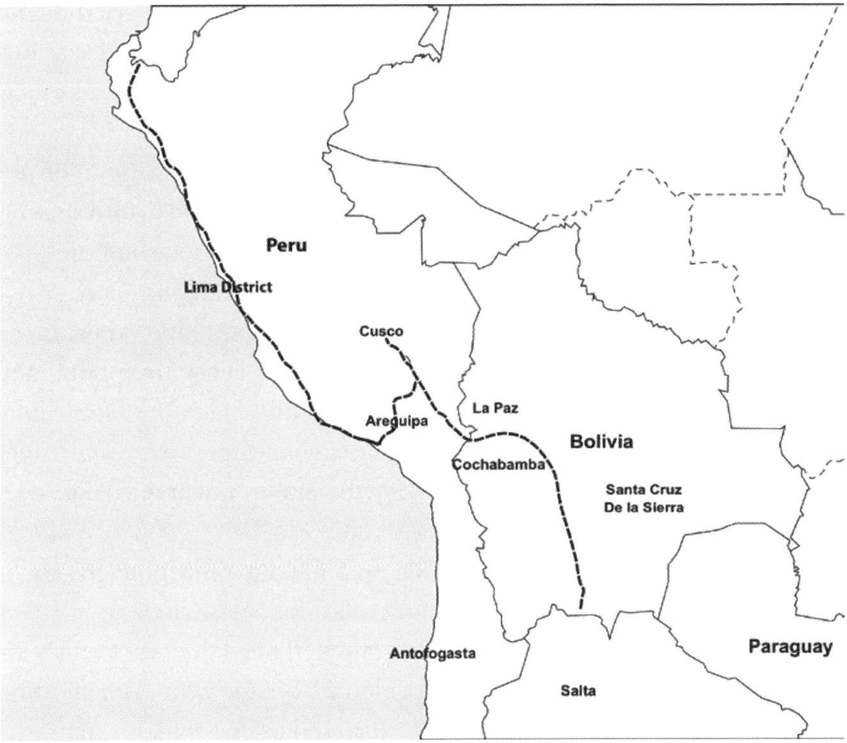

WE CROSSED THE BORDER THE NEXT DAY AND CONTINUED DOWN TO THE Pacific coast. The road meandered through banana plantations, which if I hadn't seen in Africa might have been interesting. In fact, so many of the sights and experiences I was having now reminded of ones I'd had on my journey. I'd had sub-machine guns stuck in my belly in Syria, so it was now in Ecuador. I'd ridden over deserts, and now in Peru, there was another bloody desert. At least with a road this time. Come on God, give me something new to see. I shouted at the wind as it blew the sand in my face!

But be careful what you ask for, as God might oblige, I thought later.

I had taken on a passive, aggressive form of driving. I no longer used my indicators, because they had broken off long ago, but I found pointing much more effective. At a junction, if a car was coming, I pointed at them. People associate pointing with the police and they looked at me while I waved my arms to show if I was going left or right. It seemed to work, and they stayed out of my way.

The Guzzi had hated the 9,000ft elevation of Colombia and Ecuador and was running better now, down at the coast. But I was mindful of the real test to come; I had to cross the Andes at 14,000 feet before driving down to Argentina. Moto Guzzi set the big Del Orto carburettors for 2000 feet altitude. The oxygen level at 10,000 feet is one third less.

The bike was half knackered, the throttle cables jamming, wheel bearings worn out, bald tyres, and the engine pinged with lousy petrol. My front suspension had packed in again; luckily, I had kept my Donaldson patented suspension system: two metres of nylon rope with a bent steel bar. It was running on fuel with the same octane as warm bat's piss, and it sounded like a demented donkey with hick-ups. Peruvian petrol was so crap I thought if I threw a bucket of it on a fire, the fire would go out.

Jorge and I were on a low-octane diet too. Breakfast consisted of two cups of tea at a truck stop. I drank one cup and filled the other cup with porridge oats from my bag and five teaspoons of sugar from the cafe. The idea was the uncooked porridge slowly digested in my stomach all morning while the sugar gave some energy. Lunch could be another truck stop with a bowl of white rice with a fried egg on top. Dinner would be rice with a scrawny chicken leg if I was feeling flush.

We camped by the road or stayed in the roadside truckers' hostels. They had bare concrete walls with a single dim light bulb and four or five single bedsteads in each room. I always insisted on a hostel that I could drive the bike into the bedroom, so nobody tried to steal it. My roommates didn't seem to mind.

In the West, we think people's surroundings corrupt and damage them, so if they live in an inner-city slum, the ugly environment leads them to crime. I wondered how can South America be so incredibly beautiful and yet be so awash with terror? Colombia and Guatemala are two of the most scenic places I have ever seen, with a society that is deeply religious, but in both, states-sponsored murder was rife. The land is abundant, you can put a stick in the ground, and the next day there will be a fruit tree. But there was rampant poverty, with corrupt politicians and priests who stood idly by.

One thing that tells you that you are in third world towns is the smells. The wood smoke, diesel fumes, the stench of garbage and open sewers, and the street food, all mingle to excite the senses in a way that big western cities don't.

I drove through small towns with streets of single-storey shacks, and in the middle, a splendid cathedral looked down from a great height. It's not only a place of worship, but a potent symbol to keep the people fearful of the all-powerful organization. They drive any rebellion out of the people by the realization that their beast is too big to fight.

We passed through the Atacama Desert, and the road ran between the ocean and the desert. This was not the romantic desert of the Arabian Nights, nor the Californian Big Sur. It was dusty and windswept, with the occasional shack at the side of the road. The Pacific Ocean looked devoid of any redeeming features meeting the sand with a monotonous line of rollers on a long drab beach. We camped on the beach and swam in the ocean to wash the grime off our bodies.

We passed fishing villages and small boats, and poor locals who didn't have a rowing boat stood on the beaches, throwing their fishing nets into the waves.

The towns had stinking fish processing plants that paid no heed to pollution controls. A foul-smelling red haze hung in the air over them. No tourists surfed these waves. Occasionally a river crossed our path, its waters supporting a narrow ribbon of green fields in stark contrast with the desert.

We bumped into ex-pats working as teachers, engineers, and archaeologists, and they would be glad of our company. We updated them with news of the world and stories from our trip.

This was pre-internet and in areas with no TV and poor phone lines, and it could be weeks before another westerner passed by, so they appreciated our travellers' tales. As it had been with the wandering storytellers in the middle ages. All we wanted was some food, a bed and, with any luck, a few beers.

The next stop in Peru was the ruins of Chan Chan, an adobe (mud) city, dating back 1500 years. Once home to up to 60,000 people, who abandoned it when the Spanish arrived… the locals had forgotten the city for hundreds of years. Chan Chan was now a heap of earthen mounds and tracks.

Michael was the archaeologist in charge, and happy to see us, as he only travelled to the nearest small town once a week. He had been excavating the ruins and trying to prevent farmers from ploughing up the rest.

After a barbecue and a few beers, Jorge and I raced each other, motocross-style, through the deserted city streets. Going too fast around a bend, I slid into a 1500-year-old irrigation ditch that some ancient government department had dug across the road.

"I'll sue!" I said to Jorge, laughing while I lifted the bike out of the ditch. Luckily the bike survived with a few scrapes. It was a release from the monotony of the desert roads, but not very sensible. Chan Chan is now a UNESCO World Heritage Site, so motocross racing is no longer allowed.

We visited the mysterious pyramids at Caral, which were about the same age as the Egyptian ones. They built the pyramids here with mud bricks rather than stone, and it now resembled a small brown hill, because of centuries of erosion. Not very impressive for cultural philistines like ourselves.

At the tourist centre, we chatted up a couple of cute French backpackers in the coffee shop. They said they would give us some magic mushrooms if we gave them a lift back to Lima. We had been devoid of female company for some time, so quickly agreed.

I balanced Juliet's rucksack and my tent on top of the top box and held it down with bungee cords.

"Is this safe?" Juliet asked.

I said, "I'm an expert, I'm riding around the world you know?"

"Mon Dieu!" she said!

My 'Man-of-the-World' image disintegrated when a few miles later the rucksack slipped and swung back onto my rear tyre, still hanging by the bungee cords. The tyre ripped through the bag, spinning Juliet's underwear through the air, onto the lap of an astounded Jorge following behind. By the time I stopped, I had covered a section of the Pan American Highway in French lingerie.

"I am so sorry," I said as I extricated a lacy bra from my swinging arm. "How can I make it up?"

"Leave me at the bus station!"

Jorge thought it hilarious as he swept the road for bras and knickers before the cattle trucks flattened them. But was pissed off when his passenger left him too.

"You owe me, Irish!"

"Why does she have so many knickers anyway? Two pairs do me fine!" I said.

"As long as you turn them inside out every week."

"And back to front every other week!"

That evening, we camped in the sand dunes behind a small town. I lit a fire, boiled our rice and baked beans, then ate the mushrooms for 'afters'. We wandered into the village for a beer. It was like the cowboy movies, with dirt streets and boardwalks, and everyone tied their horse or donkey up on a pole.

I saw pineapples growing on the telegraph poles, but when someone rode past on a zebra, I realised the mushrooms had kicked in. We found a bar full of farmers drinking home brew beer and sat down while some dwarfs, with huge heads and grotesque features, served us drinks. Everything was totally surreal; they had painted the walls and furniture bright reds and pinks. A man came in with a small goat and tied it to the bar.

"What breed of dog is that?" Jorge asked in hysterics.

"It's the local leisure centre," I said.

One dwarf put his fingers on his crotch and sniffed them and asked if we would like a sniff too. Another couple danced romantically until the woman punched her partner in the nose, knocking him out. We fell about the floor in stitches.

I staggered out the back to find the toilet, to find that customers literally pissed and shit in the muddy yard. In my crazed mind, I sank up to my waist in shit, wading through it, swimming in it. I struggled back and told the dwarf behind the bar to do something with the toilet.

"It's dangerous, I nearly drowned," I said.

The beer tasted of bananas; it was horrible, but we persevered and impressed the locals by singing Irish and German drinking songs. They looked at us as if we were the weird ones. Jorge told me over and over about watching the underwear fly into the air. If it was possible to die laughing, we would have done that night, but somehow, we made it back to the tents to watch the sun come up.

I was enjoying the journey now, even with the financial worry, but I was physically falling apart and had aches and pains after a hard day's drive. Jorge had a wide, 'kidney belt' that he put on every day. My kidneys took hours to settle back into position after a bumpy ride.

On Christmas Eve, we stopped at a small town that was celebrating in Christian/Indian style. We shook hands with everybody, wishing them Happy Christmas, and drank some sort hallucinogenic tequila. They had dressed everyone in the village in bright clothes with bowler hats, their faces painted different colours. Even the horses and donkeys wore long dresses, which should have indicated some potential issues!

They were having a grand old time marching up and down the dusty street banging drums and blowing trumpets. A drunk passed by with a doll sitting on the lacy saddle of a llama. Another guy came up wearing a black face mask and holding a child's negro doll which he was trying to feed with a baby bottle. His friend had an ornate dagger that he was waving at the doll.

Jorge pulled me over.

"These guys are crazy!" he said. "I think we should go."

I nodded, and we casually made our way back to the bikes, still smiling and shaking hands with those we passed.

The next thing, a drunk tried to grab something off the back of Jorge's bike and Jorge told him to clear off. The atmosphere changed, and the crowd turned aggressive, pushing and shouting, as we fought our way to the bikes. It would only take one guy to throw a punch and they would all get stuck in. We jumped on the bikes and sped off under a hail of bottles. No damage, but Jorge had his camera ripped off his neck strap.

On New Year's Day, the complete opposite happened, and in another small Peruvian town, they invited us to the Mayor's house. We hesitated, after what had happened last week, but ended up dancing and drinking to the early hours as honoured guests of the village. Every villager came in, to shake our hand. I joined in the peculiar dance, where everyone held his handkerchief in the air like it was a treasured document! But we were always on guard to make sure the bike, passports, and money concealed from prying eyes.

As I drove south, the people appeared more miserable. The Mexicans looked like a happy bunch, while the Guatemalans appeared dejected. In Peru, the peasants were completely wretched. The Indians had been trampled on since the hero or villain Christopher Columbus. Whichever way you looked at him.

A few days later we reached Lima, and I called Miriam, an Irish journalist contact. She put us up in her villa on the outskirts of town.

That night, I dreamt of the South American cities being islands in a sea full of crocodiles I had to swim across. I dragged myself out on to land to rest before plunging in again, hoping I reached the safety of the next island without being eaten.

Miriam worked for the Lima Times and interviewed me about my travels. I took her for a spin through the heart of the old town, past the cathedral and magnificent colonial buildings. Lima was a very prosperous city at one time. She took us down to the beach at Mira Flores for lunch, where I met a bunch of Irish ex-pat engineers. Patricia, Mike and Sean were working on an irrigation project in the mountains to the south, and we promised to call past on our journey over the Andes.

Now further away from home than ever, I appreciated the hospitality from these 'friends of friends'. I would never have made it past Kenya without this network.

The Guzzi was my anchor; I could take the gearbox out in a matter of hours now and dismantle the front suspension in even less. The engine was unbreakable; it took all the punishment the world could give. I imagined I was like a car in the Wacky Races cartoons with bits broken, the frame, seat, handlebars all fallen by the roadside. But the engine somehow keeping the bike rolling along. It was merely a machine, but it was where I was at home, and being on it gave me calmness and security.

The lumps of metal came to life with petrol and a spark. But we morphed into one when I started up the engine and moved off. When I was in a good mood, the bike rode well, when I felt sick the bike ran rough. It became an extension of myself, mentally and physically.

I had travelled over the mountain backbone of America. I had driven through the redwood forests in California, up the Rocky Mountains of British Columbia. Then travelled over the Mexican mountains and past volcanoes in Guatemala and Nicaragua.

Now for the grand finale, I would ride across the Andes. We made our goodbyes to Miriam and left Lima refreshed and prepared for the greatest mountain range in the world. First, we followed the coast further south and stopped at the Nazca Lines, six-inch deep marks in the gravel that ran for miles across the desert. The lines depict shapes of figures and birds, and some resemble runways.

It was a mystery who constructed them, why, or when. Someone's God, or perhaps aliens, could see them from space?

Then we hung a left, swung inland, and the Andes rose before us. My final natural obstacle to cross, and I saved the biggest to last. I looked at the map I had places like Cuzco, Machu Picchu, Lake Titicaca, and finally Rio de Janeiro ahead. My next stop was Arequipa, a fabulous old colonial town that was full of fly-in tourists. We could find a hotel for $1.50 a night bed and breakfast shared between us, and we pushed the bikes into the room.

My guidebook title claimed 'South America for $15 a day.' I had calculated that I had $2 a day after petrol if I would reach Rio. The book black-listed hostels that were too nasty, but there's where I checked in. Jorge was not much better off and so we walked the cobbled streets soaking up the atmosphere of the colourful colonial town for free. In the hostels, other down-and-out travellers shared their stories over boiled rice and beer. No one was travelling by vehicle or had much useful advice for us.

We left Arequipa and climbed up the mountain roads to Chivay, 11,000 feet above sea level. We camped in a windswept field, and in the morning both bikes refused to start, the petrol in the carburettors would not evaporate in the cold, thin air. From then on, we always pitched our tents at the top of a hill, so we push-started the bikes the next morning. They needed to freewheel up to a good 20 mph to get the engine firing.

People get altitude sickness above 6,000 feet, so this would be an extreme test for man and machine as we struggled to push start the bikes. The big Guzzi carbs sucked at the thin atmosphere like an old man gasping for breath, and I removed the air filters to help, thinking that large flies and small rodents might help the combustion process.

The mud and gravel tracks led to more Wild West towns with small wooden buildings, tethering rails for the horses and wooden boardwalks.

We were well off the main route and hand-pumped petrol from a barrel outside the grocery shops.

When the clouds rise over the Andes, they don't form rain until they are on the other side of the mountains, where the deluge created the Amazon River basin system. The Irish Engineers were blasting a huge tunnel through the mountains that took the waters back to the west to irrigate the desert sands below. The guys loved the challenge, as in Dublin they would have been building chimneys on a housing estate.

As I travelled, I got the chance to watch people living their lives. I might integrate with them for a few days, then move on to see another human story unfold. I loved watching the varied characters and situations that I touched briefly before being on my way again. It was like flicking myself into one TV documentary to the next. My hosts, the actors, didn't mind my intrusion and confided in me, as I made my way through the screenplay. They knew we wouldn't meet again. I felt privileged when they accepted me into their homes and got to know each of them.

The Irish compound was at the top of a high mountain pass, and we explored the local area and its unique Indian culture. Little changed here for centuries; the only concession to modern times was tin roofs that replaced the thatch on the stone cottages.

In the mornings, the dawn seared across the sky, lighting the peaks on top of the far side of the valley. As the sun rose higher, the light came down the side of the mountains, eventually reaching the compound and warming the chill from our bones.

In the afternoon the shadows climbed up the other valley side leaving the bottom of the canyon in the shade. The sky flaming across the valley tops, all shades from gold to pinks, oranges and reds. We were now at 15,000 feet, and when the sun's rays disappeared, the temperatures plummeted to below zero in seconds. It was spectacular.

On the farms we passed we saw strange animals like the tall alpacas and the fat guinea pigs that had adapted to live in these harsh surroundings. I was enjoying Peru, the sights, the people, and the challenge of the Andes. It was close enough to believe I could make it. I could nearly smell the South Atlantic!

We started our climb over the roof of the world, but the Irish detour had taken us well off the main roads, and onto rough muddy dirt tracks. I was in awe of the men who had built these roads over precipices a mile deep. To ride downhill was a lot worse than going up, as I braked frantically on the muddy hairpin bends, the front wheel slithered on the loose gravel overlooking precipices. We rode through the Colca Pass. The second deepest in the world, after the Grand Canyon, it stretches five miles wide and one mile deep.

It was more comfortable going uphill, as I didn't have to face the great void of the valley below, only the mountain ahead.

When I glanced behind me, I came over dizzy for an instant. It was as if I was flying up through the clouds, over the peaks on my two-wheeled flying machine. Then some mad truck driver brought me back to reality as he barrelled down towards me, missing me by inches as I wobbled on the edge of the precipice. It was truly frightening.

Giant condors soared above and below us, gliding on the air currents as we climbed the narrow tracks. The biggest flying birds in the world, they rarely flap their three-metre- wide wings, as they search for any carrion.

The Peruvians placed a metal cross on the side of the road to mark a death, and at a bad corner, there would be dozens. I saw a smashed truck or bus on the rocks below and wondered did they leave the bodies there? Retrieving them from these cliffs looked impossible.

You would think a thicket of crosses made a good road safety warning, but not for macho Peruvian truck drivers; they sped on regardless. The road was so narrow in places the trucks literally scraped together as they inched past each other. The truck one side touching the inner cliff face, and the outside truck with its wheels almost spinning in the air over the vertical drop.

At one point the mud stuck to my tyres like a rolling snowball and jammed solid against the mudguards. I stopped to scrape it off every 100 yards, then took the front mudguard off as it built up thick on the wheel; eventually, a lump of mud flew off and I bumped along with slippery, square wheels.

Then, near the top, the clouds came down and we lost the road. One moment we were driving along the mud track, and the next we were on a muddy plateau. The wind blew sleet like needles in my face. We stopped, completely lost.

"Which way?" I shouted at Jorge. He shrugged, "Go back?"

This was ridiculous: the track had disappeared in the clouds. The wind tugged at the bike trying to push it over. I panicked at the thought of a cliff opening up in front of us. We turned back and our tracks had vanished in the slippery mire but we made it back and found the trail again.

The cold wind blew through my porous waterproofs, as I shivered uncontrollably. My arms, knees and legs were numb. Cold weather on a motorcycle creeps into your bones like a virus. First, it stings your fingers and toes, but then your body cools and stops circulating blood, to conserve it for your core organs. You shiver and your teeth chatter, but all you are doing is sitting on the bike, so it's not very noticeable. It's only when you try to get off that you cannot function. If someone stuck a thermometer up my bum, it would freeze solid.

We stopped at the first town. I tried to get off, but my legs wouldn't straighten up. I wobbled into a café, my knees bent and my arms out as if I was still holding the handlebars.

The Spanish conquistadors defeated the Indians, with modern weapons, and disease. In science fiction movies, aliens wipe out our civilisation with germs. The Spanish brought smallpox, syphilis and God and decimated the Indians. They obliterated their culture, stole their gold and built churches on top of their temples.

The next town, Cuzco, was a fascinating combination of Spanish architecture, with remnants of Aztec buildings. At Machu Picchu, the Indians built a city high in the mountains above the Urubamba River to hide from the Spanish and adapted their lifestyle to survive. There was no road to Machu Picchu, only a zig-zag railway line carved into the mountain. We left the bikes and took the train to the village of Aguas Calientes. The carriage had rough wooden seats, and they advised me not to sit near the doors as bandits often jumped on when the train slowed at a bend, robbed the tourists, then jumped off again at the next bend.

The train was jam-packed with backpackers, and local Indians. I suddenly came over dizzy, and my stomach cramped and I doubled up in pain; I had to lie down under the seats. My head banged, and I had no energy. The Peruvians have a habit of chewing coca leaves and then spitting the pith out. But I was too ill to care about the masticated mess under the wooden seats. One Indian gave me a wad of coca leaves to chew. The raw material for cocaine, chewing it dulled the pain. The Inca messengers used to chew it and run a hundred miles a day. I couldn't walk to the toilet at the end of the carriage.

The railway track was the main (and only) street of the town, lined with small wooden shacks built up the valley. The hot spring, which gave Aguas Calientes its name, bubbled out of a hole in the ground outside the town. They claimed the pool of hot muddy water had magical healing qualities, but it did nothing for me apart from covering me in a thin brown slime.

Jorge helped me the hundred yards to a wooden shack hostel. I assumed I had a bad dose of the shits, but my skin and my eyes had turned a sickly yellow colour. I had no appetite, even the smell of cooking made me retch, my stomach was in cramps, and I wanted to sleep all the time. Any exertion was arduous at this altitude, but I was too tired to pick my nose.

Machu Picchu was the most dramatic archaeological site on the continent.

"You have to see it," said Jorge.

"Do I look like I give a damn?" I replied, "I wouldn't care if an Aztec Queen came into the room with a bar of gold and a blow job!"

But I loaded myself in the back of a battered truck, and it hauled us up the steep track to the lost city.

The Indians had realised that they couldn't beat the Spanish, so they retreated to this place. Rumour has it that they designed it to keep the Virgins of the Sun God safe from the Conquistadors' lust.

They built the city on the long saddle between two peaks of a mountain and it was surrounded by snow-capped 18,000 feet mountains. It is completely impossible to see it from the valley. The walls of the houses and temples were complete; they were so well-carved and well-fitted that they needed no mortar to hold them together.

I sat on the mountain like an old pensioner, while Jorge explored the maze of streets, many of which had not been cleared of vegetation.

Meanwhile, I got chatting with some Argentinian students. They were on an archaeological tour of Peru.

"Your red hair and white skin make you look very Irish," I said, Maria introduced herself.

"Many Celts settled in Argentina and some still speak Welsh," she said smiling. "Why are you not exploring the ruins?"

"I'm as sick as a dead parrot," and tried to explain who Monty Python was, in my bad Spanish. "I just want to sit, and take it in."

We shared a flask of tea, and took a few photographs, and took a group photograph with the ruins behind.

On the train trip back to Cuzco, I had to lie on the floor again as my stomach heaved.

"This is not the shits," I said to Jorge. I couldn't afford to see a doctor, but an Australian medical student looked at me and said I probably had hepatitis.

"Not so good," I said. "What's the treatment?"

"None, only rest," he replied.

"No point in paying for a doctor to tell me that, then," I groaned. This was a bloody disaster; I needed to keep moving, or I would run out of money.

Cuzco was the capital of the Inca Empire and looked like a fascinating city, but I had as much interest in architecture as the cockroaches under my bed.

I was buying some painkillers at a chemist the next evening, when an Indian beggar pulled at my sleeve. "Por favor?" he said, pointing at the aspirin.

"Por que?" I asked, expecting him to want money instead, and he moved his poncho off his shoulder. In the place where his arm should be was a raw stump, just bare flesh and exposed bone. It was black and putrid.

I jolted as if hit by an electric shock and I nearly wretched. "Accidente de coche," he said, as if a car crash made it okay.

"Jesus Christ! Go to the doctor," I said. "No dinero," he replied.

"I understand, mate," and gave him painkillers and money and scurried away, embarrassed that I couldn't do more, but life is cheap in Peru.

I dreamt of booking into a posh hotel, for crisp, clean sheets, and some good food. But it was out of the question. Sometimes, I walked into the reception, sat down and tried to look like a tourist before they threw me out. But not before I stole some super soft toilet roll.

My lack of money was always my biggest challenge. Money could buy me a doctor, spare parts, decent food, and peace of mind, as I always knew that I was a slip and a crash away from disaster.

Cuzco was the worst place in the world to get sick, located miles from any other transport. I had to get to La Paz where there would be a railway, or maybe a road with less than a 45-degree gradient.

I needed to move on, and Jorge helped me pack. By the time we loaded up, I couldn't lift the bike off its stand. It was raining, and I had to stop every ten minutes from exhaustion. Jorge patiently waited, but there wasn't much he could do. It's every man for himself on a motorcycle.

We were at an altitude of well over 11,000 feet now, and the road followed valleys through the mountains, with views to take your breath away - if I had any breath to take away. My illness sucked my energy, and I worked flat out at self- preservation, as I tried not to become another metal cross on a bend.

The engine strained red hot on the upward climb, then changed to freezing cold as I freewheeled down into the valley. We watched the trucks cross a forded river, about a hundred yards wide.

"It doesn't look too deep," I said and drove straight into the river. A sheet of solid water shot up in my face. Too fast! I slowed, but then the bike dropped into a hole mid-stream, the water swept over the upriver cylinder head, and the engine stopped dead. The water shorted the upstream spark plug as steam rose between my legs and the current wrenched at my feet trying to yank the bike away off downstream. I punched the starter, but only the downstream cylinder fired, as it was just clear of the water flow on that side, so I gave it full throttle.

The engine shuddered with just enough power from the one cylinder to get moving and slithered off the boulders and up the other bank where I fell over. Jorge followed more steadily and picked my bike up. We set up camp there on the riverbank. I shivered from the freezing water. Jorge set up camp and made dinner, but I knew I was holding him up.

When we crossed the Bolivian border, there was an air of despair about the locals. Bolivia had just had a military coup, and the drug lords now ran the country. The drug money paid off the politicians. So as usual, the peasants got nothing.

The Bolivians always looked miserable and their poverty was totally overbearing. They dressed in multiple strata of bright-coloured home-made fabrics as if trying to lift their mood from the hardships of their existence. I imagined their skinny bodies under the layers of coats and skirts. The ladies all wore black bowler hats and kept their coarse black hair in a couple of braids.

This was gaucho country, with the horse the main form of transport. They could cope with the mountain tracks better than a car and were the original all-terrain vehicle, able to ride up steep hills at will. The gauchos were lean and brown, wearing wide-brimmed hats, ponchos and leather chaps on their legs, and sat on Western saddles on their wiry steeds. I felt great empathy for them as we rode past on our steel horses, and they would look back at us with respect, or perhaps envy. I was never sure which.

A few miles over the border, the sky turned from a deep blue to a dark grey and a thunderstorm blew up in seconds. Visibility dropped to a few yards, and hailstones like concrete tennis balls smacked off my helmet and pounded my arms, then covered the ground with a treacherous carpet of ice. Lightning flashed, and the thunder roared; it was a storm the likes of which I had never seen.

I spotted a stone cottage off the road and rode towards it. The carpet of hailstones hid the potholes, which tried to slide the wheels from under me. Then as I reached the yard in front of the cottage, my front wheel dived and disappeared through the floating hailstone carpet. I plunged into an ice- covered duck pond up to the cylinder heads and the engine cut out. I howled like a drowning cat as I stood with the bike hissed steam, up to my thighs in the freezing water.

"Can this get any bloody worse!" I shouted as Jorge fell about laughing, and the water filled my boots!

Two farmers looked on, no doubt wondering why I had driven into their duck pond. But they helped push me out, and we ran for shelter inside the tiny thatched cottage. Huddled around a smoky peat fire, stood the farmer, his wife and four or five children. They were all less than five foot high.

'Jesus Christ, they're all dwarfs,' I thought, momentarily wondering if Snow White was upstairs.

I was ready to collapse. The house was deadly quiet after the crashing on my helmet; the thatched roof absorbing the noise of the hailstones and we stripped off our helmets and our leathers. Petrified at our intrusion at first, the Indians relaxed and accepted a few pennies for a bed for the night.

In the room's corner was a pile of freshly skinned alpaca fleeces, the hides hard and crusty with the dried blood. I fell into them, and they were as heavenly as a duck down quilt. Jorge pulled my boots off, and I passed out.

The next day the sun shone, and the ice disappeared. We rode along the shore of Lake Titicaca, the highest navigable lake in the world at over 12,000 feet altitude. The water was green with algae and contrasted with the deep blue of outer space a few miles up.

The lake is vast at over three thousand square miles and inhabited by the Uros tribe who live on reed islands that float on the lake. If they didn't like where they were, or they were in danger, they would slip the mooring lines and float away. They lived off fish and birds, and lake plants and superstition said that black blood kept them warm on the freezing waters. "Come see the floating islands?" said a young Bolivian at the harbour.

He owned a small open boat that had seen better days. But he said that it wasn't far, so we agreed and motored for half an hour around the lake. The island was about fifty yards across and stood six inches above the water, but apparently, the reeds go down ten feet below. As the straw gets waterlogged, they throw more on top. It felt squishy to walk on and seemed a very extreme solution to a nasty neighbour problem. The concept of tourism had not yet arrived, and the residents hid from my camera, afraid it would steal their soul. They made everything from reeds - the island, houses, boats, furniture; they even lit fires on them somehow.

On the way back, another thunderstorm suddenly blew in, the skies darkened, and the calm lake turned into a wild, windswept ocean. Then the engine stopped, we drifted into the middle of the lake, and the boat started filling up with water from the waves…

"I don't fucking believe this," I said to Jorge. "After all that we've been through, we will drown in a poxy lake on top of the world."

They had run out of petrol, so the guys started to fill the tank from a spare can. But with the wild rocking of the boat, the petrol was spilling and sizzling on the hot cylinder heads. Then I noticed he was standing with a lit cigarette in his mouth! But the petrol didn't explode, the engine started, and the day was saved. Jorge and I looked across at each other as the wind tugged our hair and rain streamed down our necks. We started to laugh like crazed maniacs.

"Just another day at the office!" I screamed.

We made it to La Paz, the highest capital city in the world, at 13,000 feet. The Spanish built it when they discovered gold here. Now skyscrapers blend with the Spanish colonial town, with ugly concrete buildings constructed with little thought of aesthetics. The gold ran out, and drugs were the new King in town.

Jorge, my faithful companion, had stuck with me since I got ill, even though I slowed him down for days. But he would leave me here. There was no point in him waiting. He was going to Tierra del Fuego, so would head south, while I should turn east for Rio. A common purpose brought us together, but we always knew that we were ultimately on our own. We helped each other if we had an accident or something, but apart from that, it was each man for himself.

He found me a cheap hotel and helped me park the bike one last time, then we awkwardly wished each other good luck, and hugged and slapped each other in the macho manly way that blokes do.

"Will you be okay?"

"Sure, I'll be well in no time!"

It was a lie, but there was nothing more Jorge could do to help.

He got on his Yamaha and drove down the cobbled lane, with a last wave.

I stood staring down the empty street for a few minutes, then went to my room on my own. I knew his departure was coming, but it was still a bitter blow and left a huge void which threatened to overwhelm me. I stayed in bed for the next few days, unable or unwilling to face the world outside and hoping, vainly, that every morning I would get better.

My money was disappearing fast, I wanted to sleep all day, and my paranoia was turning back to depression. I had a nightmare that as my journey came to a finale, it merged with real life to end together.

I had always assumed some sort of immortality and never thought I would die from my illness when I was moving, but now that I stopped, I wallowed in despair. I was like a swimmer who couldn't tread water. I needed to keep moving, or I would drown.

Soon I was down to my last 20 dollars and owed the hotel for my room.

I had no ex-pat contacts in La Paz, and my illness was not improving, I was too sick to go out to meet anyone.

If I was well, I would have hustled for sponsorship and somewhere to stay. But apart from my physical state and lack of energy, my mental dejection stopped my usual bounce back from impossible situations as I had in the past.

I was now too broke to phone home; anyway, I had as much chance of talking to God on the Bolivian telephone system. My last resort was going to the British Embassy to plead poverty. But they said they couldn't help and suggested I send a telex to ask for money from my family.

At the Post Office, I sent the telex to my brother in Ireland to transfer some money to me at the Bank of La Paz. I called at the bank every day expectantly.

"It could take a month," the bank official cheerfully explained.

"I will be dead by then," I cheerfully replied, and we both stood there wondering if I was serious or not.

It took me ten minutes to climb the stairs to my room on the first floor. My ribs were protruding and my yellow face gaunt. I was wasting away, trapped in a cockroach-infested hotel in Bolivia.

With Jorge gone, the hotel cockroaches were my only company, but like the Ancient Mariner, I didn't appreciate their presence. I threw my boots at them, using up precious energy, but getting pleasure from a crunch and smear on the lino. I wondered how my marvel of Italian motorcycle engineering and myself could be so useless, yet those wee bastards had been so successful for millions of years? I need to get out more, I decided.

So, I summoned my energy and parked the Guzzi in the main square to sit in the sun the next day.

"We don't get many UK number plates in Bolivia," said a guy with an English accent

"No, there's a good bloody reason for that," I said and told him of my predicament.

As luck would have it, Richard worked at the British Embassy as a P.A. to the Ambassador. He rode a Ducati in the UK and loved Italian bikes.

"Let me see what I can do," he offered.

By the next day, he'd got it all sorted. He rang my parents on the Embassy phone and got them to transfer money to his personal UK account, then he gave me the equivalent in cash in my hand! Whoever said that money doesn't make you happy, had obviously never been broke. But I wasn't happy; I was ecstatic!

I would have celebrated if the smell of food or alcohol didn't turn my stomach. I realised it was time to surrender to my illness and give up the journey and the Mardi Gras in Rio. With as much interest in a party as I had in having an internal examination by a fat-fingered Bolivian Customs Officer, all I needed was a good sleep and a mug of cocoa.

"Is there a train today to Rio de Janeiro?" I asked at the station.

"Next week. Today to Buenos Aires?" "That will do nicely; one way please."

I didn't care where I went; Brazil, Argentina, just get me out of Bolivia! I would go to Buenos Aires and ship the bike from there. As I settled down in my seat, the relief hit me in a tidal wave of emotion. I was so happy I was about to cry. I was finally safe, I had money in my pocket, and I didn't need to ride anywhere. It was all over. In two days, I would arrive in B.A. All I had to do was stare out the window.

I reached physical and mental rock bottom in La Paz and accepted that the trip was over. As the train left, I closed my eyes, and the journey rewound in my head. Getting sick in Peru, and the nightmare in Cuzco, the drive down South America from Colombia, flying from Panama, and the ride down Central America, then paranoid in Mexico, and how at home I was in the USA.

Then I remembered Africa; shit! The jungle, the drive through the desert, South Africa, and the yacht race, that was all me too! It all seemed so long ago and far away, but it was only last year. Then Israel and the Middle East. I seemed so young then, a lifetime ago. I thought of Austria, the girls in London, and right back to Belfast.

Belfast! I had forgotten about Ireland, where I used to live! It was such a distant memory. I would go back and get a job. Normal life would resume. It will all be okay.

With only the illness to fight, I fell asleep like a baby, holding back the urge to suck my thumb. I woke with a jolt, as the train stopped and rain ran down the outside of the windows.

"Everyone off," the guard shouted.

"What?!" I said.

"The rains have washed away the railway track; you will take a bus."

"But what about my motorbike?" I said.

"Drive it," he said as if stating the obvious.

"You must be bloody joking!" I said, but he wasn't. The train would go no further, and I sat stuck in the rain at the Argentinian border.

Just when I thought it was all over.

CHAPTER 18

Argentina & Brazil

I SAT ON THE BIKE IN THE RAIN AND WATCHED THE BUSES LEAVE, THEN RODE off in a trance. I had no Jorge to look after me now. At least the Andes were behind me, and I drove down dirt roads through the high Argentinean pampas, stopping for a rest every 30 minutes.

"You bastard," I shouted, as the river roared in a raging torrent alongside the road. Large trees, bits of houses and other debris swept past as the grey waters washed chunks of the road away. The rail track hung in mid-air where the embankment had been.

The road had washed away, so I detoured through country lanes that trucks had turned into a quagmire, and I struggled to haul the bike through the mud. After riding all the next morning, I checked in to a hotel, exhausted, and crashed out with my boots on. I woke to a bang on the door. I looked at my watch - it was 2 o'clock. I'd only been asleep for an hour. What the hell did they want now?

"Signor, are you okay?" said the owner.

"Yes," I said, "what is your problem?"

"We thought you were dead."

"I've just gone to sleep."

"No signor, you have been asleep since yesterday!" I'd slept for 25 hours, and I missed a whole day!

In the bathroom, I saw myself in the cracked mirror. I was yellow skin and bone.

'You're absolutely buggered, mate,' I said at the wizened image. I suddenly realized how sick I was and although I had as much energy as day-old roadkill, I knew I needed to keep moving to get proper medical treatment.

It was still 1500 miles to Buenos Aires, a three days ride if I was fit, but three weeks the way I was going.

I can't remember much of this time and took no notes in my diary. I was in a trance, and rode, rested and rode more. I had to keep going, as if by instinct. At a small petrol station, I stopped and, half-asleep, forgot to put my feet down and fell over. I tried to lift the bike, but it was too heavy. The attendant came over.

"Are you okay?" the teenager said, giving me a hand up. "Nope, mate, I'm buggered."

Fucked is one of those universal words you can use in any language; along with Taxi, Bar, and Beer. I guarantee that even in Outer Mongolia, you can go up to absolutely anyone and say; 'I need TAXI to BAR, I'm FUCKED and need BEER.' They will know precisely what you mean.

I rode about ten miles then stopped to rest and covered about eighty miles in a day. Then the next evening, as it got dark, suddenly the bike lurched left, and I skidded to a stop before going into the ditch. Weird, I though, must be a puncture or something. But no, the right-hand fork leg had cracked, bending the leg forward and turning the wheel to the left, and the front of the bike was about to collapse.

I was lucky the break happened now as if it had cracked on the mountain tracks, I would have flipped over the handlebars and headed down the valley a mile below. It was nearly dark, the road was deserted, and I was about thirty miles to the next village. I sat in the mud and stared forlornly at the fork leg as if this would fix it. My brain refused to take it in. I was buggered, and now the bike was buggered too.

The Guzzi fork leg was a standard size for a road bike. Off-road bikes' forks are much thicker and only half the bike weight to support. And they generally weren't asked to ride down African railways and over South American mountains. This was pure metal fatigue, but I wouldn't complain to Moto Guzzi as I was well outside the warranty terms and conditions.

A wave of exhaustion flowed over me as the cold rain ran down my neck and I started to shiver uncontrollably. I needed to do something quickly. "Shift your ass," I shouted to myself.

Then I had a brainwave; the crack was tearing open at the back of the fork leg where the 'pulling' strain was on the metal. The front of the leg was still whole as it had a compression load on it.

What if I turned the fork leg tube around 180 degrees? The 'compression load' would push the crack together. I loosened the fork yoke clamps and tried to turn it. It was dark, and I had no torch.

'Come back, Jorge,' I thought, as the old German hatchet man always had a couple of torches in his bags. My wrench gripped the leg tight and twisted it with my last remaining strength. The chrome crunched and splintered in its jaws. But it moved, and with the next couple of twists, it turned 180 degrees, and the leg was straight, the front wheel central.

I almost cried with joy. But would it take the load now the weight of the bike was pushing the crack together? There was now only a sliver of metal holding my entire world together but would it hold if I rode over a bump? My rope suspension system was all that held the wheel on. I tightened up the ropes and slid the mounts an inch down over the fork tubes. It moved the centre of pressure away from the crack, but it hid the crack behind the mounting, which made me more confident. Out of sight is out of mind.

I pushed the bike off the stand; all held good. Into first gear and moved off slowly. It was holding! The rain hissed on the exhausts, and all I wanted was to get to a town quick. But I crawled along in 2nd gear, not knowing when the front wheel would fall off.

Two freezing hours later, I trundled into the next village and stopped at a small guesthouse. I was too tired to be pleased with getting there.

"Tienes una habitación?" I pleaded.

"Si Signor." I slept for fourteen hours straight. The next morning, a mechanic put a neat weld on the crack.

"Terrible, Signor," he said. "You need a new leg."

"I need a new fucking head," I replied.

We were both right. They could both implode at any time. In San Jose, I called at a pharmacy for more painkillers, as my stomach was still cramping in agony.

"You look very ill," Eduardo, the owner, said.

"I'm quite well now," I said. "You should have seen me when I was really sick!" and then told him my story. Eduardo invited me in to have lunch and to see his old Norton.

"The train track at San Miguel is open to Buenos Aires about fifty kilometres further; my driver will take you in the van. I insist!" Eduardo said.

He explained that it was not safe to travel, as the military arrested anyone they didn't trust.

They looked for communists and their sympathizers, but they arrested teachers, students and even priests for being socialists. He said that as a foreigner, the police would view me as a potential troublemaker, and as a young guy on a motorcycle, I would stand out on the roads. "It is too dangerous," he insisted.

I later learned that over 30,000 people had 'disappeared' and that there had been some 300 secret concentration camps around the country. It would be many years before the truth about the 'disappeared' eventually emerged, and the Junta tried to deflect criticism by invading the Falklands.

They loaded the bike on the back of Eduardo's small pharmacy van, between the rows of sanitary towels and nappies. I could use them both, I thought to myself. Eduardo took a big risk; if I had been some sort of subversive, they would have arrested him. Our only connection was that we both had motorcycles. But as always, complete strangers took me in and fed me, gave me petrol and helped me on my way, as if to be part of the adventure.

Two hours later, I was at the railway station with the line open, and the next evening I arrived at Buenos Aires Central Train Station. It reminded me of London Victoria with the hustle and bustle.

When the Spanish conquistadors got to Argentina, they sorted out the Indian problem permanently - they killed them all. The station was full of European commuters It was the end of my line too; my journey was over. But I was in no mood to mark the occasion, I had no energy to look for a hotel, let alone celebrate, and I didn't know anyone in town. I parked beside a wooden bench in the station and lay down exhausted in my sleeping bag, while the din and commotion of the station carried on around me.

I dreamt of flying across Great Pampas on silk-like tarmac, but something shook me. No, no, leave me alone… I want back to my dream… I opened my eyes, expecting the police.

It was a red-haired girl!

"Chris, is that you?" She said.

"Maria?" I asked, vaguely recognizing her.

It was Maria, the Argentinian student I'd met in Machu Picchu, who was now standing over me. "What are you doing here?" I asked.

"I live here!" she laughed. "I thought you were going to Rio?"

"It's a long story!" I said, "How did you find me?"

She explained she had prepared a slide show of her trip to Peru with her family and friends that weekend. Included in the pictures was our group photo, so she had mentioned that she had met this British motorcyclist in Machu Picchu. One of her friends had been coming to work that morning and had seen me sleeping in the station beside a bike with a GB sticker on it. She rang Francesca to say how weird it was, and could it be the same guy?

Francesca rushed to see if it was really me and if I was still there, which I was, thanks to my dream. It was an incredible coincidence in this city of 10 million people.

She took me home and I spent a week being taken around Maria's family and shown off like a prize turkey. I enjoyed the fuss. With her mother's care, I got better every day. It looked like I had broken the sickness, but I only weighed about 60 kilos.

I was a minor celebrity and did a couple of local radio interviews in Spanish. I couldn't speak a word six months ago, but as long as they asked me about motorbikes and travelling, I was fluent.

It wasn't the wild celebration I had planned for in Rio, it was much better than that.

The Argentines were the friendliest of all the Latin Americans. Maria's dad organised to have the bike shipped back to the UK. I couldn't sell it now; it would be like selling my mother. Anyway, what would I say?

'One careful owner, 53,000 miles through 33 countries!' As I left the bike at the docks, I felt like I had just said goodbye to my oldest friend.

But I needed to get back to pay off my debts. I booked a flight home, via Rio and Miami.

BRAZIL

I arrived in Rio just before the Carnival as I planned, but the party didn't interest me. My liver and kidneys still weren't functioning, and the smell of beer still made me want to vomit, which, as an Irishman, meant I was very, very ill! But I stayed awake for a whole six hours straight now.

Brazil was not the destination, but it was the end of the road, and I wanted closure. I phoned Angela's mother.

"I dated your daughter in London two years ago. Can I call in and say hello?" I said.

We drank tea on her balcony near Copacabana Beach. I am sure she thought I was very strange.

I stopped in Miami; it was as if I wanted to delay going home. Jeanette was shocked at my appearance when I arrived at her door, and although I wasn't expecting a great reception, she invited me in. I apologized for dumping her. She said she understood why I did it - which was more than I did. She had got her job back, but not her boyfriend.

We wondered how the trip would have been if she had come along. Would the bike have made it over the Andes? Would our relationship have survived? Maybe.

Would a nurse have been useful? Definitely!

Jeanette said she was going to take a year off, to see the world.

I said I was glad for her. There was no passion; I didn't expect there to be.

Let's face it, I wasn't a romantic wandering motorcyclist anymore—more of a broke, sick, burnt-out bum. We promised to keep in touch.

But we never saw each other again.

Conclusion

Back in Ireland, the Troubles erupted into more violence. Maggie Thatcher was not for giving in to the hunger strikers and gave the IRA the martyrs they craved. Bobby Sands and nine other hunger strikers starved to death, and the anger increased the bloodshed.

I looked like I'd been on a hunger strike. My doctor did various tests and said that I had hepatitis E, which causes chronic liver failure and is passed on from contaminated food or water.

"Did you travel through Third World countries?" he asked.

"A few," I said.

"What did the last doctor there say?"

"You're the first I've spoken to."

There was a letter from Louis, the Austrian biker from Ecuador. It said he came down with hepatitis when he got home and spent several weeks in a hospital.

I sent him a card which said.

"You lucky bastard."

I moved in with my parents, and while I slowly recovered physically, my head was a mess.

Post-traumatic stress can result from an individual shock like a violent incident or constant danger over a long period.

I was always travelling, always on the move, never knowing what would happen around the corner. The constant danger left its mark in my head. I was restless and confused and couldn't concentrate on anything.

And did I find what I was looking for? No chance! I was too busy enjoying the good times and surviving the bad. It would be many years before I realised that I had not only found it, but I had lived it.

When Aborigines go walkabout, they don't follow an itinerary. They wander off in the wilderness and learn how to cope with the unknown, and this is what makes the man.

They know that in life we are all heading for the same destination. It is what we do along the way on the journey to that terminus in the sky that matters.

The destinations I planned - Sydney, Cape Town and Rio - they were the pots of gold at the end of my rainbow. But the anticipation of the destination was always better than the actual arrival. The real treasure was the journey, the people I met and the adventures I experienced. That was the prize. Travelling for the bragging rights, to get somewhere, is bound to disappoint.

People would ask where I had been. What should I tell them? Where would I start? If I tried, their eyes glazed over, and they changed the subject quickly; my journey was too distant from their everyday world. I didn't want to tell them, anyway; it was my own personal experience and nothing to do with them. I thought they were being nosy.

Still disconnected from everything, I got back with my girlfriend, but it didn't last. I spent most of my time staring out of the window, dreaming that I was somewhere else.

Eventually, I realised life would move on either with or without me. I started to work in the family business to pay off my debts and soon earned enough to buy a derelict house, complete with an outside toilet. I started rebuilding like a man possessed, working with my hands, doing everything from the roof to the plumbing. It was good medicine and what I needed, as it had no wheels.

The Guzzi arrived back, still covered with mud from the Andes. It had done a mighty job, over the roughest terrains in the world, the engine still running faultlessly. It would need a rebuild, but it would have to wait, as first, I needed to sort out my head.

I started to write a book, but the page was bare and words wouldn't come. I was only twenty-three years old, and English was never a strong point at school. I didn't know what to write or how to understand what really happened.

Ted Simon published his book, Jupiter's Travels, about riding a motorcycle around the world. It was excellent, but nearly every page maddened me as I thought my journey had been a unique experience, only to discover that Ted had beaten me to it. And worse, it was written more eloquently than I ever could. His story read like Shakespeare compared to my 'Noddy Goes Camping.'

But I didn't understand that while we had ridden down many of the same roads, his story differed completely from mine. The happenings in the world have a different lean when seen through my eyes as a youngster at twenty-one than through Ted's forty-five-year-old eyes. Ted had prestige and kudos from writing for the Sunday Times, and through that, met Presidents and politicians. As a young broke biker, I met Hells Angels and prostitutes.

Disillusioned, I put my notebooks and photographs in a drawer and got on with life.

Then Ewan McGregor and Charley Boorman made the Long Way films. Ewan and Charley travelled with a film crew, a doctor, a security expert, mechanics, and spare bikes. He had two back-up trucks with a support crew, and twenty-four people in his team photo. When they broke their suspension in Sudan, they flew in a mechanic with a replacement. When I broke mine, I got a rope from a man with a goat.

As you watch them on TV, it looks like they are on their own. But they were no more on their own than Michael Caine was fighting the African warriors in the movie Zulu.

However, I understand that as a film star, Ewan had no choice; he couldn't just disappear off on his own. And if I had had the money, I would have done it his way too! They rode their motorbikes around the world, and that is no easy feat, but I don't see what they got from the journey other than a couple of sore bottoms.

It was like we had been smoking the same joint, but they didn't inhale. A story of riding a motorcycle around the world is not about motorcycles, nor is it about seeing the world. That's only the backdrop. It's about how these experiences impact the rider. It's about your ability to adapt to face the challenges.

My journey was so intense that, practically every day, something happened that I would remember. Some forty years later, I can still look at my maps and remember how hot it was, where I slept.

I recently spent a few days with Ted Simon, and he taught me about writing and French red wine. I taught him about Italian motorcycles and 80s American drug culture. We were like old soldiers from the same war, we just fought in different trenches.

The Iranian Revolution stopped me riding to Australia, but I should thank the Ayatollah, as the chaos it plunged me into was what made the magic happen. I travelled up, down and all about the world, like a demented ant.

I left for a four-month, 10,000-mile trip to Australia, and having gone the wrong way, I spent twenty months riding 39,000 miles through 33 countries. I did it by living like a native, staying in hostels or sleeping rough in the fields, or on concrete floors, public toilets, and garage forecourts.

But it wasn't the danger that was my biggest challenge; it was my lack of money. With money, you can live easy. Can't find a campsite? Book into a Hilton. You've had a hard day in the saddle? Well, sit in a Jacuzzi.

Was I brave or foolhardy? There's a fine line between them. My traveller's intuition served me well. I turned down offers of hospitality if I didn't like the circumstances. I didn't question it. If it didn't feel right, I didn't go.

I experienced many things we don't do in the Western world. When I took the train from Khartoum to Wau, I was hungry and thirsty, which, for me, was a novelty, but quite normal for my native companions. It scared me lots of times and fear is so far gone from our lives that we go to amusement parks to find some adrenalin.

I had left home a boy and returned a man. Somewhere under the searing sun of Sudan, I made the metamorphosis; everything before was just a test, everything after, was just a chance to use my newfound powers.

I have known middle-aged men who never made this transition. They probably work all their lives for the civil service and end up married to a strong-willed woman who took over from their mothers.

I do not claim my way is the right way. It is just… my way.

Western society encourages everyone to follow a civilised path, to do the right thing.

From when I crossed the English Channel to when I arrived in Argentina, I had four days' insurance in Rhodesia. The policy there covered careless driving but excluded getting your balls cut off by terrorists.

But sometimes it's good to throw caution aside and take a chance or five. You know you shouldn't and it's wrong; you know the odds are against you. But isn't there a sense of accomplishment doing something out of your comfort zone? Just don't come back to complain when you break your neck!

I have worked in many industries: furniture, property, fitness, I.T. Each time I started a new job, I plunged myself into a situation that was way over my head, and out of my depth.

But it was nowhere near as difficult as riding across the Sahara, or over the Andes. After those experiences, I believed I could do anything. It might just hurt while I learned what to do!

When the Ulster Bank put my businesses into receivership in 2013, they stole everything I owned. I had to learn about property law and self-litigated against them for three years. While it was terrifying standing up before a Judge in the High Court, against the banks of QCs, the slimy lawyers and bankers were fluffy puppies compared to the child soldiers in Uganda.

They didn't stand a chance.

I rebuilt Le Mans SOI 222 and still ride it. In 2004, and nearing classic bike status, I headed east with my future wife Julie, on the pillion. We made it as far as Moscow, then like Napoleon and Hitler before us, we retreated to Europe through Poland and Berlin. I wonder, at 40-plus, is there another trip left in the Guzzi?

By staying with strangers and trusting them with yourself, you can discover what people are really like. When you put yourself in danger, when you are on your own, you find out what drives you.

I stayed with Arab villagers and enjoyed their hospitality without the threat of beheading or being held for ransom. This is not something you can do now. I only had to worry about thieves and a bit of good old-fashioned buggery.

Not unlike the great Victorian explorers in Africa, I travelled, cut off from home. There was no 'phone home' option, no life insurance, no spare parts. I had only myself to get me out of trouble and many places have not changed since Livingstone and General Gordon travelled.

This travel is gone forever, for better or for worse.

As I drove from one Third World village to another, I watched the people go about their existence, living, breeding and dying. But their lives had a simple innocence and honesty.

Snowflake travellers now follow a laid-out itinerary, with routes planned and hotels booked, then send daily updates home on Facebook.

To plan every stop and every train ride saves time and money but loses out on the whole point of the exercise. And you return as you left, a child of your society.

Mobile phones, GPS, and Internet access have changed the world forever. Those villagers now are online and understand how we live and they want it for themselves, and they are envious of our lifestyles.

I've been told the road from Wau is now tarmac and they can do the trip to Juba in 8 hours instead of the 5 days it took me. The village chief who swapped my underwear for a bow and arrow is probably running a car wash.

YouTube makes Westerners a valuable target for kidnappers. All I had was the cash in my pocket, but now the baddies can demand thousands of dollars in ransom online.

When we are young, we have dreams and ambitions that get left behind as we grow up. Our dreams can't fight the pressure of life and get replaced by things that don't matter, like bigger houses, and new furniture. We consign our aspirations to oblivion. Such a waste of desire, to be forgotten about until, in old age, you stop to wonder what it was all about, and realise it's too late.

You've missed it.

I've been lucky and had many of my dreams fulfilled. I've done crazy things and challenged myself, and still go the wrong way, sometimes by mistake, sometimes by design. I've had two beautiful children and finally found a wonderful wife and soulmate.

But I still dream and will always strive to achieve them. For when you stop dreaming, the journey is over…And you may as well be dead.

Soon, virtual reality will arrive, and kids will ride around the world through a headset, rather than getting into the action for real.

I don't need a headset.

I just need to close my eyes. And dream.

If you enjoyed the book, I would really appreciate it
if you would write an online review.

Thanks!

A poem for Bikers, Travellers and youngsters just trying to find their way.

ITHAKA BY C. P. CAVAFY

As you set out for Ithaka
hope your road is a long one,
full of adventure, full of discovery.
Laistrygonians, Cyclops,
angry Poseidon—don't be afraid of them:
you'll never find things like that on your way
as long as you keep your thoughts raised high,
as long as a rare excitement
stirs your spirit and your body.
Laistrygonians, Cyclops,
wild Poseidon—you won't encounter them
unless you bring them along inside your soul,
unless your soul sets them up in front of you.

Hope your road is a long one.
May there be many summer mornings when,
with what pleasure, what joy,
you enter harbours you're seeing for the first time;
may you stop at Phoenician trading stations
to buy fine things,
mother of pearl and coral, amber and ebony,
sensual perfume of every kind—
as many sensual perfumes as you can;
and may you visit many Egyptian cities
to learn and go on learning from their scholars.

Keep Ithaka always in your mind.
Arriving there is what you're destined for.
But don't hurry the journey at all.
Better if it lasts for years,
so you're old by the time you reach the island,
wealthy with all you've gained on the way,
not expecting Ithaka to make you rich.